# THE LAW
# OF RIGHTS
# OF LIGHT

# THE LAW
# OF RIGHTS
# OF LIGHT

Jonathan Karas MA (Oxon)
Of the Middle Temple
One of Her Majesty's Counsel

With technical appendices
by Point 2 Surveyors

Wildy, Simmonds & Hill Publishing

Contains public sector information licensed under the Open Government Licence v3.0.

ISBN: 9780854901647

British Library Cataloguing in Publication Data

A catalogue record for this book is available from the British Library.

First published in 2016 by

Wildy, Simmonds & Hill Publishing
58 Carey Street
London WC2A 2JF
England
www.wildy.com

Typeset by Heather Jones, North Petherton, Somerset.
Printed in Great Britain by CPI Antony Rowe, Chippenham, Wiltshire.

*Dedicated to my family*

# Contents

**Appendices**

# Preface

The law of rights of light is part of the law of easements. Despite this, it has often been treated warily by land lawyers.

If this book has a purpose, it is to show that 'rights of light' is simply just another legal subject. It considers how rights can be established, what constitutes an infringement of those rights and what remedies can be provided for the infringement of those rights. This does not mean that there are no technical difficulties nor that there are no differences between the law of rights of light and that relating to other easements. The aim, however, is to show that there is no problem in the law of rights of light with which a competent lawyer cannot grapple.

Some of the wariness of lawyers can perhaps be explained by the complex ways in which light and its loss have been measured. The surveyors who undertake this measurement and assess losses deal with many more cases than any lawyer ever could. This undoubted practical experience of the subject has meant that many lawyers have been cautious about questioning the methodology adopted by surveyors, and how it has been applied to specific cases. These days, the measurement is no less complex than it used to be. In practice, however, the complexity is hidden behind computer modelling. This means that the results can be presented in a straightforward manner, but the models sometimes hide assumptions. These assumptions, however, are often surprising to the uninitiated. I am indebted to Point 2 Surveyors, and in particular to Liam Dunford, Paul Fletcher, Dr Martin Howarth and Dr Malcolm Macpherson for writing two technical appendices (Appendix A and Appendix B) which unpick some of these assumptions and explain some of the basic concepts which surveyors adopt. These appendices will, I hope, provide lawyers with the tools with which to ask intelligent questions of their technical witnesses.

They also highlight some of the difficulties of the current methods which surveyors may face, and suggest how practice may develop in the future.

I am also indebted to my colleague Jonathan Gaunt QC, with whom I discussed some of the problems with the measurement of light from the perspective of lawyers, and to Jerome Webb of GIA, who referred me to the body of research which supports the comparative value of natural light over artificial light. Any errors in the text, however, are all my own.

The law is stated as at 1 January 2016.

# List of Figures

# Table of Cases

*References are to page numbers.*

# Table of Legislation

*References are to page numbers. Page numbers in bold refer to where legislation is set out in the Appendices.*

# Table of Statutory Instruments

*References are to page numbers. Page numbers in bold refer to where legislation is set out in the Appendices.*

# Chapter 1

# The Legal Nature of a Right of Light

## NATURE OF A RIGHT OF LIGHT

1.1    A 'right of light' is an easement. In other words, it is a right enjoyed by one parcel of land (the 'dominant tenement') over another parcel of land (the 'servient tenement'). A right of light is one where the dominant tenement carries with it the right to receive light in a lateral direction to an aperture in a building[1] on that land without interruption from the servient tenement.

1.2    Like other easements, rights of light can be acquired by grant (either express or implied).[2] More usually they are acquired by prescription. As with other easements, there are three sorts of prescription:[3]

(a)    common law prescriptive rights deriving (at least notionally) from user since time immemorial, i.e. since 1189;

(b)    rights arising under the doctrine of 'lost modern grant', i.e. 20 years' uninterrupted user of light (for any period) 'as of right';[4]

(c)    prescription under the Prescription Act 1832.

In the case of rights of light, the Prescription Act 1832 contains provisions which differ from those applicable to other forms of easement.

---

[1]    See paras 2.62 and 2.67. A right to receive light to vacant land is not recognised as an easement.

[2]    See paras 2.14, 2.62 and 2.71 ff.

[3]    See para 2.44 ff.

[4]    See generally *Tehidy Minerals v Norman* [1971] 2 QB 528 at 552.

1.3    Rights of light may take effect as legal or equitable easements. A legal easement is one created for an interest equivalent to:

(a)   a fee simple absolute in possession; or

(b)   a term of years absolute.[5]

The formalities for creation of legal easements are considered below.[6] Where an easement is established by prescription,[7] it also takes effect as a legal easement.[8] The circumstances in which an equitable easement may arise are considered at para 2.7 ff.

1.4    The extent to which each sort of easement endures through changes in title is considered at para 5.1 ff. Because an easement benefits a 'dominant tenement' it does not exist 'in gross', i.e. it cannot be separated from the land which benefits from it.

## DISTINCTION FROM RESTRICTIVE COVENANT

1.5    Landowners can agree between themselves as a matter of contract what they may or may not do on their respective lands. Light may thus be protected by covenants given by the owner of 'servient land'. Such restrictions might give the owner of the 'dominant land' a right to protection of his light because of the restrictions agreed which stop or restrict building on the 'servient' land. This is not what one usually refers to as a 'right of light' (which, as we explain above,[9] is commonly regarded as a sort of easement).

1.6    Further, the rules by which such agreements benefit and bind successors to the original contracting parties are not straightforward. If successors in title to freehold land are to benefit from, or to be burdened by, this sort of covenant, certain conditions must be met. The principles

---

5    Law of Property Act 1925, s 1(2)(a).

6    See para 2.4 ff.

7    See para 2.44 ff.

8    See paras 2.77 and 5.2.

9    See para 1.1.

by which a covenant may be enforced against a successor to the original covenantor may be summarised as follows:[10]

(a) For a subsequent purchaser of the land subject to the covenant to be bound by the covenant there are three requirements:

    (i) the covenant must be negative in nature;

    (ii) the covenant must be either:

        (1) for the protection of land retained by the covenantee; or

        (2) part of a scheme; and

    (iii) the subsequent purchaser must have notice of the covenant. In the modern context, registration has taken the place of notice.

(b) For the subsequent purchaser of the other land to be able to enforce the covenant, there are also three requirements:

    (i) the covenant must, to use the old expression, touch and concern his land;

    (ii) the benefit of the covenant must have passed to him by:

        (1) annexation;

        (2) assignment; or

        (3) pursuant to a scheme; and

    (iii) there must be no good grounds for depriving him of the right to enforce the covenant.

As between landlord and tenant, covenants may be enforced under the general law of landlord and tenant whether such covenants are positive or negative.[11]

1.7    As the law stands, restrictive covenants may be modified by the Upper Tribunal (Lands Chamber) under the provisions of section 84(1) of

---

[10]   See *Whitgift Homes Ltd v Stocks* [2001] EWCA Civ 1732 at [12].

[11]   See Landlord and Tenant (Covenants) Act 1995; Law of Property Act 1925, ss 141 and 142.

the Law of Property Act 1925. These statutory provisions do not at present[12] apply to easements and thus are not applicable to rights of light.

1.8    This sort of protection of light is generally outside the scope of this book but is considered briefly below.[13]

## STATUTORY PROTECTION OF LIGHT: THE PLANNING SYSTEM?

1.9    While the impact on amenity due to loss of light to a building adjoining proposed development can be relevant to deciding whether or not planning permission for that development should be granted, the planning system is entirely separate from the law of rights of light. The planning system does not create enforceable rights to light as such. The following points should be noted.

1.10    The impact on amenity of residents and neighbours to development is plainly a potentially material consideration in deciding whether or not planning permission should be granted,[14] but the impact on private legal rights is not such a material consideration.[15]

1.11    Conversely, the grant of planning permission will, in general, be of no relevance in determining whether or not a right of light would be infringed by a permitted development. In this context, three points should be noted:

(a)    The grant of planning permission for development does not in itself authorise an interference with a right of light (but it is a necessary pre-condition to the overriding of rights of light under the statutory procedures available under section 237 of the Town and Country Planning Act 1990, which are dealt with at para 9.6 ff).

---

[12]    However, the Law Commission has recommended that the Upper Tribunal will have jurisdiction to discharge or modify rights of light: see para 11.5.

[13]    See para 4.11.

[14]    *Stringer v Minister for Housing and Local Government* [1971] 1 All ER 65.

[15]    See e.g. *Brewer v Secretary of State for the Environment* [1998] JPL 480.

(b) 'Public benefit' may be relevant in determining whether to restrain an interference with rights of light by injunction. This is considered further at para 10.39 ff. But the fact that a local planning authority considered that a proposed development would enhance a neighbourhood will not *in itself* determine whether or not the court will intervene to prevent or cure an infringement of a right of light by that development.[16]

(c) The methods of assessing the impact of development on 'sunlight' and 'daylight' for town planning purposes are not those used for determining whether or not a private right of light is interfered with. The usual method of assessment for planning purposes is found in the *Site Layout Planning for Daylight and Sunlight: A Guide to Good Practice*,[17] which incorporates the British Standards Institution's *Code of practice for daylighting*.[18] The criteria employed are different from those usually deployed for deciding whether or not rights of light would be infringed. This is considered further in Appendix A.[19]

## STATUTORY PROTECTION OF LIGHT: HIGH HEDGES

1.12   Under Part 8 of the Anti-Social Behaviour Act 2003, owners and occupiers of 'domestic property' may complain to local authorities if a hedge is over 2 m high, mostly evergreen or semi-evergreen and acts as a barrier to light so that the reasonable enjoyment of that domestic property is adversely affected. In such circumstances, local authorities have powers to serve a remedial notice requiring work to the hedge (with the possibility of an appeal to the Secretary of State). Failure to comply with notices may lead to prosecution. While the entitlement of residential occupiers to make a complaint together with the powers of local authorities to take action does protect the amenity of residential occupiers, these provisions do not create a 'right of light' strictly so called. The entitlement gives the owner

---

[16]   See para 10.42.

[17]   Littlefair, P (2011), *Site Layout Planning for Daylight and Sunlight: A Guide to Good Practice* (2nd edn), BR209, BRE Press.

[18]   British Standards Institution (2008), *Lighting for buildings. Code of practice for daylighting*, BS 8206-2:2008, British Standards Institution.

[19]   See Appendix A30 ff.

of land with the benefit of light no directly enforceable right against a person who blocks that light. The relevant statutory provisions are found in Appendix C9.

# Chapter 2

# Rights of Light: Creation

## INTRODUCTION

2.1    As with other easements, there are three ways in which a right of light may be created:

(a)  by statute;

(b)  by act of the parties, which may give rise:

    (i)   to express rights; or

    (ii)  to implied rights;

(c)  by long enjoyment (prescription).

This chapter considers each method of creating a right of light.

## STATUTE

2.2    Easements can be created by statute.[1] In contexts other than rights of light, there are numerous statutes under which rights may be created for the benefit of land. In practice, such statutes are unlikely in a normal case to be applicable when considering the existence of a right of light. The statutes most likely to be of potential relevance are those which give rights to tenants. First, there are statutes under which a lessee or groups of lessees are entitled to acquire the freehold of the premises of which they are

---

[1]    See Gaunt, J and Morgan, Mr Justice (eds) (2012), *Gale on Easements* (19th edn), Sweet & Maxwell, at para 3-02.

tenants or to acquire long leases.[2] These statutes make provision for the grant and reservation of easements.[3] Secondly, under Part II of the Landlord and Tenant Act 1954 business tenants have security of tenure and are entitled to seek new leases of premises to which the Act applies.[4] On the face of things, new leases will include rights granted to or reserved over the demised premises except as otherwise agreed between the parties or determined by the court.[5] Thirdly, in the absence of agreement to the contrary, section 62 of the Law of Property Act 1925 imports words into conveyances by which rights of light may be granted: these provisions are considered at para 2.39 ff in the context of easements created by grant.

## CREATION BY ACT OF PARTIES

2.3    A landowner may agree expressly or impliedly that his land is subject to an easement of light benefitting the land of another. Such rights of light can take effect as legal or equitable easements. What is required to create each differs.

### Creation of legal easements

2.4    A legal easement over land can exist only as an interest equivalent to an estate in fee simple absolute in possession or a term of years absolute.[6] Thus, for instance, the grant of an easement for life cannot take effect as a legal easement but only as an equitable easement. There is nothing, however, to preclude the owner of a servient tenement granting a legal easement to a leasehold owner of the dominant land.

---

[2]    Primarily, the Leasehold Reform Act 1967; the Housing Act 1985; the Leasehold Reform, Housing and Urban Development Act 1993.

[3]    Leasehold Reform Act 1967, ss 8 and 9; see *Kent v Kavanagh* [2006] EWCA Civ 162, [2007] Ch 1; Housing Act 1985, Sch 6; Leasehold Reform, Housing and Urban Development Act 1993, s 57, Schs 7 and 9.

[4]    Landlord and Tenant Act 1954, ss 23, 24 and 29.

[5]    See Landlord and Tenant Act 1954, s 32(3).

[6]    Law of Property Act 1925, s 1(2)(a). See also para 1.3.

2.5    To create a legal easement by a grant, it is necessary for the grant to be by deed.[7]

2.6    Where an easement is established by prescription,[8] it also takes effect as a legal easement.[9] As explained below, the law of prescription originates from the presumption of a grant by deed.

2.7    The effect of a legal easement on successors to the original servient owner is considered below.[10]

## Creation of equitable easements

2.8    An equitable easement may be created otherwise than by deed. An equitable easement may be created otherwise than for an interest equivalent to a fee simple absolute in possession or for a term of years absolute.

2.9    An agreement to grant an easement is a disposition of an interest in land and, until completed, may take effect as the grant of an equitable easement. To be an enforceable agreement, however, the requirements of section 2 of the Law of Property (Miscellaneous Provisions) Act 1989 must be fulfilled. Under these provisions, a contract for the sale or other disposition of an interest in land can only be made in writing and only by incorporating all the terms which the parties have expressly agreed in one document or, where contracts are exchanged, in each.[11] The terms may be incorporated in a document either by being set out in it or by reference to some other document.[12] The document incorporating the terms, or where contacts are exchanged, one of the documents incorporating them (but not necessarily the same one), must be signed on behalf of each party to the

---

[7]    Law of Property Act 1925, s 52. See Law of Property (Miscellaneous Provisions) Act 1989, s 1 for the formalities required.

[8]    See para 2.44 ff.

[9]    See para 2.77.

[10]    See para 5.1 ff.

[11]    Law of Property (Miscellaneous Provisions) Act 1989, s 2(1). These requirements do not apply to contracts to grant short leases under Law of Property Act 1925, s 54(2), contracts made in the course of public auctions or contracts regulated under the Financial Services and Markets Act 2000 (subject to certain exceptions: see s 2(5)).

[12]    Law of Property (Miscellaneous Provisions) Act 1989, s 2(2).

contract.[13] These provisions, however, do not affect the creation or operation of resulting, implied or constructive trusts.[14]

2.10 In limited cases, it is possible for an agreement which does not comply with these provisions to be enforceable in equity by operation of the doctrine of proprietary estoppel. This may be so in:

> those cases in which a supposed bargain has been so fully performed by one side, and the general circumstances of the matter are such, that it would be inequitable to disregard the claimant's expectations, and insufficient to grant him no more than a restitutionary remedy.[15]

2.11 The principles of proprietary estoppel have applied in the context of the law of easements.[16] In *Crabb v Arun District Council*,[17] the defendants, knowing of the plaintiff's intention to sell his land in separate portions, led the plaintiff to believe that he would be granted a right of access and encouraged him to act to his detriment in selling part of his land without reserving a right of way over it. It was held that there was an estoppel and an equity in the plaintiff's favour and that the plaintiff was entitled to a right of way. Scarman LJ[18] said that the law was correctly stated by Lord Kingsdown in *Ramsden v Dyson*[19] (in the context of a landlord and tenant dispute):

> The rule of law applicable to the case appears to me to be this: If a man, under a verbal agreement with a landlord for a certain interest in land, or what amounts to the same thing, under an expectation, created or encouraged by the landlord, that he shall have a certain interest, takes possession of such land, with the consent of the landlord, and upon the

---

[13]  Law of Property (Miscellaneous Provisions) Act 1989, s 2(3).

[14]  Law of Property (Miscellaneous Provisions) Act 1989, s 2(5).

[15]  *Yaxley v Gotts* [2000] Ch 162 at 180, per Robert Walker LJ. See also generally *Cobbe v Yeoman's Row Management Ltd* [2008] UKHL 55, [2008] 1 WLR 1752.

[16]  See *Crabb v Arun District Council* [1976] Ch 179; *Ward v Kirland* [1967] Ch 194; *Valentine v Allen* [2003] EWCA Civ 915; *Sweet v Sommer* [2004] EWHC 1504 (Ch), [2005] EWCA Civ 227; *Bexley LBC v Maison Maurice Ltd* [2006] EWHC 3192 (Ch); [2007] 1 EGLR 19.

[17]  *Crabb v Arun District Council* [1976] Ch 179.

[18]  *Crabb v Arun District Council* [1976] Ch 179 at 193–194.

[19]  *Ramsden v Dyson* (1866) LR 1 HL 129 at 170.

faith of such promise or expectation, with the knowledge of the landlord, and without objection by him, lays out money upon the land, a Court of equity will compel the landlord to give effect to such promise or expectation.

There is no reason why these principles should not in appropriate circumstances apply in relation to a right of light.

2.12 The requirements for registration and the extent to which equitable easements are binding on successors to the servient owner are considered below.[20] The topic is far from straightforward.

## The nature of the rights which can be the subject matter of a grant (express or implied)

2.13 Where parties enter into an agreement or transaction relating to property, easements may be granted expressly or implicitly. It is necessary to construe the terms of a particular transaction in its circumstances to discern whether such a grant has been made. The principles by which contractual arrangements are construed are now well known. They are considered further in Chapter 4.[21]

2.14 Whether express or implied, however, a right can only be granted as an easement if the law will recognise the right as such. Thus, there is no easement of view[22] or privacy.[23] Still more pertinently, it has been held that a right to light cannot be acquired by prescription in respect of vacant land.[24] It seems, therefore, that to be the subject matter of an easement of light, the light must be enjoyed with a building or structure on the dominant land and *ex hypothesi* the light must be able to enter the building

---

[20] See para 5.1 ff.

[21] See in particular para 4.2 ff.

[22] *Aldred's Case* (1610) 9 Co Rep 57(b); *Dalton v Angus* (1881) 6 App Cas 740 at 824; *Harris v De Pinna* (1886) 33 ChD 238 at 262; *Browne v Flower* [1911] 1 Ch 219 at 225; *Campbell v Paddington Corp* [1911] 1 KB 869 at 875 and 876.

[23] *Chandler v Thompson* (1811) 3 Camp 80; *Dalton v Angus* (1881) 6 App Cas 740 at 764; *Browne v Flower* [1911] 1 Ch 219 at 225.

[24] *Roberts v Macord* (1832) 1 Mood & R 230; see paras 2.62 and 2.67 ff.

through an aperture.[25] Of course, there is nothing to prevent parties entering into restrictive covenants to keep servient land undeveloped.[26]

2.15   There is no reason, however, why in appropriate circumstances a right of a specific extent should not be granted beyond that which might, for instance, be acquired by prescription. Thus in *Browne v Flower*,[27] Parker J stated a:

> ... lease of a building to be used for a special purpose requiring an extraordinary amount of light might well be held to preclude the grantor from diminishing the light passing to the grantee's windows, even in cases where the diminution would not be such as to create a nuisance within the meaning of recent decision.

The extent of an expressly or impliedly granted right of light will depend on the construction of each grant in its context. General principles of construction are considered in more detail at para 4.2 ff.

## Express grants

2.16   Express grants of rights of light between owners of adjoining parcels of land are sometimes made. Such grants often occur to compromise disputes between parties about their respective rights. This sort of dispute often happens when one party wishes to develop its land in a way to which the other objects.[28] Sometimes, express grants of rights of light are found coupled with restrictive covenants.[29]

2.17   As mentioned above,[30] section 62 of the Law of Property Act 1925 imports general words in conveyances as if these words were *expressly* set out in the conveyance.[31] These words have been held to apply to rights of light and are considered in detail at para 2.39 ff.

---

[25]   See para 2.62 and 2.71 ff; and see para 7.10 for circumstances in which an aperture may be blocked.

[26]   See paras 1.5 and 4.11.

[27]   *Browne v Flower* [1911] 1 Ch 219 at 226.

[28]   See para 4.1 ff concerning deeds.

[29]   See para 4.1.

[30]   See para 2.2.

[31]   See para 2.40.

## Implied grants: generally

2.18 An easement may be implied into a document which does not expressly refer to the grant of a right.[32] As with express grants, there is no reason, in principle, why in appropriate circumstances there might not be implied a right of light of a specified extent (beyond that which might, for instance, be acquired by prescription).[33] This might occur where the parties contemplated that premises were to be used for a specific purpose for which the maintenance of a certain level of light was necessary.

2.19 While there are specific principles which are applicable to easements and these are considered below, there is nothing to exclude the general principles of contractual construction when determining whether an easement is implicit in a transaction. These general principles of construction are considered in more detail in Chapter 4. In practice, however, implied terms may arise in a number of ways consistently with the general approach to the construction of contracts.[34]

2.20 First, where land granted or retained would be rendered completely unusable without the implication of an easement, then an easement of 'necessity' may be implied (albeit that the law takes a stricter approach in relation to implied reservations).[35] While light may be important to the use of land, its absence is unlikely to render land wholly unusable (as it would, for instance, be rendered unusable if it were landlocked without any right of way). A right of light, therefore, is unlikely to be implied as an easement of 'necessity'.

2.21 Secondly, where the grant contains particular words of description or other words, then a right may be implied from those words even though express words of grant are not used. Such implications have been made in

---

[32] See e.g. *Roberts v Karr* (1809) 1 Taunt 495 (description of land released as abutting road implicitly precluded grantor from denying access from road over retained verge). See also *Lyttleton Times Co Ltd v Warners Ltd* [1907] AC 476; *Yankwood Ltd v Havering LBC* [1998] EGCS 75.

[33] See para 2.15 and *Browne v Flower* [1911] 1 Ch 219 at 226.

[34] See para 4.4 ff.

[35] See generally *Nickerson v Barraclough* [1981] Ch 426; *Adealon International Litd v Merton LBC* [2007] EWCA Civ 362; [2007] 1 WLR 1898.

a number of cases concerning rights of way,[36] and there is no reason why a right of light could not be implied into a grant in a similar way.

2.22    Thirdly, if it is concluded that a particular use of land by a grantee was intended by the parties, then an easement may be implied.[37] In *Pwllbach Colliery Co v Woodman*,[38] Lord Parker said:

> The law will readily imply the grant or reservation of such easements as may be necessary to give effect to the common intention of the parties to a grant of real property, with reference to the manner or purposes in and for which the land granted or some land retained by the grantor is used.

Thus, if it were concluded that it was the common intention of the parties that land was to be used for artists' studios or greenhouses (for instance, if restrictive covenants were imposed limiting how the land was to be used), then an easement of light sufficient to make the land usable for those purposes might be inferred: such a right to light would be necessary to give effect to that common intention.

2.23    Fourthly, an easement may be implied where if one were not, the grantor would be in derogation from what he has granted.[39]

2.24    Fifthly, as a particular application of the principle that a grantor may not derogate from his grant, an easement may be implied under the 'rule in *Wheeldon v Burrows*'. This sort of implication is commonly found in the cases concerning rights of light and is considered further at para 2.26 ff.

2.25    Sixthly, by section 62 of the Law of Property Act 1925, conveyances are 'deemed' to include easements and rights unless an

---

[36]  See e.g. *Roberts v Karr* (1809) 1 Taunt 495; *Espley v Wilkes* (1872) LR 7 Exch 298; *Rudd v Bowles* [1912] 2 Ch 60.

[37]  See e.g. *Hall v Lund* (1863) 1 H & C 676; *Lyttleton Times Co Ltd v Warners Ltd* [1907] AC 476; *Jones v Pritchard* [1908] 1 Ch 630.

[38]  *Pwllbach Colliery Co v Woodman* [1915] AC 634 at 646. See also *Re Walmsley and Shaw's Contract* [1916] 1 Ch 93 at 98; *Stafford v Lee* (1993) 65 P & CR 172; *Donovan v Rana* [2014] EWCA Civ 99 at [30].

[39]  See *Browne v Flower* [1911] 1 Ch 219 at 224–225, per Parker J.

intention to the contrary is found. This occurs because general words are imported by statute into the conveyance and is not strictly 'implication' of the sort discussed above. This sort of 'implication' also requires particular consideration in relation to rights of light. It is considered further at para 2.39 ff.

## Implied grants: *Wheeldon v Burrows*

2.26 The 'rule' in *Wheeldon v Burrows*[40] pre-dates the modern exposition of when terms will be implied and how documents must be construed in their contexts. However, it can be seen as an early acknowledgment that the circumstances surrounding a grant are an important factor in determining how the grant is to be construed and its extent. It is part of the principle that a person cannot derogate from his grant.

2.27 *Wheeldon v Burrows* concerned a workshop and an adjacent piece of land belonging to the same owner. First, the piece of land was sold at auction and soon afterwards conveyed to the purchaser. A month after this, the vendor agreed to sell the workshop to another person and subsequently conveyed it to him. The workshop had windows overlooking and receiving light from the piece of land. It was held that as the vendor had not, when he conveyed the piece of land, reserved the right of access of light to the windows, no right of light passed to the purchaser of the workshop, and that the purchaser of the land could obstruct the workshop.

2.28 The principle was summarised by Thesiger LJ as follows:[41]

> ... on the grant by the owner of a tenement of part of that tenement as it is then used and enjoyed, there will pass to the grantee all those continuous and apparent easements (by which, of course, I mean quasi-easements), or in other words all those easements which are necessary to the reasonable enjoyment of the property granted, and which have been and are at the time of the grant used by the owners of the entirety for the benefit of the part granted.

---

[40] *Wheeldon v Burrows* (1879) 12 ChD 31.

[41] *Wheeldon v Burrows* (1879) 12 ChD 31 at 49.

The problem for the owner of the workshop was that when the workshop was sold to him, his vendor had retained no rights over the land which could be enjoyed with the workshop (implied reservations are considered further below).[42] However, the case reiterated that on a disposal of a building deriving light from adjoining land owned by the disposing party, there will be implied a right for the building to enjoy light over the adjoining land (in the absence of something indicating the contrary).[43]

2.29 In principle, the implication may arise on any conveyance or transfer of land. It does not matter that the disposition is by a mortgagee pursuant to its powers of sale.[44] This applies equally to the grant of a lease of land where the landlord retains land as it does to freehold land.[45] It is important, therefore, that in a lease the lessor should reserve the right to build on adjoining land if it wishes to ensure that it is entitled so to do without infringing the tenant's rights. The manner in which lessors and other grantors may reserve to themselves the right to build on adjoining land is considered at para 3.8 ff.

2.30 In principle, if the *mortgagor* makes a disposition which is authorised by the mortgagee or under statutory powers so as to bind the mortgagee, then there is nothing to preclude the implication of a right into such disposition also binding the mortgagee. On the other hand, if the mortgagor makes a disposition *not* binding on the mortgagee, in principle any implication would not bind the mortgagee[46] (albeit that it would bind the mortgagor and his successors[47]).

2.31 Whether or not the 'rule' in *Wheeldon v Burrows* will result in the implication of a right of light will depend on the circumstances. Thus, the 'rule' will apply where at the time of the disposition (or prior agreement to dispose) it is known that the land is being acquired for building purposes in circumstances where the enjoyment of light over the grantor's land is

---

[42]  See para 2.35.

[43]  See *Swansborough v Coventry* (1832) 9 Bing 305 at 309; *Leech v Schweder* (1874) 9 Ch App 463 at 472.

[44]  *Born v Turner* [1900] 2 Ch 211.

[45]  *Leech v Schweder* (1874) 9 Ch App 463 at 472.

[46]  *Davies v Thomas* [1899] WN 244.

[47]  *Beddington v Atlee* (1877) 35 ChD 317 at 322, per Chitty J.

necessary for the reasonable enjoyment of the buildings to be so constructed: in such a case the right will attach to the buildings when constructed.[48]

2.32   On the other hand, an implication will not be made where such an implication would deprive the grantor of the benefit of something which at the date of the grant (or preceding agreement) it was contemplated he was to have following the grant. So in the case of *Birmingham, Dudley and District Banking Co v Ross*,[49] it was held that where at the time of the grant of a lease the land retained by the grantor was laid out for building, the grantee could not complain about an interference with his rights by that building.

2.33   The onus, however, of establishing factual circumstances which negative an implicit grant will fall on the (putative) grantor.[50] The mere fact that the retained land was contemplated as being built on will not in itself preclude the implication of a right of light.[51] What was contemplated on the retained land, however, will determine the precise extent of any right to be implied. Thus, in *Swansborough v Coventry*,[52] where the retained land was described as 'a piece of freehold building ground' and there had stood a low building recently demolished, the vendor and his successors were entitled to build to the extent of the former building but not beyond. Similarly, in *Myers v Catterson*,[53] where a railway company sold a piece of land near a railway line including a viaduct for the construction of a house, it was held that the retained land could be used for railway purposes but it was held that the company was obliged not to interfere with the plaintiff's lights by anything not required for those purposes. Accordingly, the grantee was entitled to enjoy the light through

---

[48]   *Miles v Tobin* (1868) 17 LT 432; *Robinson v Grave* (1873) WR 569; *Bailey v Icke* (1891) 64 LT 789; *Pollard v Gare* [1901] 1 Ch 834; *Frederick Betts Ltd v Pickfords Ltd* [1906] 2 Ch 87.

[49]   *Birmingham, Dudley and District Banking Co v Ross* (1888) 38 ChD 295; see also *Godwin v Schweppes Ltd* [1902] 1 Ch 926.

[50]   *Broomfield v Williams* [1897] 1 Ch 602 at 610 (a case decided on the implication of general words under Conveyancing Act 1881, s 6).

[51]   See e.g. *Pollard v Gare* [1901] 1 Ch 834.

[52]   *Swansborough v Coventry* (1832) 9 Bing 305.

[53]   *Myers v Catterson* (1890) 43 ChD 470.

arches in the viaduct, and the grantor's lessee was not entitled to block them up.

2.34   The rule in *Wheeldon v Burrows*, however, operates only to the extent that it is not inconsistent with the intention of the parties which might be inferred from the circumstances.[54] So where words are imported into a conveyance by section 62 of the Law of Property Act 1925, there is perhaps little or no scope for an implication under *Wheeldon v Burrows*.[55]

## Implied reservations on the disposal of part?

2.35   In general, when a landowner disposes of part of his land, no reservation of an easement in favour of his retained land will be implied.[56] Likewise, if the landowner grants a lease of part of his land but fails to reserve an easement of light over the part demised, the retained land will normally enjoy no right to light during the term of the lease.[57] On the face of things, the reservation would be inconsistent with an outright grant.[58] Each case, however, needs to be viewed in its particular circumstances. Thus, for instance, where the retained land is landlocked, then rights of way may be impliedly reserved. It is unlikely, however, in most ordinary situations that an implied right of light would be reserved on the disposal of part.[59]

2.36   The position, however, is different where an owner of two adjoining properties (A and B) grants to someone a tenancy of A with the benefit of an easement over land retained by him and then subsequently grants to someone else a lease of B. In such a case, the lease of B is subject to a

---

[54]   *Selby District Council v Samuel Smith Old Brewery (Tadcaster)* (2000) 80 P & CR 466. See para 2.32.

[55]   See e.g. *Wood v Waddington* [2015] EWCA Civ 538 at [36].

[56]   See *Suffield v Brown* (1864) 4 De G J & S 185 at 195; *Crossley & Sons Ltd v Lightowler* (1867) 2 Ch App 478 at 486; *Wheeldon v Burrows* (1879) 12 Ch 31 at 49.

[57]   *Re Webb's Lease* [1951] Ch 808.

[58]   *Wheeldon v Burrows* (1879) 12 Ch 31. See also *Suffield v Brown* (1864) 4 De G J & S 185.

[59]   See para 2.20 (easements of necessity).

reservation of the easement in favour of the tenant of A.[60] Clearly, in such a situation it must have been intended that the lease of B would be subject to a reservation to enable the rights of the tenant of A to continue to be enjoyed.

2.37 Sometimes, conditions of sale contained in contracts expressly provide that where the vendor retains land, it will enjoy the benefit of reservations over the land sold as if the land retained had been simultaneously conveyed to a different purchaser. This by express terms effectively reserves to the vendor rights equivalent to those which would pass on a conveyance under *Wheeldon v Burrows*.[61] However, as with *Wheeldon v Burrows*, whether a quasi-easement will pass will depend on the circumstances and the implication of a right may be negatived. Thus, where an option to repurchase land was granted in circumstances where the parties intended to restore the position as it was before the original purchase, the vendor was not entitled to easements of the 'rights' which his retained property had enjoyed over the land reconveyed, but over which he had not acquired easements at the date of the original grant.[62]

## Implied easements on simultaneous dispositions?

2.38 On the other hand, where a landowner disposes of two plots of land simultaneously, each part enjoys by implication the same easements over the other part as if that other part had been retained.[63] 'Simultaneity' in this context does not necessarily require precise temporal simultaneity of the two transactions; 'ultimately the question is whether they are to be regarded as in effect part and parcel of a single transaction'.[64] Where dispositions are preceded by contracts, the question will be determined by the dates of the contracts rather than the dates of completion of the conveyances or transfers.[65]

---

[60] See *Thomas v Owen* (1888) 20 QBD 225; *Aldridge v Wright* [1929] 2 KB 117 at 130–131; see generally Gaunt, J and Morgan, Mr Justice (eds) (2012), *Gale on Easements* (19th edn), Sweet & Maxwell, at para 3-108 ff.

[61] But without the necessity that the rights must be necessary for the reasonable enjoyment of the dominant land: see *Wood v Waddington* [2015] EWCA Civ 538.

[62] *Selby District Council v Samuel Smith Old Brewery (Tadcaster)* (2000) 80 P & CR 466.

[63] *Russell v Watts* (1884) 25 ChD 559 at 584.

[64] *Donaldson v Smith* [2007] 1 P & CR D4 at [16]. See also *Wood v Waddington* [2014] EWHC 1358 (Ch) at [105], per Morgan J.

[65] *White v Taylor (No 2)* [1969] 1 Ch 150.

## Words imported by Law of Property Act 1925, section 62

2.39    Section 62 of the Law of Property Act 1925 provides:

(1)    A conveyance of land shall be deemed to include and shall by virtue of this Act operate to convey, with the land, all buildings, erections, fixtures, commons, hedges, ditches, fences, ways, waters, water-courses, liberties, privileges, easements, rights, and advantages whatsoever, appertaining or reputed to appertain to the land, or any part thereof, or, at the time of conveyance, demised, occupied, or enjoyed with, or reputed or known as part or parcel of or appurtenant to the land or any part thereof.

(2)    A conveyance of land, having houses or other buildings thereon, shall be deemed to include and shall by virtue of this Act operate to convey, with the land, houses, or other buildings, all outhouses, erections, fixtures, cellars, areas, courts, courtyards, cisterns, sewers, gutters, drains, ways, passages, lights, watercourses, liberties, privileges, easements, rights, and advantages whatsoever, appertaining or reputed to appertain to the land, houses, or other buildings conveyed, or any of them, or any part thereof, or, at the time of conveyance, demised, occupied, or enjoyed with, or reputed or known as part or parcel of or appurtenant to, the land, houses, or other buildings conveyed, or any of them, or any part thereof.

(3)    A conveyance of a manor shall be deemed to include and shall by virtue of this Act operate to convey, with the manor, all pastures, feedings, wastes, warrens, commons, mines, minerals, quarries, furzes, trees, woods, underwoods, coppices, and the ground and soil thereof, fishings, fisheries, fowlings, courts leet, courts baron, and other courts, view of frankpledge and all that to view of frankpledge doth belong, mills, mulctures, customs, tolls, duties, reliefs, heriots, fines, sums of money, amerciaments, waifs, estrays, chief-rents, quitrents, rentscharge, rents seck, rents of assize, fee farm rents, services, royalties jurisdictions, franchises, liberties, privileges, easements, profits, advantages, rights, emoluments, and hereditaments whatsoever, to the manor appertaining or reputed to appertain, or, at the time of conveyance, demised, occupied, or enjoyed with the same, or reputed or known as part, parcel, or member thereof.

For the purposes of this subsection the right to compensation for manorial incidents on the extinguishment thereof shall be deemed to be a right appertaining to the manor.

(4)  This section applies only if and as far as a contrary intention is not expressed in the conveyance, and has effect subject to the terms of the conveyance and to the provisions therein contained.

(5)  This section shall not be construed as giving to any person a better title to any property, right, or thing in this section mentioned than the title which the conveyance gives to him to the land or manor expressed to be conveyed, or as conveying to him any property, right, or thing in this section mentioned, further or otherwise than as the same could have been conveyed to him by the conveying parties.

(6)  This section applies to conveyances made after the thirty-first day of December, eighteen hundred and eighty-one.

2.40  The effect of this section (which re-enacts section 6 of the Conveyancing Act 1881) is that words are imported automatically into conveyances unless the contrary intention is expressed. This is a sort of 'implication' but can be distinguished from easements implied as a result of construing agreements in their surrounding circumstances in the way considered above.[66] The statute removes the need for 'general words' which were commonly set out in conveyances making express provision for the grant of rights. When the words are imported into a conveyance in this way, one is dealing with an express grant of the rights in question.[67]

2.41  A 'conveyance' includes a mortgage, charge, lease, assent, vesting declaration, vesting instrument, disclaimer, release and every other assurance of property or an interest therein by any instrument, except a will.[68] Therefore, it includes instruments which transfer or create a legal estate in freehold land. This includes a tenancy agreement for a term not exceeding 3 years.[69] It does not apply to agreements which create only equitable interests such as an agreement for a lease exceeding 3 years.[70]

---

[66]  See para 2.18 ff.

[67]  *Broomfield v Williams* [1897] 1 Ch 602 at 610; *Gregg v Richards* [1926] 1 Ch 521 at 534; *Wood v Waddington* [2014] EWHC 1358 (Ch) at [104], [2015] EWCA Civ 538.

[68]  Law of Property Act 1925, s 205(1)(ii).

[69]  *Wright v Macadam* [1949] 2 AC 744.

[70]  *Borman v Griffith* [1930] 1 Ch 493. See also paras 2.3–2.12, 5.2 and 5.3 for the distinction between legal and equitable easements.

Because this provision applies to conveyances it does not apply to oral tenancies.[71]

2.42   So far as relevant, the effect and limits of section 62 of the Law of Property Act 1925 can be summarised as follows:

(a)   Section 62 is not relevant to existing easements appurtenant to the land conveyed. This is because such easements pass with the land automatically and without the need for any words in the conveyance.[72]

(b)   The words imported by section 62 have the effect of creating by express grant new easements out of 'quasi-easements'.[73] Quasi-easements are rights habitually exercised by someone over part of his own land which, if the part in question were owned and occupied by another, would be easements.[74] The question is not one of title, but the question of *fact* of enjoyment.[75]

(c)   Unlike former quasi-easements implied as easements on a conveyance under the rule in *Wheeldon v Burrows*,[76] quasi-easements within the ambit of a grant under section 62 need not be continuous and apparent (if there is diversity of occupation of the relevant tenements) nor need they be reasonably necessary to the enjoyment of the property granted; they can be simply convenient.[77]

---

[71]   *Rye v Rye* [1962] AC 496.

[72]   *Godwin v Schweppes Ltd* [1902] 1 Ch 926 at 932. Where a person is registered as proprietor of land easements appurtenant to the land of which he is proprietor vest in him by statute: see Land Registration Act 2002, ss 11(3) and 12(3) (the estate is vested in the proprietor together with all interests subsisting for the benefit of the estate).

[73]   See *Crow v Wood* [1971] 1 QB 77.

[74]   *Wheeldon v Burrows* (1879) 12 ChD 31 at 49; Harpum, C, Bridge, S and Dixon, M (2012), *Megarry & Wade: The Law of Real Property* (8th edn), Sweet & Maxwell, at para 27-03.

[75]   *International Tea Stores v Hobbs* [1903] 2 Ch 165 at 172; *Wall v Collins* [2007] EWCA Civ 444, [2007] Ch 290 at [24].

[76]   See para 2.26 ff.

[77]   See *Goldberg v Edwards* [1950] 247. See *Long v Gowlett* [1923] 2 Ch 17; *Wood v Waddington* [2014] EWHC 1358 (Ch), [2015] EWCA Civ 538.

(d) So, where at the time of a conveyance a right was enjoyed under a licence,[78] or was customarily exercised but of unknown origin,[79] or reputed to be exercised,[80] or was continuous and apparent,[81] it could be granted as an easement by the words imported into the conveyance by section 62.

(e) Accordingly, section 62 will apply if at the time of the grant there was either:

    (i)    prior diversity of occupation of the dominant and servient tenements with the advantage being enjoyed with the former over the latter;[82] or

    (ii)   if there was no diversity of occupation the 'right' was continuous and apparent.[83]

The ultimate question is whether the advantage in question was, on the facts, 'enjoyed with' the land conveyed.[84] It is settled that quasi-easements of light will pass under the general words.[85] This has been described as an exception,[86] but it is now established that continuous and apparent easements pass under the general words either because they are enjoyed with the land or because they appertain or are reputed to appertain to it.[87] The light enjoyed by a parcel conveyed

---

[78]   *International Tea Stores Co v Hobbs* [1903] 2 Ch 164; *Wright v Macadam* [1949] 2 KB 744; see also *Commission for New Towns v J J Gallagher Ltd* [2002] EWHC 2668 (Ch), [2003] 2 P & CR 3 at [61].

[79]   *White v Williams* [1922] 1 KB 727; *Crown v Wood* [1971] 1 QB 77 at 87.

[80]   *Handel v St Stephens Close Ltd* [1994] 1 EGLR 70 at 71.

[81]   *Bayley v Great Western Railway* (1884) 26 ChD 434.

[82]   *Sovmots Investments Ltd v Secretary of State for the Environment* [1979] AC 144 at 176.

[83]   *Long v Gowlett* [1923] 2 Ch 177 at 198–199; *P & S Platt Ltd v Crouch* [2003] EWCA Civ 11; *Wood v Waddington* [2014] EWHC 1358 (Ch) at [131] and [133]; see also [2015] EWCA Civ 538.

[84]   *Wood v Waddington* [2014] EWHC 1358 (Ch) at [133]; see also [2015] EWCA Civ 538.

[85]   See *Broomfield v Williams* [1897] 1 Ch 602; *Sovmots Investments Ltd v Secretary of State for the Environment* [1979] AC 144 at 176.

[86]   *Sovmots Investments Ltd v Secretary of State for the Environment* [1979] AC 144 at 176.

[87]   *P & S Platt Ltd v Crouch* [2003] EWCA Civ 110 at [42]; *Alford v Hannaford* [2011] EWCA Civ 1099 at [36].

over another can properly be said to be an 'advantage' enjoyed with the land conveyed within the meaning of section 62.[88]

(f)   Section 62 will only apply to rights which are capable of existing as an easement if granted[89] and will only operate where the grantor has power to make a grant.[90] A grant can only apply where the owner of the land over which the right is impliedly granted has a sufficient estate to support making such a grant. Section 62 is concerned with what is granted and it cannot include something which at the time of the relevant conveyance the grantor had no power to grant.[91]

(g)   Inchoate 'rights' in course of acquisition by prescription under the Prescription Act 1832 (but before they have been established) have been held to be within the scope of section 62 of the Law of Property Act 1925.[92] So, it was held that the benefit of the enjoyment of light over another's land (which in due course could be relied upon to establish a prescriptive right) passed upon the grant of a lease of the dominant land by operation of the words imported into the lease by section 62 and could be relied upon by the tenant subsequently to establish a prescriptive right under the 1832 Act. This might be justified on the basis that the enjoyment of light which might eventually be relied upon to establish a prescriptive right can be described to be an 'advantage ... appertaining or reputed to appertain to the land'. Unlike prescription arising by lost modern grant, all that needs to be established for a prescriptive right of light under the 1832 Act is that 'access and use of light to and for ... any ... building shall have been actually enjoyed therewith for the full period of 20 years'.[93] This suggestion, however, is inconsistent with the proposition that section 62 does not apply to a 'right' which the grantor has no power to grant. Since a right under the 1832 Act remains inchoate and is not crystallised until proceedings are commenced, until proceedings are commenced a landlord has no right capable of being granted.

---

[88]   See *Wood v Waddington* [2014] EWHC 1358 (Ch) at [111].

[89]   See *International Tea Stores Co v Hobbs* [1903] 2 Ch 164 at 172.

[90]   *Quicke v Chapman* [1903] 1 Ch 659.

[91]   *MRA Engineering Ltd v Trimster Co Ltd* (1988) 56 P & CR 1.

[92]   *Midtown Ltd v City of London Real Property Co Ltd* [2005] EWHC 33 (Ch) at [23].

[93]   See para 2.63 ff.

(h)  Importantly, section 62 operates 'only if and as far as a contrary intention is not expressed in the conveyance'. Plainly it is open to the parties by express and direct words to exclude the application of section 62. Clear words are required to negative the importation of the words of section 62 into a grant.[94] An intention, however, may in some circumstances be sufficiently clearly expressed by the parties where other express provisions are directly contradictory to a grant being made under the general words of section 62. Thus, a fencing covenant may negative the grant of a right of way pursuant to imported general words.[95] Similarly, in *Birmingham, Dudley & District Banking Co v Ross*,[96] it was held that where plots were sold as part of a building scheme, the purchaser of a plot could not assert a right of light 'under such circumstances as to show that there could be no expectation of its continuance'. On the other hand, the mere description of adjoining land as 'building land' was held not in itself sufficient to oust the importation of the general words and with it the benefit of a right of light.[97] Further, the express grant of a limited right is not in itself inconsistent with the importation of general words.[98] While the matter may be open to argument (depending on the context of any particular conveyance), it is commonly understood that an express provision excluding 'implied rights' from a conveyance will be sufficient to exclude the importation of the general words under section 62 even though (technically) these words are imported into a conveyance by statute rather than 'implied' by construction.[99]

---

[94]  *Gregg v Richards* [1926] Ch 531 at 535; *Commission for New Towns v J J Gallacher Ltd* [2002] EWHC 2668 (Ch) at [59]; *Wood v Waddington* [2015] EWCA Civ 538 at [59]–[67].

[95]  *Hillman v Rogers* [1997] EWCA Civ 3069; *Alford v Hannaford* [2011] EWCA Civ 1099 at [50].

[96]  *Birmingham, Dudley & District Banking Co v Ross* (1888) 38 ChD 295. See also *Selby District Council v Samuel Smith Old Brewery (Tadcaster) Ltd* (2000) 80 P & CR 466.

[97]  *Broomfield v Williams* [1897] 1 Ch 606 at 610.

[98]  *Snell and Prideaux Ltd v Dutton Mirrors Ltd* [1995] 1 EGLR 259 at 264M; see also *Alford v Hannaford* [2011] EWCA Civ 1099 at [39]; *Wood v Waddington* [2015] EWCA Civ 538.

[99]  Cf Gaunt, J and Morgan, Mr Justice (eds) (2012), *Gale on Easements* (19th edn), Sweet & Maxwell, at para 3-161.

## Restrictions on grants

2.43   In considering whether an instrument creates an easement of light it may be necessary to consider the capacity of the putative grantor. The Crown,[100] local authorities[101] and the Church of England[102] are limited in what they can grant. So, for instance, a grant can only be made in relation to church land by licence or faculty. This therefore restricts the extent to which the right of an easement can be made, and the nature of any contract purporting to grant a right will need to be construed in that context.[103]

# CREATION OF RIGHT OF LIGHT BY LONG ENJOYMENT: PRESCRIPTION

## Introduction: principles of prescription

2.44   As with other easements, rights of light may be acquired by 'prescription'. Prescription is a legal title acquired by long use. As mentioned above,[104] there are three sorts of prescription:

(a)   common law prescriptive rights deriving (at least notionally) from user since time immemorial, i.e. since 1189;

(b)   rights arising under the doctrine of lost modern grant, i.e. 20 years' uninterrupted user of light (for any period) 'as of right';[105]

(c)   prescription under the Prescription Act 1832.

---

[100]   Crown Lands Act 1702, and see para 2.78 ff.

[101]   E.g. Local Government Act 1972, s 123.

[102]   See generally Clashfern, Lord (2003) (re-issue), Vol 8(1), *Halsbury's Laws of England*, LexisNexis.

[103]   See *Re St Martin le Grand, York* [1990] Fam 63 at 76–77 (a faculty could not have conferred a right of way on a churchyard as it was consecrated land, but long use did confer a licence of infinite duration which could be terminated only by the faculty if the ordinary was put on notice that it was being abused and the consistory court determined that it should be terminated); cf *Re St Clement's, Leigh-on-Sea* [1988] 1 WLR 720 at 728.

[104]   See para 1.2.

[105]   *Tehidy Minerals v Norman* [1971] 2 QB 528 at 552.

The provisions relating to light in the 1832 Act, however, differ from the provisions relating to other easements, as explained below. It is convenient, first, to deal with common prescription and 'lost modern grant' together but to note the differences between them.

## Common law prescription and lost modern grant

### *Generally*

2.45 The basis of the doctrine of prescription is that if long enjoyment of a right is shown, the court will uphold the right by presuming that it has a lawful origin. Thus, at common law, as with other easements, if light has been enjoyed 'as of right'[106] from time immemorial, then it will be deemed to have been lawfully acquired.[107]

2.46 The difficulties inherent in establishing a claim to an easement based on user from time immemorial were mitigated by development of the presumption that if user as of right continued for a sufficient period then it would be presumed (as a legal fiction) that the origin of the user was lawful and derived from a modern grant that had been lost.[108] There is no reason why this doctrine should not apply to rights of light as it does to other easements.[109]

### *Length of enjoyment*

#### *Time immemorial*

2.47 User from time immemorial means use since 1189, the first year of the reign of Richard I. Such long enjoyment, however, will be presumed if it can be shown that it has continued for as long as anyone alive can remember and an origin subsequent to that date could not be proved.[110]

---

[106] See below for what constitutes use 'as of right'.

[107] See generally *R v Oxfordshire County Council ex parte Sunningwell Parish Council* [2001] 1 AC 335 at 349G–350B.

[108] See generally *R v Oxfordshire County Council ex parte Sunningwell Parish Council* [2001] 1 AC 335, per Lord Hoffmann for a history of the law of prescription. See also *Tehidy Minerals Ltd v Norman* [1971] 2 QB 528.

[109] See *Marlborough (West End) Ltd v Wilks Head and Eve*, 1996, unreported, ChD, per Lightman J.

[110] *Angus v Dalton* (1877) 3 QBD 85 at 89, per Lush J.

Further, the evidence to establish enjoyment since time immemorial need not cover any particular continuous period provided that it can be shown to have existed over a period extending as far back as living memory goes.[111] Since in practice and with diligence nearly every building that might enjoy a right of light can be shown to have been constructed after 1189, an origin subsequent to that date should usually be capable of proof. In *Aynsley v Glover*,[112] however, evidence of an elderly witness showed the building had enjoyed light since before living memory and the date of the building of the dwelling receiving the light was not proved.

## *Lost modern grant*

2.48    The period of enjoyment which needs to be proved for this presumption to arise is 20 years.[113] The 20-year period was adopted by analogy with the 20-year limitation period introduced for possessory claims under the Limitation Act 1623.[114] So, where it was proved that light through windows was enjoyed by the dominant tenement for a period of 20 years, proof that they did not exist 22 years previously was insufficient to disprove the existence of a right of light.[115]

## **Presumed grantors and grantees: fee simple owners**

2.49    In order to rely upon common law prescription and the doctrine of lost modern grant, however, the user must be by or on behalf of the owner in fee simple against the owner in fee simple, 'The whole theory of prescription at common law is against presuming any grant or covenant not to interrupt, by or with anyone except an owner in fee'.[116] Accordingly, where the fee simple in both the servient and the dominant tenement is in

---

[111]   *RPC Holding Ltd v Rogers* [1953] 1 All ER 1029 at 1031 and 1032.

[112]   *Aynsley v Glover* (1875) 10 CH App 283; see also *RPC Holding Ltd v Rogers* [1953] 1 All ER 1029 at 1031 and 1032 (a right of way case).

[113]   See generally *R v Oxfordshire County Council ex parte Sunningwell Parish Council* [2000] 1 AC 335, per Lord Hoffmann for a history of the law of prescription. See also *Tehidy Minerals Ltd v Norman* [1971] 2 QB 528.

[114]   See *R v Oxfordshire County Council ex parte Sunningwell Parish Council* [2000] 1 AC 335.

[115]   *Penwarden v Ching* (1829) Moo & Mal 400.

[116]   *Wheaton v Maple & Co* [1893] 3 Ch 48 at 63; see also *Kilgour v Gaddes* [1904] 1 FB 467; *Fear v Morgan* [1906] 2 Ch 415 at 416.

the same ownership no easement can be acquired at common law or by lost modern grant.[117]

2.50   Likewise, it follows:

(a)   if the owner of the servient tenement does not have sufficient capacity to make a grant, then the prescription period cannot run during that time;[118] and

(b)   if there was no competent grantee, then the prescription period cannot run.[119]

2.51   On the other hand, while time will not run where the fee simple in both the servient and dominant tenements are in the same ownership,[120] unity of possession without unity of ownership may not prevent a claim to possession at common law.[121]

2.52   There is nothing in principle to preclude a freeholder claiming a right of light where a tenant is in occupation of the dominant tenement since the tenant has 'seisin in his lessor'.[122] Thus in *Gayford v Moffatt*,[123] in holding that a tenant could not obtain an easement by prescription against his own landlord, Lord Cairns said,[124] 'the possession of the tenant

---

[117]   *Cory v Davies* [1923] 2 Ch 95. This rule does not apply where the lessee had at the material time a unilateral right to enfranchise his leasehold interest into the fee simple under Law of Property Act 1925, s 152 without anyone else's consent: see *Bosomworth v Faber* (1992) 69 P & CR 63 at 69. See also para 7.4 (extinguishment of easements).

[118]   See e.g. *Oakley v Boston* [1976] QB 270 (lost modern grant). See para 2.78 and para 2.83 for the position of the Crown and Church.

[119]   See e.g. *National Guaranteed Manure Co v Donald* (1859) 4 H & N 8. See also *Traill v McAllister* (1890) 25 LR Ir 524.

[120]   *Cory v Davies* [1923] 2 Ch 95.

[121]   Co. Litt. 114B; cf also *Morris v Edgington* (1810) 3 Taunt 24 at 30 (where 'possession' seems to be used synonymously with 'ownership'; see Gaunt, J and Morgan, Mr Justice (eds) (2012), *Gale on Easements* (19th edn), Sweet & Maxwell, at para 4-07. See also para 7.4 (extinguishment of easements).

[122]   *A-G v Gauntlett* (1829) 3 Y & J 93.

[123]   *Gayford v Moffatt* (1869–69) LR 4 Ch App 133.

[124]   *Gayford v Moffatt* (1869–69) LR 4 Ch App 133 at 135.

of the demised close is the possession of the landlord'. So, consistently with this, in *Pugh v Savage*,[125] Cross LJ stated:

> a tenant cannot by user gain a prescriptive right of way for himself as tenant; but by user over land of a stranger he can gain a prescriptive right of way in fee for his landlord which he can use while he is tenant and which his landlord can grant to a subsequent tenant.

There is nothing in principle which precludes this from applying to the context of rights of light.

2.53   On the other hand, consistently with the proposition that the user to establish a prescriptive right must be by or on behalf of the owner in fee simple *against the owner in fee simple*, the traditional view is that a tenant cannot acquire an easement by lost modern grant on his own behalf against an adjoining servient tenement.[126]

2.54   Conversely (subject to the qualification described in the next section[127]), if the servient tenement is subject to a tenancy which is inconsistent with the freehold owner being able to grant a right of light over the servient tenement, then time will not run for the duration of that tenancy because the tenant would not be competent to grant a right binding the fee.

### Common law and lost modern grant: summary of position where tenements are subject to tenancies

2.55   Where tenements are subject to tenancies, the position may be summarised as follows.

2.56   Where the freehold dominant tenement is demised by D (dominant owner) to T (tenant), T's enjoyment of rights over S's (servient owner's) land enures for the benefit of D's estate. This is explained above.[128]

---

[125]  *Pugh v Savage* [1970] 2 QB 373 at 380G–H. See also *Midtown Ltd v City of London Real Property Co Ltd* [2005] EWHC 33 (Ch) at [15].

[126]  *Simmons v Dobson* [1991] 1 WLR 720 at 725.

[127]  See para 2.55 ff.

[128]  See para 2.52.

2.57 Where the freehold dominant tenement is demised by D to T and T enjoys use over the servient land which is also owned by D, no easement is acquired for T's enjoyment.[129]

2.58 Where both the dominant and the servient land are subject to tenancies, it is settled law that prescriptive title to an easement over the freehold land cannot be acquired.[130]

2.59 Where the servient land alone is subject to a tenancy, prescriptive rights cannot be acquired over that land if the freehold owner would not be able to grant such rights during the currency of the tenancy. This, however, is subject to an important qualification. In *Pugh v Savage*,[131] as explained in *Williams v Sandy Lane (Chester) Ltd*,[132] it was held that the following principles are applicable to cases where the servient land is, or has been, subject to a tenancy. In the latter case, Chadwick LJ summarised the position as follows:[133]

> First, in a case where the grant of the tenancy of the servient land predates the user by or on behalf of the owner of the dominant land, it is necessary to ask whether, notwithstanding the tenancy, the freehold owner of the servient land could take steps to prevent user during the tenancy. The answer to that question is likely to turn on the terms of the tenancy.
>
> Second, if (notwithstanding the tenancy) the owner of the servient land could take steps to prevent the user, it is necessary to ask whether (and, if so, when) the freehold owner had knowledge (actual or imputed) of that user by the owner of the dominant land. The fact that the freehold owner of the servient land was out of possession when the user began and throughout the term of the tenancy may well lead to the conclusion that knowledge of that user should not be imputed. However, if, on the facts, the owner of the servient land does have knowledge of the user and

---

[129] *Wheaton v Maple & Co* [1893] 3 Ch 48; *Kilgour v Gaddes* [1904] 1 KB 457 (a Prescription Act 1832 case).

[130] See generally *Kilgour v Gaddes* [1904] 1 KB 457; *Simmons v Dobson* [1991] 1 WLR 720 at 725.

[131] *Pugh v Savage* [1970] 2 QB 373.

[132] *Williams v Sandy Lane (Chester) Ltd* [2006] EWCA Civ 1738.

[133] *Williams v Sandy Lane (Chester) Ltd* [2006] EWCA Civ 1738 at para [24], per Chadwick LJ.

could (notwithstanding the tenancy) take steps to prevent that user, but does not do so, then (prima facie) acquiescence will be established.

Third, in a case where user of the servient land by the owner of the dominant land began before the grant of the tenancy, it is necessary to ask whether the freehold owner of the servient land had knowledge (actual or imputed) at or before the date of the grant. If so, it is likely to be immaterial whether the terms of the tenancy are such that the owner of the servient land could (or could not) take steps to prevent that user. That is because if (with knowledge of the user) the owner of the servient land grants a tenancy of that land on terms that put it out of its power to prevent that user, it can properly be said to have acquiesced in it.

Fourth, if the owner of the servient land did not have knowledge of the user at the date of the grant, the position is the same as it would be if the grant had predated the user. It is necessary to ask whether (notwithstanding the tenancy) the freehold owner can take steps to prevent the user; and, if so, whether (and if so when) the owner had knowledge of the user.

Different considerations, however, arise in relation to rights of light under the Prescription Act 1832.[134]

2.60   The rule that lost modern grant does not apply between leaseholders has been criticised: 'It is not easy to see to see why, if a grant can be made expressly, it cannot be presumed'.[135] Similarly, the rule that a tenant of a dominant tenement cannot acquire a right by lost modern grant and that a prescriptive right by lost modern grant cannot be acquired (subject to the qualifications set out above)[136] against a servient tenement where that tenement is subject to a tenancy has been criticised:

> The rule is both counterintuitive and contrary to the policy of the law. It is counterintuitive because it is difficult to see why it should be impossible to presume a lost grant of an easement by or to a lessee for the term of his lease when such a grant may be made expressly. The grant cannot prejudice the reversion to the servient land, for the right granted must expire with the term of the grantor's lease; and user during the

---

[134]   See para 2.63 ff.

[135]   *China Field Ltd v Appeal Tribunal (Buildings)* [2009] 5 HKC 231 at [50], per Lord Millett.

[136]   See para 2.55 ff.

currency of the lease will not bind the reversion unless the reversioner knew of or acquiesced in it. It is contrary to the policy of the law, for if the disturbance of long established de facto enjoyment of a right is contrary to legal policy, then this is equally the case whether the enjoyment is by or against a freeholder or a leaseholder.[137]

Despite this criticism, the Law Commission has not recommended reform in this respect despite making other recommendations.[138]

## *Quality of enjoyment: enjoyment as of right*

2.61   If an easement of light is to be acquired at common law or under the doctrine of lost modern grant, the light must have been enjoyed for the requisite time 'as of right'.[139] Enjoyment 'as of right' means enjoyment *nec vi nec clam nec precario*. In other words, it must be without force, openly ('not secretly') and without consent. Looking at each of these concepts in more detail, the following points should be noted:

(a)   Enjoyment of light which continues to be enjoyed as a result of the forcible removal of an obstruction to the light to the dominant tenement would not continue *nec vi*, i.e. without force. Further, enjoyment which is merely contentious might also be treated as continuing 'forcibly'.[140]

(b)   In the context of rights of light, it is difficult to envisage circumstances in which enjoyment would not have taken place openly. As explained below, enjoyment must be of light across the servient tenement to an aperture in a building on the dominant tenement. The enjoyment of light in this way would always on the face of things be 'open' (*nec clam*).

(c)   The question whether light has been enjoyed by consent (*nec precario*) is the one which arises most frequently when considering

---

[137]   *China Field Ltd v Appeal Tribunal (Buildings)* [2009] 5 HKC 231 at [50], per Lord Millett.

[138]   See para 11.2.

[139]   See para 2.47 for the duration of enjoyment for common law prescription; see para 2.48 for lost modern grant.

[140]   See, in the context of rights of way, *Newnham v Willison* (1987) 56 P & CR 8; *Smith v Brudenell-Bruce* [2002] 2 P & CR 51.

whether enjoyment has been 'as of right'. Accordingly, this is
something which is considered in some detail below.[141]

## Quality of enjoyment: enjoyment in the nature of an easement – buildings and apertures

2.62   To acquire a prescriptive right to an easement by prescription, the
right must be one capable of subsisting as an easement. As explained
above,[142] a right to light cannot be acquired by prescription in respect of
vacant land.[143] Accordingly, when considering whether a right to light has
been acquired at common law, one is considering light enjoyed by some
form of *building* and *ex hypothesi* through an aperture in a building. Thus,
the use of open ground in a particular way requiring light and air does not
give rise to a right of light.[144] This is considered in more detail at
para 2.67 ff.

## Prescription Act 1832

### Generally

2.63   The Prescription Act 1832 deals with rights to light differently from
other easements, and the rules are significantly different from those
applicable to prescription by user from time immemorial and under the
doctrine of lost modern grant. In essence, to establish a prescriptive right
under section 3 of the 1832 Act, it is necessary to establish the following:

(a)   access and user of light to a building;

(b)   'actually enjoyed therewith';

(c)   for a full period of 20 years.

2.64   Particular points to note are:

(a)   the right may be acquired by tenants;[145]

---

[141]  See para 3.2 ff.

[142]  See para 2.14.

[143]  *Roberts v Macord* (1832) 1 Mood & R 230.

[144]  *Roberts v Macord* (1832) 1 Mood & R 230.

[145]  See para 2.75.

(b)  the period of 20 years runs back from the commencement of the action; accordingly, until the action is commenced, the right is inchoate;

(c)  the acquisition of a right will be defeated if there is an interruption for a year;[146] but enjoyment for a period exceeding 19 years which is then obstructed can be protected if proceedings are brought after 20 years have run and before the obstruction has lasted one year;[147]

(d)  the acquisition of the right can be defeated if there is consent or agreement in writing to the enjoyment.[148]

## *Length of enjoyment*

2.65   Twenty years' enjoyment is required for the purposes of establishing a prescriptive right to light under section 3 of the Prescription Act 1832. The period of 20 years runs back from the commencement of the action: until the action is commenced, however, the right is merely inchoate, i.e. in the course of being acquired but not yet acquired. So, if proceedings are brought before the 20 years have run, the claimant's right is still inchoate and he cannot protect his light by injunction.[149] But it should be noted that under section 4, the acquisition of a right will be defeated if there is an interruption for one year. So enjoyment for a period exceeding 19 years which is then obstructed can be protected if proceedings are brought: (a) after 20 years have run; but (b) before the obstruction has lasted one year. What constitutes interruption is considered further below.[150]

## *Quality of enjoyment: generally*

2.66   There is no requirement that the enjoyment of light is 'as of right' for a right to light to be acquired under section 3 of the Prescription Act 1832. However:

---

[146]  Prescription Act 1832, s 4.

[147]  See para 2.65.

[148]  Consents may be contained in conveyances and transfers. How they will be construed will depend upon the precise words used. See in particular para 3.1 ff. Issues may arise over the extent to which a consent can bind successors in title to the original parties; see para 3.13. See also para 5.3.

[149]  *Bridewell Hospital (Governors) v Ward Lock Bowden & Co* (1893) 62 JJ Ch 270; *Lord Battersea v London City Sewers Commissioners* [1895] 2 Ch 708.

[150]  See para 3.23 ff.

(a)  enjoyment must be 'continuous';[151]

(b)  a claim will be defeated if there is consent or agreement in writing to the enjoyment;[152] and

(c)  the light must be enjoyed by a building;[153] but

(d)  it is not necessary that there should be physical benefit from the light provided that an aperture in the building exists.[154]

Whether there has been actual enjoyment for a full period of 20 years for the purposes of the Prescription Act 1832 is a question of fact. In a case where there has been a radical alteration of a building during the 20-year period so that light does not continually pass through a defined aperture, it is difficult to see how there could be the requisite enjoyment. See further para 6.8 ff (Alteration of apertures: 'transferred rights'). What constitutes a 'building' and the apertures within it are considered at para 2.68 ff. What might constitute 'consent' or 'agreement' is considered further at para 3.2 ff.

## *Prescription: buildings and apertures*

2.67   As mentioned above,[155] an easement of light created by prescription at common law or under the doctrine of lost modern grant is a right of enjoyment of light for a building. Similarly, section 3 of the Prescription Act 1832 applies where there has been access and user of light to and for a 'building'.[156] For a light to be enjoyed by a building, there must be some aperture through which the light passes.

---

[151]  See para 6.10 ff.

[152]  Consents may be contained in conveyances and transfers. How they will be construed will depend upon the precise words used. See in particular para 3.1. Issues may arise over the extent to which a consent can bind successors in title to the original parties; see para 3.13. See also para 5.33.

[153]  See para 2.68 ff.

[154]  See para 2.71 ff.

[155]  See paras 1.1 and 2.62.

[156]  See para 2.66.

## *Buildings*

2.68    The answer to the question whether a structure is a building will turn on the facts. The word 'building' has been held to include a church or chapel,[157] a greenhouse[158] and (in particular circumstances) an open-sided garage.[159] On the other hand, in *Harris v De Pinna*[160] at first instance, the word 'building' was held not to extend to a timber store (comprising simply of upright baulks of timber or standards fixed in stone bases built on brick piers with cross beams and braces, divided into stagings).

2.69    The following have been suggested as being relevant criteria for determining whether a structure is a 'building' for the purposes of the Prescription Act 1832:

(a)    Did the structure give substantial shelter from the elements?

(b)    Was it one which ordinarily required light by means of windows or fixed apertures?

(c)    Did it have windows?

(d)    Was it so attached to the soil as to pass under a conveyance of the land without specific mention?[161]

---

[157]    See *Ecclesiastical Commissioners v Kino* (1880) 14 ChD 213; *A-G v Queen Anne Gardens & Mansion CO* (1889) 60 LT 213. Cf *Duke of Norfolk v Arbuthnot* (1880) 5 CPD 390 (Bramwell LJ doubted whether a church could be a building, but this does not appear to be part of the *ratio* and was not mentioned by the other members of the court).

[158]    *Clifford v Holt* [1899] 1 Ch 698; *Allen v Greenwood* [1980] Ch 119.

[159]    *Smith & Co (Orpington) v Morris* (1962) 112 LJ 702 (county court).

[160]    *Harris v De Pinna* (1886) 33 ChD 238 at 249, per Chitty J at first instance. The decision of the Court of Appeal, however, seems to have turned on the structure not having a defined aperture, the wood being stored in different ways at different times that no aperture could be defined: (1886) 33 ChD 238, see at 257, per Cotton LJ.

[161]    *Smith & Co (Orpington) v Morris* (1962) 112 LJ 702 (county court). See Bickford-Smith, S, Francis, A and Weekes, T (2015), *Rights of Light: The Modern Law* (3rd edn), Jordan Publishing, at p 50. See also *Elitestone Ltd v Morris* [1997] 1 WLR 687 for consideration of when a structure is treated as a fixture; and *Maberley v Dowson* (1827) 5 LJ (os) KB 261 cited by Gaunt, J and Morgan, Mr Justice (eds) (2012), *Gale on Easements* (19th edn), Sweet & Maxwell, at para 4-23.

2.70   A 'building' exists as soon as the exterior walls with spaces for windows are completed and properly roofed even if the window sashes and glass and the interior may not be finished until some time after.[162]

## Apertures

2.71   For light to be enjoyed in a manner sufficient to give rise to a prescriptive right, however, an aperture in the building must be defined.[163] As explained below, it is by reference to the aperture through which light passes that the extent of a prescriptive right to light is defined.[164] An aperture may be sufficiently definite even if has yet to be glazed – as mentioned in the last paragraph.

2.72   There seems no reason in principle why to be enjoyed for the purposes of establishing a prescriptive right light should not pass through part of a building before reaching an aperture in the dominant tenement: nor is there any reason why apertures through which light may pass to give rise to a right of light need be placed in the external envelope of a building. So, in *Tisdall v McArthur & Co (Steel & Metal) Ltd*[165] it was held that the existence of a glass roof over a yard did not amount to an obstruction to light to windows forming part of the dominant tenement to prevent a prescriptive right of light arising.

2.73   Further, it is not necessary to show that the dominant tenement was used in such a way that the light had any practical benefit provided that a defined aperture has existed.[166] Accordingly, the internal arrangement of the building does not affect the nature of the enjoyment necessary to establish a prescriptive right to light[167] (albeit it may be relevant to the

---

[162]   *Coutauld v Legh* (1869) LR 4 Ex 126; followed in *Collis v Laugher* [1894] 3 Ch 659.

[163]   *Harris v De Pinna* (1886) 33 ChD 238, at 257, per Cotton LJ.

[164]   See paras 6.3 and 6.7.

[165]   *Tisdall v McArthur & Co (Steel & Metal) Ltd* [1951] IR 228 (considered in *Marine & General Life Assurance Society v St James Real Estate Co* [1991] 2 EGLR 178); cf *Duke of Norfolk v Arbuthnot* (1880) 5 CPD 390 (where light passed through an arch for the common benefit of two buildings, Bramwell LJ doubted whether there was a right of light (although, in any event, there was interruption for more than a year)).

[166]   See *Coutauld v Legh* (1869) LR 4 Ex 126.

[167]   See para 6.14.

issue of whether there is an infringement of such a right,[168] and it might be highly relevant to the question of the relief which the court might be willing to grant for any infringement of the right[169]). To establish a right, it does not matter that the windows are shuttered[170] or obscured by shelves,[171] but if the aperture is completely boarded up, then there will be insufficient in the enjoyment and time will stop running for the purposes of prescription.[172]

## *Grantors, grantees and tenants: Prescription Act 1832*

2.74  In general, while a prescriptive easement must be claimed as appurtenant to the fee simple of the dominant tenement,[173] it is sufficient in pleading a claim under the Prescription Act 1832 to claim it on the ground of an enjoyment as of right by the occupiers of such tenement.[174] Enjoyment by the tenant in possession of the dominant tenement, therefore, will enure for the benefit of the fee simple.

2.75  Section 3 of the Prescription Act 1832 provides that the *actual* enjoyment of light to a 'dwelling-house, workshop or other building' for 20 years without interruption shall make the right 'absolute and indefeasible' unless enjoyed by written consent or agreement.[175] This has been construed so that despite the general position described above:[176]

(a)  a tenant can acquire a right to light enuring for the benefit of the tenancy against an adjoining landowner;[177]

(b)  a tenant can acquire such a right to light even against his own landlord;[178]

---

[168]  See para 6.15 ff (not only current uses need be considered).

[169]  See para 10.20 ff.

[170]  *Cooper v Straker* (1888) 40 Ch 21.

[171]  *Smith v Baxter* [1900] 2 Ch 138.

[172]  *Smith v Baxter* [1900] 2 Ch 138; *Tamares Ltd v Fairpoint Properties Ltd* [2006] EWHC 3589 (Ch) at [12]; and see para 6.5.

[173]  See para 2.49 ff.

[174]  See Prescription Act 1832, s 5.

[175]  See para 3.3 ff for consent or agreement.

[176]  See para 2.55 ff.

[177]  *Fear v Morgan* [1906] 2 Ch 406; *Morgan v Fear* [1907] AC 425.

[178]  *Fear v Morgan* [1906] 2 Ch 406; *Morgan v Fear* [1907] AC 425.

(c)  a tenant can acquire a right to light against another tenant of his own landlord;[179]

(d)  where the easement is acquired against another tenant and the lease of the servient land expires first, the easement binds the landlord (and subsequent occupiers of the servient tenement).[180]

2.76  Unlike prescription for other easements under section 2 of the Prescription Act 1832, there is no exclusion for periods of 'disability' by the owner of the servient tenement: section 7 of the 1832 Act (which contains a proviso for cases where the owner of the servient tenement is under a disability) does not apply to cases such as claims under section 3 which are 'absolute and indefeasible' when the period of enjoyment is established.

## Prescriptive easements take effect as legal easements

2.77  Where an easement is acquired by prescription it takes effect as a legal easement and its lawful origin is presumed. For the treatment of such easements under the Land Registration regime, see para 5.1 ff.

## The Crown and prescription

2.78  There is nothing in principle to prevent common law prescription and lost modern grant applying to the Crown.[181] The doctrine will certainly not prevent the inference of a grant arising by reference to a period *before* the Crown acquired its interest, provided that the other conditions are satisfied. If prior to the Crown acquiring its title there was sufficient enjoyment to give rise to the application of the doctrine, then the fact that the Crown has subsequently acquired its interest will not prevent reliance on this doctrine.

2.79  It should be noted, however, that the general rule is that the enjoyment of land as against an owner of the servient tenement who is unable to dispose of the fee is not sufficient to give rise to a prescriptive

---

[179] *Fear v Morgan* [1906] 2 Ch 406; *Morgan v Fear* [1907] AC 425.

[180] *Fear v Morgan* [1906] 2 Ch 406; *Morgan v Fear* [1907] AC 425.

[181] See paras 2.43 and 2.50.

title (except under section 3 of the Prescription Act 1832[182]). If the Crown has no capacity to grant an easement, then no grant will be presumed. Thus in *Mill v New Forest Commissioner*,[183] a *profit à prendre* was enjoyed against the Crown for 30 years and a claim made under section 1 of the 1832 Act was defeated on the ground that the Crown was by statute incapacitated from making a grant. The Crown Lands Act 1702 still limits the capacity of the Crown to make grants. In order for the Crown to have capacity to grant an easement of light, the land would have to have been held for a statutory purpose which enables the grant. Therefore, if the land vests in a Crown body for statutory purposes, it is necessary to find a power under which a grant could be made. The question is whether while land was appropriated for a statutory purpose, the Crown body could grant an interest over its land. It will be necessary to consider the history of the title to the land and in whom the title vested at various stages and the statutory powers which that person or body had at each stage.

2.80 The conventional view, however, is that section 3 of the Prescription Act 1832 does *not* apply to the Crown. The general rule of construction is that a statute will not bind the Crown unless it is expressly provided that it will do so. In any event, sections 1 and 2 expressly refer to the Crown but section 3 does not. This reinforces the conclusion that section 3 does not bind the Crown. On this basis, in relation to land comprised within the freehold title of the Crown, reliance cannot be placed upon the 1832 Act.[184]

2.81 The conventional view that section 3 of the Prescription Act 1832 does not bind the Crown might be challenged on the following basis:

(a) It might be argued that section 3 should be read as a qualification to the general provisions for the acquisition of easements by prescription under the Act contained in section 2, section 3 expressly applying to 'any dwelling house, workshop or other building' (including those which enjoy light over Crown land mentioned in section 2).

---

[182] See paras 2.43, 2.50 and 2.74–2.76.
[183] *Mill v New Forest Commissioner* (1856) 18 CB 60.
[184] See *Wheaton v Maple & Co* [1893] 3 Ch 48.

(b)   In support of this interpretation it may be possible to pray in aid the
      Human Rights Act 1998. It might be argued that a person would be
      discriminated against in relation to his enjoyment of property under
      Article 1 of the First Protocol to the European Convention for the
      Protection of Human Rights and Fundamental Freedoms 1950 on the
      ground of his 'status' if he enjoys light over Crown property and if
      section 3 is read as not applying to the Crown.

(c)   It seems likely that Article 1 of the First Protocol is 'engaged' where
      one is considering the acquisition of easements appurtenant to land.

(d)   There would seem to be a difference in treatment between those
      enjoying light over Crown land and those who do not. This might be
      characterised as discrimination under Article 14 as respects
      Convention rights, i.e. Article 1 of the First Protocol.[185]

(e)   It might thus be argued that the discrimination is on one of the
      grounds within Article 14, i.e. 'other status'.

(f)   It is difficult to see what objectively justifiable rationale there is for
      such discrimination.

2.82   Against such an argument, however, the following points seem
decisive:

(a)   The 'traditional' approach to construction favouring section 3 *not*
      applying to the Crown is consistent with the natural reading of
      sections 2 and 3 together.

(b)   Even if Article 1 of the First Protocol and Article 14 are engaged, it
      is difficult to describe the difference in treatment as being determined
      by the status of the person who receives the light. The difference in
      treatment stems from the specific nature of the land over which the
      light is enjoyed (land held by the Crown which in general is held for
      the public benefit) rather than by reference to the particular status of
      the person who enjoys the light.

---

[185] Cf e.g. *Larkos v Cyprus* [1999] ECHR 11.

## Ecclesiastical property and prescription

2.83   As explained above, if the person in whom land is vested has no capacity to grant an easement, then no grant will be presumed under the doctrine of lost modern grant.[186] Thus, when considering the application of the doctrine of lost modern grant, it is necessary to consider whether there are limitations on the freeholder's right to make a grant. In the case of incumbents, their ability to deal with land is limited.[187] In the case of section 3 of the Prescription Act 1832, however, there is no reason in principle why this provision should not apply to ecclesiastical land as it does to any other land where the servient owner would otherwise be disabled from making a grant.[188]

2.84   Conversely, there is nothing to prevent ecclesiastical land acquiring the benefit of an easement by prescription.[189]

## The City of London and prescription

2.85   The custom of the City of London limits the application of the principles of common law prescription and of the doctrine of lost modern grant. The extent of that limit is a matter of debate.

2.86   In *Plummer v Bentham*,[190] it was declared (in summary)[191] that it was the custom of the City of London that a man might rebuild his house upon the ancient foundation to what height he pleased even though he thereby stopped another's light if there were no agreement in writing to the contrary. The court, however, refused to declare the custom more widely in relation to any erection or building.

---

[186]   See para 2.50 and para 2.78 ff (Crown land).

[187]   See Church Property (Miscellaneous Provisions) Measure 1960, s 9 (as amended) and Pastoral Measure 1983, s 60. See *Re St Martin le Grand, York* [1990] Fam 63 at 76–77. See para 2.43.

[188]   See para 2.76.

[189]   *Ecclesiastical Commissioners v Kino* (1880) 14 ChD 213.

[190]   *Plummer v Bentham* (1757) 1 Burr 248.

[191]   See *Bowring Services Ltd v Scottish Widows Fund & Life Assurance Society* [1995] 1 EGLR 158, citing Maurice, SG (1986), *Gale on Easements* (15th edn), Sweet & Maxwell.

2.87    This was followed in the case of *Wynstanley v Lee*,[192] in which an injunction to restrain an interference with lights to a house in the City of London was refused because the presumption of right from 20 years' undisturbed enjoyment of light was excluded by this custom.

2.88    In *Perry v Eames*,[193] Chitty J on the authority of *Wynstanley v Lee* held that the:

> custom was that a man might rebuild his house or other edifice upon the ancient foundation to what height he pleased, though thereby the ancient windows or lights of the adjoining or opposite house were obstructed, if there were no agreement in writing to the contrary

and applied this to the site of the former Bankruptcy Court. Chitty J was not, however, referred to *Plummer v Bentham* in which the custom was plainly confined only to 'messuages and houses'.

2.89    In *Bowring Services Ltd v Scottish Widows Fund & Life Assurance Society*,[194] the deputy judge referred to these authorities including the judgment of Chitty J and decided that he would:

> not depart from the decision of that judge made over 100 years nearer to the time when the custom was of more practical relevance, before the 1832 Act.

2.90    Given that Chitty J had not been referred to *Plummer v Bentham*, and given the court in that case had expressly declined to declare the wider custom, it must remain open to argument that the custom of London is narrower than suggested by Chitty J and is limited to excluding only 'messuages and houses' from the application of the doctrine of lost modern grant.[195]

---

[192]    *Wynstanley v Lee* (1818) 2 Swan 33.

[193]    *Perry v Eames* [1891] 1 Ch 658 at 667.

[194]    *Bowring Services Ltd v Scottish Widows Fund & Life Assurance Society* [1995] 1 EGLR 158.

[195]    See Gaunt, J and Morgan, Mr Justice (eds) (2012), *Gale on Easements* (19th edn), Sweet & Maxwell, at paras 7-32–7-33.

2.91 Whatever its extent, however, the custom only applies to prescription at common law and under the doctrine of lost modern grant. Section 3 of the Prescription Act 1832 applies 'any local custom or usage notwithstanding'.

## Illegality and prescription

2.92 Where an express grant would be contrary to the common law or statute, no presumed grant by prescription can arise.[196] Thus, where use would be illegal even if a grant had been made, this cannot give rise to a prescriptive right. On the other hand, if a grant could lawfully be made, there is nothing to preclude prescription being relied upon.[197] It is difficult, however, to envisage the circumstances in which this principle will be applicable in the context of the enjoyment of light.[198]

---

[196] See *Neaverson v Peterborough Rural District Council* [1902] 1 Ch 557; *Bakewell Management Ltd v Brandwood* [2004] UKHL 14, [2004] 2 AC 519.

[197] *Bakewell Management Ltd v Brandwood* [2004] UKHL 14, [2004] 2 AC 519.

[198] See generally *R (on the application of Best) v Chief Land Registrar* [2015] EWCA Civ 17.

# Chapter 3

# Preventing a Right of Light Arising by Prescription: Consent and Obstruction

## GENERALLY

3.1    This chapter considers in detail two ways in which prescriptive rights of light may be prevented from arising: consent and obstruction.

## CONSENT

3.2    The *consent* of the servient owner to the enjoyment of light may prevent a putative dominant owner acquiring a right by prescription either: (a) at common law or by lost modern grant since enjoyment by consent is not 'as of right';[1] or (b) under the Prescription Act 1832 because of the express terms of that Act.[2] Under section 3 of the Prescription Act 1832, the consent or agreement must be 'in writing'[3] to prevent a prescriptive right arising.

### Original parties to consent or agreement

#### *Servient owners' consent or agreement*

3.3    It seems clear that the consent or agreement of the servient owner is sufficient to prevent enjoyment of light being 'as of right' at common

---

[1]    See para 2.61.

[2]    See para 2.66.

[3]    *London Corp v Pewterers' Co* (1842) 2 Moo & R 409; *Plasterers' Co v Parkish Clerks Co* (1851) 6 Exch 630; *Judge v Lowe* (1873) IR 7 CL 291; *Mallam v Rose* [1915] 2 Ch 222.

law or under the doctrine of lost modern grant or under the Prescription Act 1832. It is not necessary for the servient owner to sign such consent or agreement for it to be 'in writing' for the purposes of the 1832 Act.[4]

## Agreement to consensual use by owner or occupier of dominant land

3.4　　In principle, the agreement of the dominant owner that his own enjoyment of light is consensual is sufficient to prevent the prescription period from running. In *Hyman v Van den Bergh*,[5] Parker J pointed out that the acquisition of rights of light at common law or by lost modern grant resulted from enjoyment by the occupier (albeit that, as explained above,[6] any easement established by lost modern grant accrued to the freehold). He indicated[7] that in the context of common law prescription and lost modern grant, if the occupier had asked for some consent or entered into some agreement with the effect that the enjoyment was by consent, then the owner of the land could be in no better position. He concluded that this was also the position under section 3 of the Prescription Act 1832. So, while the owner of the dominant tenement may agree that his enjoyment of light is consensual, it also appears that a person in possession claiming through the dominant owner can agree that enjoyment is consensual to preclude rights of light arising both at common law, under the doctrine of lost modern grant and by prescription under the 1832 Act. Accordingly, an agreement made and signed by the tenant of the dominant tenement for the purpose of securing the access and use of light to windows and to which such access and use is actually due, is sufficient in writing within the meaning of section 3 if signed by the tenant in possession of the dominant tenement. This reasoning appears to have been approved by the Court of Appeal.[8]

---

[4]　*Bewley v Atkinson* (1879) 13 ChD 283.

[5]　*Hyman v Van den Bergh* [1907] 2 Ch 516 at 530.

[6]　See paras 2.49 and 2.52.

[7]　*Hyman v Van den Bergh* [1907] 2 Ch 516 at 530.

[8]　*Hyman v Van den Bergh* [1908] 1 Ch 167 at 172, per Cozens-Hardy MR; see also 175, per Fletcher Moulton LJ; but Farwell LJ, at 177, did not consider the position 'independently of the Act'.

## Consent or agreement between landlord and tenant of dominant land sufficient to preclude tenant's rights?

3.5     Section 3 of the Prescription Act 1832 does not expressly state that 'consent or agreement' must be that of the servient owner to preclude enjoyment of light giving rise to a prescriptive right under that section. On the reasoning of Parker J in *Hyman v Van den Bergh* (which equated the position under section 3 with that at common law and under lost modern grant), it would appear to follow that it is the consent or agreement of the servient owner that is intended: the position would mirror that at common law or under the doctrine of lost modern grant where it was the servient owner's consent which precluded enjoyment being 'as of right' against the servient land.

3.6     A different conclusion was reached at first instance in *Paragon Finance plc v City of London Real Property Co Ltd*.[9] It is was held that, because section 3 of the Prescription Act 1832 does not expressly require the consent of the servient owner, it is within the power of the owner of a building which had enjoyed a right for more than 20 years to agree with the person to whom he grants an interest in such building that he should not be entitled to assert such a right, and this is sufficient to prevent a prescriptive right from arising in favour of that person. This conclusion is perhaps surprising given the analysis in *Hyman v Van den Bergh*,[10] but it is also intelligible: if a landlord wishes to preclude his tenant acquiring rights of light by prescription against an adjoining, servient owner, there seems to be no good reason in principle to prevent him from doing so. The point, however, remains unresolved.

3.7     As indicated above,[11] an agreement may be made by a freeholder of the dominant land with the owner of the servient land so that enjoyment of light is by consent for the purposes of the doctrine of lost modern grant or by agreement for the purposes of section 3 of the Prescription Act 1832. However, if the dominant land is subject to a tenancy, such an agreement cannot bind the tenant (unless the terms of the lease provide for the tenant

---

[9]     *Paragon Finance plc v City of London Real Property Co Ltd* [2002] 1 P & CR 36 at [35] ff.

[10]    See para 3.4.

[11]    See para 3.3.

to be so bound) to prevent the tenant from enjoying light for the purposes
of establishing a right to light under section 3.

## Construing agreements and consents

3.8    Consent to the enjoyment of light may be found in freestanding
agreements, conveyances and transfers or in the terms of leases. The
extent of such consent and its effect will be a matter of construction. The
principles for construing agreements relating to light are considered in
more detail below.[12]

3.9    In some instances, clauses seeking to preclude rights of light will
simply stop the acquisition of extant rights. In other instances, they will
be wide enough to amount to consents which will prevent rights being
acquired in the future.

3.10   This distinction is illustrated by *RHJ Limited v FT Patten
(Holdings) Ltd.*[13] In that case, the lease of an office block contained a
provision excepting or reserving:

> All rights to the access of light or air from the said adjoining property
> known as Victoria House and Graham House to any of the windows of
> the demised property.

The lease also reserved to the landlord:

> The full and free right to erect, build, re-build and/or alter as they think
> fit at any time and from time to time any buildings or bays or projections
> to buildings on any land adjoining the demised property and/or on the
> opposite sides of the adjoining streets and access ways.

Both Lewison J and the Court of Appeal held that the provisions of this
lease had the effect of triggering the proviso to section 3 of the Prescription
Act 1832, i.e. that subsequent enjoyment of light was by consent. Lewison

---

[12]   See para 4.2 ff for a discussion of the principles of construction.

[13]   *RHJ Limited v FT Patten (Holdings) Ltd* [2007] EWHC 1665 (Ch), [2007] 4 All
ER 744.

J reviewed a long line of authorities concerning the effect of section 3. He said this:[14]

> The real distinction that the cases draw is, as it seems to me, between clauses that deal with the position as it exists at the date of the lease, and clauses that deal with what might happen in the future. Clauses of the first kind are effective only to prevent the creation of easements by express or implied grant; and do not prevent the subsequent acquisition of a right of light by prescription. Clauses of the second kind may prevent the acquisition of a right of light by prescription if what they authorise would interfere with light. If, on a fair reading of the clause they do, then it is not necessary, in my judgment, for the clause to use the word 'light'. Nor, in my judgment, is it necessary for the clause to provide that the enjoyment of light is 'permissive'. What is needed is that the clause makes it clear that the enjoyment of light is not absolute and indefeasible. The court must 'find out the substance of the contract': in other words it is a question of interpretation of the clause in question. Once the clause has been interpreted, that interpretation will have been 'expressly' agreed. A clause in a lease which authorises the landlord to build as he pleases is likely to satisfy the test.

In the Court of Appeal,[15] Lloyd LJ gave the principal judgment with which Lawrence Collins and Mummery LJJ agreed. Lloyd LJ reviewed the authorities on section 3. Lloyd LJ stated,[16] with reference to the last part of section 3:

> I consider that the phrase 'expressly made or given for that purpose' can be satisfied by an express provision in the relevant document which, on its true construction according to normal principles, has the effect of rendering the enjoyment of light permissive or consensual, or capable of being terminated or interfered with by the adjoining owner, and is therefore inconsistent with the enjoyment becoming absolute and indefeasible after 20 years.

---

[14] *RHJ Limited v FT Patten (Holdings) Ltd* [2007] EWHC 1665 (Ch), [2007] 4 All ER 744 at [34].

[15] *RHJ Limited v FT Patten (Holdings) Ltd* [2008] EWCA Civ 151, [2008] Ch 341.

[16] *RHJ Limited v FT Patten (Holdings) Ltd* [2008] EWCA Civ 151, [2008] Ch 341 at [44].

In contrast, in *Salvage Wharf Limited v G&S Brough Limited*,[17] the Court of Appeal held that an agreement between a developer and a property owner whereby the property owner agreed not to enforce its right of light in relation to the proposed development did not amount to a consent or agreement under section 3. On a fair reading of the agreement, the property owner consented to a development that could cause some reduction in the amount of light entering its premises. It did not consent to a completely different development that would block all light.

3.11 Cases where the words considered have been sufficient to amount to consent or agreement which precluded an easement of light arising by prescription include the following:

(a) *Bewley v Atkinson*[18] – declaration signed only by dominant owner that:

> windows and lights above mentioned are put out and remain upon the leave of the [servient owner] and that I will, upon the request of him or his heirs or assigns to be made at any time hereafter, wall or block up the same, and in the meantime, until such request is made as aforesaid, I hereby promise to pay the said [servient owner], his heirs and assigns, the sum of sixpence per annum.

(b) *Haynes v King*[19] – lease granted with declaration that:

> notwithstanding anything contained herein, the lessors shall have power, without obtaining any consent from or making any compensation to, the lessee, to deal as they may think fit with any of the premises adjoining or contiguous to the hereditaments hereby demised and to erect, or suffer to be erected, on such adjoining or contiguous premises, any buildings whatsoever, whether such building shall or shall not affect or diminish the light or air which may now, or at any time during the term hereby granted, be enjoyed by the lessee, or the tenants or occupiers of the hereditaments hereby demised.

---

[17] *Salvage Wharf Limited v G&S Brough Limited* [2009] EWCA Civ 21.

[18] *Bewley v Atkinson* (1879) 13 ChD 283.

[19] *Haynes v King* [1893] 3 Ch 439.

(c) *Hyman v Van den Bergh*[20] – letter in writing that 'I will give you one shilling per annum for the use of those eight lights you have boarded up in my cowshed' stamped as an agreement.

(d) *Foster v Lyons & Co Ltd*[21] – lease containing reservation:

> to the lessor, and his lessees and tenants, full right to build to any height upon the land adjoining the land and premises hereby demised, notwithstanding such building may obstruct any light on the land hereby demised.

(e) *Willoughby v Eckstein*[22] – lease:

> subject to the adjacent buildings or any of them being at any time or times rebuilt or altered according to plans both as to height elevation extent or otherwise as shall or may be approved of the ground landlord for the time being.

(f) *Blake and Lyons Ltd v Lewis Berger & Sons*[23] – lease:

> subject to the adjacent buildings being at any time or times rebuilt or altered according to plans both as to height elevation extent and otherwise as shall or may be approved by the ground landlord for the time being.

(g) *Marlborough v Wilks Head & Eve*:[24]

> it is hereby agreed and declared that notwithstanding that the Building Owners have placed windows in that part of their new buildings which overlook the premises occupied by the adjoining owner no right or easement of light or air exists in respect thereof or has been or shall at any future time be acquired by the Building Owners or anyone deriving title through or under them and the adjoining owner and the freeholders and all persons deriving title through or under them or either of them shall have the right to intercept light and air coming to the said windows.

---

[20] *Hyman v Van den Bergh* [1907] 2 Ch 516.

[21] *Foster v Lyons & Co Ltd* [1927] 1 Ch 219.

[22] *Willoughby v Eckstein* [1937] 1 Ch 167.

[23] *Blake and Lyons Ltd v Lewis Berger & Sons* [1951] 2 TLR 605.

[24] *Marlborough v Wilks Head & Eve*, 20 December 1996, unreported, Lightman J.

(h)  *RHJ Limited v FT Patten (Holdings) Ltd*[25] – lease of an office block contained a provision excepting or reserving:

> All rights to the access of light or air from the said adjoining property known as Victoria House and Graham House to any of the windows of the demised property

and reservation to the landlord of:

> The full and free right to erect, build, re-build and/or alter as they think fit at any time and from time to time any buildings or bays or projections to buildings on any land adjoining the demised property and/or on the opposite sides of the adjoining streets and access ways.[26]

3.12    Cases in which words have been held to be insufficient to preclude prescriptive rights arising subsequent to the grant:

(a)  *Mitchell v Cantrill*[27] – a lease demised land:

> except rights, if any, restricting the free use of any adjoining land or the conversion or appropriation at any time thereafter of such land for building or other purposes, obstructive or otherwise.

(b)  *Ruscoe v Grounsell*[28] – stone table set in a wall in 1816 stating:

> this stone is placed by John Atkin [the purchaser] to perpetuate John Musgrave's [the vendor and owner of adjoining land] right to build within nine inches of this and any other building

The Court (assuming that the tablet contained an agreement in writing) held that it was unable to say whether this was to deal with the enjoyment of light so it concluded that it was unable to conclude that this fell within section 3 of the Prescription Act 1832.

---

[25]  *RHJ Limited v FT Patten (Holdings) Ltd* [2007] EWHC 1665 (Ch), [2007] 4 All ER 744.

[26]  See also the more complicated clauses in *Paragon Finance plc v City of London Real Property Co Ltd* [2002] 1 EGLR 97 and *Midtown Ltd v City of London Real Property Co Ltd* [2005] EWHC 33 (Ch).

[27]  *Mitchell v Cantrill* (1887) 37 ChD 56.

[28]  *Ruscoe v Grounsell* (1903) 89 LT 426; but cf cases in para 3.11 where reservation of right to build appears sufficient to amount to 'consent'.

(c)   *Salvage Wharf Limited v G&S Brough Limited*[29] – agreement not to
enforce 'subsisting rights to light to or enjoyed by the property' did
not preclude prescriptive rights arising thereafter.

## Prescription, consent and successors in title

3.13   An agreement which prevents the acquisition of rights of light or air
for the benefit of the registered estate may be entered in the property
register of that estate where the land is registered.[30] It has long been
considered that such agreements can endure through title and will not
infringe the rule against perpetuities.[31] There is, however, some juridical
difficulty in analysing the basis on which the 'benefit' and 'burden' of
such arrangements can pass from the original parties to their successors
and when it might do so. One possible analysis is that once 'consent or
agreement' has been 'expressly made or given' for the purpose of access
and use of light to a building by deed or in writing, that is sufficient for
the purposes of section 3 of the Prescription Act 1832, and the consent has
statutory force and endures against the putative dominant tenement
regardless of changes in title. This analysis has the advantage of
simplicity. However, this argument would not apply to common law
prescription and prescription under the doctrine of lost modern grant.
Further, the reference to an 'agreement in writing' in section 3 suggests
that there is a consensual arrangement binding between the servient owner
and the person enjoying the light for the time being. This in turn suggests
that the usual principles for determining whether successors to original
parties are bound come into play. On that basis, the following points
suggest themselves.

3.14   First, in some instances, on its proper construction a permission can
be personal to the original parties. In such instances, no question will arise
of its burden or benefit passing to successors.[32]

---

[29]   *Salvage Wharf Limited v G&S Brough Limited* [2009] EWCA Civ 21; see para 3.10.

[30]   See Land Registration Rules 2003 (SI 2003/1417), rr 36 and 76. See also para 5.33 ff.

[31]   See *Bewley v Atkinson* (1879) 13 ChD 283 at 289.

[32]   Cf *London Tara Hotel Ltd v Kensington Close Hotel Ltd* [2011] EWCA Civ 1356
(licence to use way granted to dominant owner's predecessor was personal to the
predecessor and was not implicitly renewed on acquisition of land by dominant owner).

3.15   Secondly, in the case of agreements and reservations in leases, such agreements and reservations will be enforceable between the parties to the lease and their successors as landlord and tenant in accordance with the usual principles of landlord and tenant law.[33]

3.16   Thirdly, a successor to an owner of the 'dominant' land, who has entered into an agreement that he enjoys light by the licence of the owner of the 'servient' land, is likely to be regarded implicitly as having the benefit of the agreement unless he 'denounces' or repudiates it.[34] Accordingly, in the absence of such denunciation or repudiation, enjoyment of light will be by consent of the servient owner granting the licence.

3.17   Fourthly, however, if a 'servient' owner grants a licence to the 'dominant' owner enabling the enjoyment of light over the servient land, then on the face of things the servient owner's successors will not be bound by the licence over the servient land. In the absence of the imposition of a constructive trust or the operation of the doctrine of estoppel, the burden of a licence over land does not pass to successors of the grantor of the licence.[35] Following a transfer of the servient land, therefore, continued enjoyment of light by the dominant owner would be 'as of right' (for the purposes of lost modern grant) or without consent (for the purposes of the Prescription Act 1832). On the other hand, following a transfer of the 'dominant' land, the 'benefit' of the licence might pass to the transferee as a 'licence' or 'advantage' under the general words imported into a conveyance under section 62 of the Law of Property 1925 so that light would continue to be enjoyed by licence. This conclusion is counter-intuitive: while the 'servient' land is subject to a licence, the purpose of the licence is invariably to permit building on the servient land by preventing the prescription period from running. Rather than being a burden, the licence is in fact beneficial to the servient land. However, if the substance of the agreement is that the servient owner has granted a licence over the servient land, then a successor to the servient owner will not be bound by the licence in accordance with usual principles and (consistently with this) it is difficult to see how he could rely on it.

---

[33]   See para 3.5 ff.

[34]   See Gaunt, J and Morgan, Mr Justice (eds) (2012), *Gale on Easements* (19th edn), Sweet & Maxwell; see also *Bewley v Atkinson* (1879) 13 ChD 283; *Greenhalgh v Brindley* [1901] 2 Ch 324; *Smith v Colbourne* [1914] 2 Ch 533.

[35]   *Ashburn Anstalt v Arnold* [1989] Ch 1.

3.18    Fifthly, if an agreement is not construed simply as a licence in this way, then there seem to be three possible ways in which it might bind successors to the owner of the 'dominant' land to prevent him taking advantage of a prescriptive right.

3.19    If the right is contained in a lease, then it might be enforceable between the parties in accordance with usual principles of landlord and tenant law.[36]

3.20    If the right relates to freehold land, then the right might expressly provide or be construed as a covenant by the grantor not to assert a prescriptive right to obstruct development. Thus it might extend to successors in title by virtue of section 79 of the Law of Property Act 1925 and bind them as a restrictive covenant if duly registered.[37] This was the conclusion in the case of *CGIS City Plaza v Britel Find Trustees Ltd*.[38] However, the correctness of the analysis in this case is doubtful. In general, the burden of a covenant will not pass with freehold land. For the burden of the covenant to pass at law, it would be necessary to find that the burden was conditional upon the enjoyment of some benefit.[39] Unless the provision could be construed as being a condition for the continued enjoyment of some other right, the burden of the covenant could not pass under this principle. For the burden of the covenant to pass in equity, it is generally considered that the covenant must be restrictive of the *use* of the land burdened.[40] A restriction on asserting a right over adjoining land does not restrict the *use* of the burdened land as such. Such restriction seems akin to a restriction on alienation or dealing with the burdened land rather than on how it is used or developed.

---

[36]    See para 3.15 and the examples at para 3.11.

[37]    See Land Registration Act 2002; Land Charges Act 1972, ss 2(5) and 4(6).

[38]    *CGIS City Plaza v Britel Find Trustees Ltd* [2012] EWHC 1594 (Ch) at [55].

[39]    See *Halsall v Brizell* [1957] Ch 169; *Rhone v Stephens* [1994] 2 AC 310.

[40]    See para 1.6. See also *University of East London Higher Education Corpn v Barking and Dagenham LBC* [2004] EWHC 2710 (Ch), [2005] Ch 354 at [28]; *Crestfort Ltd v Tesco Stores Ltd* [2005] EWHC 805 (Ch), [2005] 3 EGLR 25 at [58]–[59]. See also Land Charges Act 1972, s 2(5)(ii); Law of Property Act 1925, s 84. Cf *Test Valley BC v Minilec Engineering Ltd* [2005] 2 EGLR 113 at [162] ff. See also *Langevad v Chiswick Quay Freeholds Ltd* [1999] 1 EGLR 61 at 62.

3.21 The right might be construed as an easement. This is a suggestion made by the editors of *Gale on Easements*.[41] A right to commit that which would otherwise constitute a nuisance can be an easement.[42] While it is difficult to acquire such a right to commit a nuisance by *prescription*,[43] in principle it seems quite possible that such a right could be acquired by express grant or reservation. So, if the effect of the grant or reservation is to authorise a building which would otherwise constitute a nuisance, then it might take effect as an easement. Depending on the words used in any particular case, this seems to be a sound suggestion.

3.22 In the case of registered land, if the right is an easement, then where the title of the land burdened by the right is registered, an easement which is expressly created after the Land Registration Act 2002 came into force will only take effect at law if registered.[44] On the other hand, a legal easement created before the Act came into force took effect as an overriding interest[45] and there are transitional provisions by which an easement that was an overriding interest when the 2002 Act came into force retains that status.[46] If the right is not registered, it may still take effect in equity. In the case of unregistered land, there is no need to register a legal easement.

## PREVENTING A RIGHT OF LIGHT ARISING BY PRESCRIPTION: PHYSICAL INTERRUPTION

3.23 It is axiomatic that to establish a right of light by prescription, there must have been enjoyment for the requisite length of time.[47] Accordingly, physical interruption of the enjoyment of light can prevent the enjoyment light sufficiently to stop a prescriptive right.

---

[41] Gaunt, J and Morgan, Mr Justice (eds) (2012), *Gale on Easements* (19th edn), Sweet & Maxwell, at para 4-36.

[42] *Elliottson v Feetham* (1835) 132 ER 53; *Crump v Lambert* (1867) LR 3 Eq 409 at 413; *Sturges v Bridgman* (1879) 11 ChD 852; *Coventry v Lawrence* [2014] UKSC 13.

[43] *Pwllbach Colliery Co Ltd v Woodman* [1915] AC 634 at 646, 647 and 649; *Coventry v Lawrence and Shields* [2012] EWCA 26 Civ at [91], [2014] UKSC 13 at [32]–[34].

[44] See Land Registration Act 2002, s 27(1). See also paras 5.20ff, 5.34 and 5.35.

[45] Land Registration Act 1925, s 70(1)(a).

[46] See Land Registration Act 2002, Sch 12, para 9.

[47] See para 2.44 ff.

## Physical interruption of light: common law and lost modern grant

3.24  If it can be shown that light has been physically interrupted during the period relied upon by a person claiming a prescriptive right at common law or by lost modern grant, then this can defeat the claim. As explained above, however, to establish a right based on lost modern grant, it is sufficient to establish 20 years' enjoyment as of right at any time, so if there has been 20 years' enjoyment of light as of right *before* an interruption, then a prescriptive right might still be established under the doctrine of lost modern grant.[48] Accordingly, even if an interruption prevents reliance on the Prescription Act 1832 (as explained in the next paragraph), it might not preclude reliance on the doctrine of lost modern grant.

## Physical interruption of light: Prescription Act 1832

3.25  As explained above,[49] under section 3 of the Prescription Act 1832, the 20-year period of enjoyment of light which needs to be shown runs back from the commencement of an action. Until the action is commenced, however, the right is inchoate. Because of the operation of section 4, the acquisition of a right will be defeated if there is an interruption which has been acquiesced in for one year.[50] If the enjoyment of light has been obstructed for one year, a potential claim to a right of light under the 1832 Act will be defeated. But enjoyment for a period exceeding 19 years which is then obstructed can be protected if proceedings are brought after 20 years have run and before the obstruction has lasted one year.[51]

---

[48]  See para 2.48.

[49]  See para 2.65.

[50]  See *Davies v Du Paver* [1953] 1 QB 184 (concerning a profit claimed by prescription) in which Birkett and Morris LJJ were of the view that acquiescence in an interruption needed to be evidenced by conduct and was not to be inferred by nothing being done; Singleton LJ dissented and was of the view that if nothing was done, then this was sufficient interruption. See also *Seddon v Bank of Bolton* (1882) 19 ChD 462 in which Fry J suggested that written notice of the interruption had to be proven if acquiescence was to be inferred.

[51]  See para 2.65.

3.26   For an interruption to be sufficient to preclude the prescription period running under the Prescription Act 1832, the obstruction may be by the servient owner[52] or by a stranger.[53] The mere commencement of proceedings,[54] however, is not an interruption within section 4 because to be an interruption sufficient to stop time running the dominant owner must have *submitted to or acquiesced in* the interruption of his light for one year.[55] In general, in the law of prescription, submission to or acquiescence in an interruption is a state of mind evidenced by the conduct of the parties and is not to be decided merely by saying that there was in fact a period of one year in which nothing was done.[56] Accordingly, the dominant owner must have some notice of the existence of the interruption. There has been a suggestion that written notice of the interruption is required.[57] However, written notice is not expressly required by the statute. If light is physically interrupted, this is likely to be enough to bring the interruption to the notice of the owner of the dominant tenement given the continuous nature of a right of light.

3.27   Whether or not the dominant owner has in fact acquiesced or submitted to the interruption will be a question of fact. If the dominant owner commences proceedings to vindicate his right, then plainly he will not be acquiescing in the interruption.[58] Protests[59] or other acts inconsistent with acquiescence or submission[60] may also be sufficient.

3.28   The ability to defeat a right of light by obstructing its enjoyment led to the practice of screens being erected to prevent the acquisition of rights of light. This practice, however, has fallen into desuetude because planning controls following the Town and Country Planning Act 1947 meant that buildings and 'engineering operations' (such as the erection of screens) required planning permission.

---

[52]   See *Plasterers' Co v Parish Clerks' Co* (1851) 6 Exch 630.

[53]   *Davies v Williams* (1851) 16 QBD 558.

[54]   *Reilly v Orange* [1955] 2 QB 112.

[55]   *Glover v Coleman* (1874) LR 10 CP 108.

[56]   *Davies v Du Paver* [1953] 1 QB 184 at 203; *Ward v Kirkland* [1967] 1 Ch 194 at 231.

[57]   See *Seddon v Bank of Bolton* (1882) 19 ChD 462 at 464, per Fry J.

[58]   *Glover v Coleman* (1874) LR 10 CPO 108.

[59]   *Davies v Du Paver* [1953] 1 QB 184.

[60]   *Ward v Kirkland* [1967] 1 Ch 194 at 231G–232F.

# PREVENTING A RIGHT OF LIGHT ARISING BY PRESCRIPTION: LIGHT OBSTRUCTION NOTICES

## Introduction

3.29 As mentioned in para 3.28, since 1947 the restriction on development without planning permission has made it impracticable to erect screens physically to interrupt light in order to stop prescriptive rights from arising. There is now, however, an alternative to physical obstruction of light. The Rights of Light Act 1959 introduced a scheme under which a *notional* obstruction of a right of light could be effected in order to stop the prescription period from running and to stop prescriptive rights of light being acquired.[61]

3.30 In summary, registering a light obstruction notice following the procedure under the Rights of Light Act 1959 results in the light crossing the servient owner's land being treated as having been interrupted as if an opaque structure had been erected. If the light obstruction notice is unchallenged then, for the purposes of the Prescription Act 1832, the passage of light is treated as having been interrupted and the clock is 'reset'. A light obstruction notice can also prevent the acquisition of an easement of light by stopping the continuous enjoyment of light necessary to establish a right under doctrine of lost modern grant.[62]

## The right to register a light obstruction notice

3.31 Under the Rights of Light Act 1959, any person who is the owner of land ('the servient land') over which light passes to a building[63] ('the dominant building') may apply to the local authority in whose area the dominant building is situated for the registration of a notice.[64] Such a notice is commonly referred to as a 'light obstruction notice'.

---

[61] See generally *Bowring Services Ltd v Scottish Widows Fund & Life Assurance Society* [1995] 1 EGLR 158.

[62] Barnes, M and Bignell, J (2009), 'The Rights of Light Act 1959 and a fiction too far?' *Conveyancer and Property Lawyer*, p 474 at 483.

[63] The phrase used is 'dwelling-house, workshop or other building' as in Prescription Act 1832, s 3: see para 2.68 and Appendix C1; and Rights of Light Act 1959, s 2(1): see Appendix C3.

[64] Rights of Light Act 1959, s 2(1).

3.32   The 'owner' of servient land means a person who:

(a)   is the estate owner in respect of the fee simple thereof; or

(b)   is entitled to a tenancy thereof (within the meaning of the Landlord and Tenant Act 1954) for a term of years certain of which, at the time in question, not less than 7 years remain unexpired; or

(c)   is a mortgagee in possession (within the meaning of the Law of Property Act 1925) where the interest mortgaged is either the fee simple of the land or such a tenancy thereof.[65]

## Certification

3.33   Before applying to register a light obstruction notice, the applicant must obtain one of two sorts of certificate from the Upper Tribunal. The certificate must either:

(a)   certify that adequate notice of the proposed application has been given to all persons who, in the circumstances existing at the time when the certificate is issued, appear to the Upper Tribunal to be persons likely to be affected by the registration of a notice in pursuance of the application; or

(b)   certify that, in the opinion of the Upper Tribunal, the case is one of exceptional urgency, and that accordingly a notice should be registered forthwith as a temporary notice for such period as may be specified in the certificate.[66]

Rules have been made for regulating the issue of certificates. These are contained in Part 7 of the Tribunal Procedure (Upper Tribunal) (Lands Chamber) Rules 2010 (SI 2010/2600).[67]

3.34   An application for a certificate by the Tribunal is made by sending or delivering to the Tribunal an application which must be signed and dated. The application must state:

---

[65]   Rights of Light Act 1959, s 7(1).

[66]   See Rights of Light Act 1959, s 2(3).

[67]   See Appendix C10.

(a)   the name and address of the applicant;

(b)   the name and address of the applicant's representative (if any);

(c)   whether the applicant is—

    (i)   the owner;

    (ii)   the tenant for a term of years certain and, if so, when the term will expire; or

    (iii)   the mortgagee in possession of the servient land;

(d)   a description of the servient land;

(e)   the name of the local authority that keeps the relevant register of local land charges;

(f)   the names and addresses of all persons known by the applicant, after conducting all reasonable enquiries, to be occupying the dominant building or to have a proprietary interest in it; and

(g)   if the application is for a temporary certificate, the grounds upon which it is claimed that the case is of exceptional urgency.[68]

The application must be accompanied by three copies of the application which the applicant proposes to make to the local authority in whose area the dominant building is situated.[69]

3.35   Upon receipt of the application, the Tribunal determines what notices are to be given, by when, and whether by advertisement or otherwise to persons who appear to have an interest in the dominant land.[70]

3.36   Then, the notices that the Tribunal directs shall be given must be given by the applicant. Once this has been done and as soon as reasonably

---

[68]   Tribunal Procedure (Upper Tribunal) (Lands Chamber) Rules 2010 (SI 2010/2600), r 41(1).

[69]   Tribunal Procedure (Upper Tribunal) (Lands Chamber) Rules 2010 (SI 2010/2600), r 41(2).

[70]   Tribunal Procedure (Upper Tribunal) (Lands Chamber) Rules 2010 (SI 2010/2600), r 42(1).

practicable the applicant must notify the Tribunal in writing and set out full particulars of the steps taken.[71]

3.37   Once the Tribunal is satisfied that the required notices have been given, the Tribunal issues a 'definitive certificate'.[72]

3.38   In cases of exceptional urgency, after an application has been made, as described above,[73] where the Tribunal is satisfied that exceptional urgency requires the immediate registration of a temporary notice in the register of local land charges, the Tribunal issues a temporary certificate in a prescribed form.[74] A temporary certificate lasts for no longer than 4 months.[75] This limited duration is necessary to prevent temporary certificates being used to circumvent the requirements for obtaining a definitive certificate. The temporary certificate holds the position until a definitive certificate can be obtained.

3.39   The need for a temporary certificate will arise where the period of enjoyment is about to expire and it would not be practicable to notify the servient landowners in time to stop the prescription period from running.

## Application for registration of light obstruction notice

3.40   The application for registration of a light obstruction notice is made to the local authority in whose area the dominant building is situated.[76] The application must be in the prescribed form.[77] It must:

---

[71]   Tribunal Procedure (Upper Tribunal) (Lands Chamber) Rules 2010 (SI 2010/2600), r 42(2).

[72]   Tribunal Procedure (Upper Tribunal) (Lands Chamber) Rules 2010 (SI 2010/2600), r 44.

[73]   Tribunal Procedure (Upper Tribunal) (Lands Chamber) Rules 2010 (SI 2010/2600), r 43.

[74]   Tribunal Procedure (Upper Tribunal) (Lands Chamber) Rules 2010 (SI 2010/2600), r 23(1).

[75]   Tribunal Procedure (Upper Tribunal) (Lands Chamber) Rules 2010 (SI 2010/2600), r 43(2).

[76]   Rights of Light Act 1959, s 2(1).

[77]   Rights of Light Act 1959, s 2(2).

(a)  identify the servient land and the dominant building in the prescribed manner; and

(b)  state that the application is intended to be equivalent to the obstruction of the access of light to the dominant building across the servient land which would be caused by the erection, in such position on the servient land as may be specified in the application, of an opaque structure of such dimension (including, if the application so states, unlimited height) as may be so specified.[78]

The application must also be accompanied by a certificate from the Upper Tribunal obtained as described above.[79]

## Registration of light obstruction notice

3.41  Where the application is duly made to a local authority for registration of a light obstruction notice, the authority is under a duty to register the notice in the appropriate local land charges register.[80] Any notice so registered takes effect as a local land charge.[81] However, the provisions of the Local Land Charges Act 1975 are modified: in particular, the provisions for compensation for non-registration or a defective official search certificate do not apply.[82]

3.42  The requirement for registration means that successors to the original dominant owner should have notice of a light obstruction notice. The provisions for certification should bring the intended registration of the light obstruction notice to the attention of the original dominant owner.

## The effect of registration

3.43  A light obstruction notice has effect until the earliest of:

---

[78]  Rights of Light Act 1959, s 2(2)(b).

[79]  See para 3.33; Rights of Light Act 1959, s 2(3).

[80]  Rights of Light Act 1959, s 2(4).

[81]  Rights of Light Act 1959, s 2(4)(a).

[82]  Rights of Light Act 1959, s 2(4)(b): Local Land Charges Act 1975, ss 5(1) and (2) and 10 do not apply.

(a)  the date when it is cancelled; or

(b)  the expiration of the period of one year beginning with the date of registration; or

(c)  in a case where the Upper Tribunal has certified urgency, the date specified in the notice.[83]

3.44   Where a notice is registered, then for the purposes of determining whether a person is entitled by virtue of the Prescription Act 1832 *or otherwise* to a right of access of light to a dominant building across the servient land, the access of light to that building across that land shall be treated as obstructed to the same extent, and with the like consequences, as if an opaque structure, of the dimensions specified in the application:

(a)  had, on the date of registration of the notice, been erected in the position on the servient land specified in the application; and
(b)  had been so erected by the person who made the application; and
(c)  had remained in that position during the period for which the notice has effect; and
(d)  had been removed at the end of that period.[84]

Accordingly, there will be deemed to be interruption in the enjoyment of access of light both for the purposes of deciding whether or not a prescriptive right has been acquired under the 1832 Act *and* for the purposes of prescription at common law or by lost modern grant.

3.45   Where a light obstruction notice is registered, any person who would have had a right of action in respect of the erection of such a structure as is specified in the application, as infringing a right of access of light to the dominant building, has the same right of action in respect of the registration of the notice.[85] Any such action cannot be begun after the notice has ceased to have effect.[86]

---

[83]  Rights of Light Act 1959, s 3(2).

[84]  Rights of Light Act 1959, s 3(1).

[85]  Rights of Light Act 1959, s 3(3).

[86]  Rights of Light Act 1959, s 3(3).

3.46   The remedies available to a claimant who brings an action under the Rights of Light Act 1959 are:

(a)   such declaration as the court may consider appropriate in the circumstances; and

(b)   an order directing the registration of the notice to be cancelled or varied, as the court may determine.[87]

3.47   Since the 20-year prescription period under the Prescription Act 1832 is the period 'next before' the commencement of proceedings as described above,[88] a dominant owner needs to commence proceedings to crystallise his inchoate right where a notional obstruction takes place under the Rights of Light Act 1959. The dominant owner's enjoyment, however, is treated as commencing one year earlier than it actually did[89] – this deeming provision was presumably intended to avoid problems for the dominant owner where a notice is registered in the final year of the prescription period for the purposes of the 1832 Act.[90] It is expressly provided that for the purposes of section 4 of the 1832 Act (under which a period of enjoyment of any of the rights to which the 1832 Act applies is not to be treated as interrupted except by a matter submitted to or acquiesced in for one year after notice thereof):

(a)   as from the date of registration of a light obstruction notice, all persons interested in the dominant building or any part thereof are shall be deemed to have notice of the registration and of the person on whose application it was registered;

(b)   until such time as an action is brought under the 1959 Act in respect of the registration of a light obstruction notice, all persons interested in the dominant building or any part thereof shall be deemed to acquiesce in the obstruction which is deemed to result from the registration of the notice;

---

[87]   Rights of Light Act 1959, s 3(5). See *Hawker v Tomalin* (1969) 20 P & CR 550.

[88]   See para 2.65.

[89]   Rights of Light Act 1959, s 3(4).

[90]   See para 2.65, but see Barnes, M and Bignell, J (2009), 'The Rights of Light Act 1959 and a fiction too far?', *Conveyancer and Property Lawyer*, p. 474 at 484 for the problematic nature of this deeming.

(c)  as from the date on which such an action is brought, no person shall
     be treated as submitting to or acquiescing in that obstruction;

provided that if, in any such action, the court decides against the claim of
the claimant the court may direct that these provisions shall apply in
relation to the notice as if that action had not been brought.

3.48  However, as explained above,[91] for the purposes of the doctrine of
lost modern grant a prescriptive right can be acquired by a dominant owner
relying on 20 years' use *at any time.* Accordingly, the interruption by
reason of the notional obstruction under the Rights of Light Act 1959 will
not defeat a right which could be established by 20 years' enjoyment at
some time prior to the registration of the notice. Thus, an owner who
enjoys light by a pre-existing right which can be established by lost
modern grant will not lose his right if he does not commence proceedings.

## Other challenges to light obstruction notices?

3.49  The possibility of challenging a decision of the Upper Tribunal is
very limited. In theory, a decision by the Upper Tribunal to issue a
certificate is susceptible to judicial review. However, given the right of a
dominant owner to challenge the light obstruction notice itself on
substantive grounds, in most cases the dominant owner will have an
alternative remedy which is likely to make judicial review inappropriate.
It is not open to a dominant owner to commence proceedings by writ
challenging the issue of the certificate by the Tribunal and the registration
of the notice on grounds which could have been put forward on an
application for judicial review.[92] Further, it is not possible to appeal by
way of case stated against the issue of a certificate by the Upper Tribunal.[93]

## Application to Crown land

3.50  The Rights of Light Act 1959 applies to land in which there is an
interest belonging to the Queen in right of the Crown or the Duchy of

---

[91]  See para 2.48.

[92]  *Bowring Services Ltd v Scottish Widows Fund & Life Assurance Society* [1995] 1
      EGLR 158.

[93]  *Bowring Services Ltd v Scottish Widows Fund & Life Assurance Society* [1995] 1
      EGLR 158.

Lancaster or belonging to the Duchy of Cornwall or belonging to a government department or held in trust for the Queen for the purposes of a government department.[94] However, section 3 of the Prescription Act 1832 is not to be construed as applying to land to which (by reason of there being a Crown or Duchy interest) that section would not apply apart from the 1959 Act.[95] The extent to which section 3 of the 1832 Act applies to Crown land is considered above.[96]

---

[94] Rights of Light Act 1959, s 4(1) and (3).

[95] Rights of Light Act 1959, s 4(2).

[96] See para 2.80.

# Chapter 4

# Agreements Dealing with Light

## INTRODUCTION

4.1    The formalities for express grants of rights of light,[1] how they may be granted by implication[2] (and how implications may be excluded[3]) and agreements which can prevent prescriptive rights arising[4] are considered above. In practice, however, it is possible to find one transaction in which the parties try to achieve a number of things. They may also contain a number of provisions with the same objective, for example defining precisely the parties' respective rights by a combination of licences or rights to carry out work together with restrictive covenants limiting work to specified parameters.[5] It is important in construing the document or documents embodying the transaction to read the document(s) as a whole yet to disentangle the various different provisions and their objectives. It is, therefore, useful at this point to draw together some of the things previously said and to make some additional points about agreements which expressly deal with light.

---

[1]    See paras 2.3 ff and 2.16 ff.

[2]    See para 2.18 ff.

[3]    See paras 2.34 and 2.40(h).

[4]    See para 3.3 ff.

[5]    See e.g. *Mayor and Commonalty and Citizens of the City of London v Intercede (1765) Ltd* [2005] EWHC 1691 (Ch).

## CONSTRUING DEEDS GENERALLY

4.2    Deeds dealing with light are no different to any other contract. In essence, in the words of Lord Bingham in *BCCI v Ali*,[6] the general approach to construing a contract is as follows:

> To ascertain the intention of the parties the court reads the terms of the contract as a whole, giving the words used their natural and ordinary meaning in the context of the agreement, the parties' relationship and all the relevant facts surrounding the transaction so far as known to the parties. To ascertain the parties' intentions the court does not of course inquire into the parties' subjective states of mind but makes an objective judgment based on the materials already identified.

4.3    The influence which such material will have on construction will be determined by asking what weight the reasonable person with all the background knowledge of the parties would attribute to it.[7] Accordingly, where the document in question is a document which requires registration on a public register, documents collateral to the registered document which would not be available to the public will not in practice influence the process of interpretation.[8]

4.4    While there are specific principles which are applicable to easements which are considered at para 2.18 ff, there is nothing to exclude the general principles of contractual construction when determining whether an easement is implicit in a transaction. Indeed, the specific cases in which easements are implied can properly be considered to be specific examples of these principles or at least to be consistent with the general approach to the implication of terms into contracts.

---

[6]    *BCCI v Ali* [2001] UKHL 8 at [8], [2001] 1 AC 251; see also *Investors Compensation Scheme v West Bromwich Building Society* [1998] 1 WLR 896; *Chartbrook Limited v Persimmon Homes Limited* [2009] UKHL 38; *Rainy Sky SA v Kookmin Bank* [2011] UKSC 50.

[7]    *Cherry Tree Investments Ltd v Landmain* [2012] EWCA Civ 735, [2013] Ch 305, in particular per Lewison LJ.

[8]    *Cherry Tree Investments Ltd v Landmain* [2012] EWCA Civ 735, [2013] Ch 305, in particular per Lewison LJ. See also, generally, *Arnold v Britton* [2015] UKSC 36.

4.5   In *BP Refinery (Westport) Pty Limited v Shire of Hastings*,[9] the Privy Council set out five conditions (which may overlap) for implication of terms, Lord Simon saying:

> (1) [The proposed implied term] must be reasonable and equitable; (2) it must be necessary to give business efficacy to the contract, so that no term will be implied if the contract is effective without it; (3) it must be so obvious that 'it goes without saying'; (4) it must be capable of clear expression; (5) it must not contradict any express term of the contract.

4.6   In *Marks and Spencer plc v BNP Paribas Securities Services Trust Company (Jersey) Limited*,[10] Lord Neuberger indicated that the observations in the *BP Refinery* case represented a clear approach, and that terms will only be implied into a contract where strictly necessary to give efficacy to the contract. He added the following six comments:[11]

> First, in *Equitable Life Assurance Society v Hyman* [2002] 1 AC 408, 459, Lord Steyn rightly observed that the implication of a term was 'not critically dependent on proof of an actual intention of the parties' when negotiating the contract. If one approaches the question by reference to what the parties would have agreed, one is not strictly concerned with the hypothetical answer of the actual parties, but with that of notional reasonable people in the position of the parties at the time at which they were contracting. Secondly, a term should not be implied into a detailed commercial contract merely because it appears fair or merely because one considers that the parties would have agreed it if it had been suggested to them. Those are necessary but not sufficient grounds for including a term. However, and thirdly, it is questionable whether Lord Simon's first requirement, reasonableness and equitableness, will usually, if ever, add anything: if a term satisfies the other requirements, it is hard to think that it would not be reasonable and equitable. Fourthly, as Lord Hoffmann I think suggested in *Attorney General of Belize v Belize Telecom Ltd* [2009] 1 WLR 1988, para 27, although Lord Simon's requirements are otherwise cumulative, I would accept that business

---

[9]   *BP Refinery (Westport) Pty Limited v Shire of Hastings* (1977) 180 CLR 266 at 282–283.

[10]   *Marks and Spencer plc v BNP Paribas Securities Services Trust Company (Jersey) Limited* [2015] UKSC 72.

[11]   *Marks and Spencer plc v BNP Paribas Securities Services Trust Company (Jersey) Limited* [2015] UKSC 72 at [21]

necessity and obviousness, his second and third requirements, can be alternatives in the sense that only one of them needs to be satisfied, although I suspect that in practice it would be a rare case where only one of those two requirements would be satisfied. Fifthly, if one approaches the issue by reference to the officious bystander, it is 'vital to formulate the question to be posed by [him] with the utmost care', to quote from Lewison, *The Interpretation of Contracts* 5th ed (2011), para 6.09. Sixthly, necessity for business efficacy involves a value judgment. It is rightly common ground on this appeal that the test is not one of 'absolute necessity', not least because the necessity is judged by reference to business efficacy. It may well be that a more helpful way of putting Lord Simon's second requirement is, as suggested by Lord Sumption in argument, that a term can only be implied if, without the term, the contract would lack commercial or practical coherence.

The court emphasised that although the implication of terms might be regarded as part of the process of construing a document in a wider sense, the process of implication is distinct from the narrower process of construing the words used. It is only after construction (in the narrow sense) has been considered that the question of implication can arise.

4.7    In some cases, it is possible to 'correct' an apparent error in an agreement by the process of construction or implication. For this to occur:

> [t]wo conditions must be satisfied: first, there must be a clear mistake on the face of the instrument; secondly, it must be clear what correction ought to be made in order to cure the mistake. If those conditions are satisfied, then the correction is made as a matter of construction.[12]

This statement is 'no more than an expression of the common sense view that we do not readily accept that people have made mistakes in formal documents', and was endorsed by the House of Lords in *Chartbrook Limited v Persimmon Homes Limited.*[13] In that case Lord Hoffmann made two qualifications, namely:

---

[12]   *East v Pantiles (Plant Hire) Ltd* (1981) 263 EG 61, per Brightman J.

[13]   *Chartbrook Limited v Persimmon Homes Limited* [2009] UKHL 38 at [22]–[25], per Lord Hoffmann. See also *Arnold v Britton* [2015] UKSC 15; *LBG Capital No 1 PLC v BNY Mellon Corporate Trustee Services Ltd* [2015] EWCA Civ 1257.

(a)  that:

> 'correction of mistakes by construction' is not a separate branch of the law, a summary version of an action for rectification. As Carnwath LJ said [in *KPMG LLP v Network Rail Infrastructure Ltd*[14]]:
>
>> 'Both in the judgment, and in the arguments before us, there was a tendency to deal separately with correction of mistakes and construing the paragraph "as it stands", as though they were distinct exercises. In my view, they are simply aspects of the single task of interpreting the agreement in its context, in order to get as close as possible to the meaning which the parties intended.'

(b)  that:

> in deciding whether there is a clear mistake, the court is not confined to reading the document without regard to its background or context. As the exercise is part of the single task of interpretation, the background and context must always be taken into consideration.
>
> … What is clear from these cases is that there is not, so to speak, a limit to the amount of red ink or verbal rearrangement or correction which the court is allowed. All that is required is that it should be clear that something has gone wrong with the language and that it should be clear what a reasonable person would have understood the parties to have meant.

## EXPRESS AND IMPLIED GRANTS OF RIGHTS OF LIGHT

4.8    As explained above, a right of light may be the subject of a grant, express[15] or implied.[16] The extent of the right granted will be a matter of construction in the context. There is no reason, in accordance with these principles, why in appropriate circumstances a right of light might not be granted of a specific extent (beyond that which might, for instance, be acquired by prescription). Whether express or implied, however, a right

---

[14]   *KPMG LLP v Network Rail Infrastructure Ltd* [2007] Bus LR 1336 at 1351 at [50].

[15]   See para 2.16 ff.

[16]   See para 2.18 ff.

can only be granted as an easement if the law will recognise the right as such.[17]

4.9    The specific situations in which easements have historically been implied are considered in detail above.[18] These situations (save where words are imported by statute under section 62 of the Law of Property Act 1925) can be regarded as consistent with the approach to construction described above, dependent as they are on the factual circumstances in which land is transferred or let.

## PERMISSION, AGREEMENT OR CONSENT TO ENJOY LIGHT

4.10    The grant of a right of light (as an easement) must be distinguished from *permission* to enjoy light. Permission to enjoy light is usually granted with the intention of preventing a right to light arising by prescription. This is explained above.[19]

## RESTRICTIONS ON BUILDING WHICH INTERFERES WITH LIGHT: RESTRICTIVE COVENANTS

4.11    Covenants in conveyances and leases often restrict building or building of a certain form or for a certain use. The essence of such covenants might not depend on whether or not the restricted form of building interferes with light (though such covenants might, in practice, protect light), but might be aimed at protecting amenity more generally. Sometimes, however, covenants will be formulated so that building is not permitted beyond a certain envelope (usually identified by an elevation and plan) with the clear intention of protecting light enjoyed by the 'dominant' land.[20] Such covenants are not only found in conveyances and

---

[17]    See para 2.13–2.15.

[18]    See para 2.18 ff.

[19]    See para 3.2 ff and see also para 5.33 ff (land registration).

[20]    See e.g. *Cemp Properties (UK) Limited v Dentsply Research and Development Corporation (No 2)* [1989] 2 EGLR 196 (on appeal [1991] 2 EGLR 197); cf also *Mayor and Commonalty and Citizens of the City of London v Intercede (1765) Ltd* [2005] EWHC 1691 (Ch).

leases but are sometimes imposed as part of a transaction in which existing rights of light are released to ensure that no additional interference with light will be caused in the future. The rules for the extent to which such covenants bind successors to the original parties are considered above.[21]

## RIGHTS TO CONSTRUCT BUILDINGS WHICH INTERFERE WITH LIGHT

4.12 Covenants which authorise building that interferes with light can take a number of forms. They might authorise a specified building. They might authorise a specified building and the rebuilding of the specified building. They might authorise any building within a specified envelope (or in such a way that the new building will not interfere with light any more than the existing building).[22] Such covenants are often found together with covenants which expressly or implied restrict development outside the specified envelope.[23]

4.13 Authority to build may take effect as a consent or agreement which will preclude the acquisition of prescriptive rights of light.[24] It is necessary, therefore, to distinguish between:

(a) clauses which provide the authority only for the construction of a particular scheme so that the acquisition of rights by prescription thereafter is not precluded;[25] and

---

[21] See para 1.6. See also paras 5.11, 5.19 and 5.28.

[22] See e.g. *Cemp Properties (UK) Limited v Dentsply Research and Development Corporation (No 2)* [1989] 2 EGLR 196 (on appeal [1991] 2 EGLR 197). Deed providing 'servient' owner should 'have full liberty and power to erect the new building in accordance with plan annexed hereto *but not otherwise*'.

[23] See e.g. the provisions under consideration in *Mayor and Commonalty and Citizens of the City of London v Intercede (1765) Ltd* [2005] EWHC 1691 (Ch).

[24] See para 3.2 ff.

[25] See paras 3.9–3.10; *Salvage Wharf Limited v G&S Brough Limited* [2009] EWCA Civ 21.

(b)   clauses which permit future redevelopment of the 'servient' tenement
      so that light is enjoyed by the 'dominant' owner permissively and the
      acquisition of prescriptive rights precluded.[26]

This is explained more fully above.[27]

## EXCLUSION OF IMPLIED RIGHTS ON TRANSACTION

4.14   As explained above, deeds may preclude implied rights being
granted. Such exclusion may be express or implied.[28] Plainly, where an
express authorisation to build is granted and such authorisation is
inconsistent with an implied right, then implied rights will be implicitly
excluded.[29]

---

[26]   See paras 3.9–3.10; *RHJ Limited v FT Patten (Holdings) Ltd* [2007] EWHC 1665 (Ch),
       [2007] 4 All ER, [2008] EWCA Civ 151, [2008] Ch 341.

[27]   See para 3.8 ff.

[28]   See paras 2.34 and 2.40(h).

[29]   See paras 4.12–4.13 generally; but see para 2.40(h) for the position for the exclusion
       of the application of Law of Property Act 1925, s 62.

# Chapter 5

# Successors in Title and Registration of Rights

## INTRODUCTION

5.1    Where agreements and rights concerning light are contained in, or arise under, a contract between two or more parties, the obligations may be enforced between the original parties to the contract by reason of the doctrine of privity of contract. Where, however, there has been a transfer of the dominant or servient land, questions arise about the extent to which successors to the original parties may enforce, and may be subject to, the rights and obligations contained in the contract.

5.2    A legal easement is one created for an equivalent to a fee simple absolute in possession or a term of years absolute.[1] Because a legal easement benefits a 'dominant tenement' it does not exist 'in gross', i.e. it cannot be separated from the land which benefits from it. The benefit of such an easement, however, will in general pass on the transfer of the dominant tenement to the owners of that tenement unless excluded from the transfer. In general, a legal easement over a servient tenement will bind successors to the original servient owner. The formalities which are necessary for the grant of a legal easement are described above.[2] Easements arising by prescription are also legal easements[3] and are treated in this way.

5.3    Equitable easements are different. They may be created otherwise than for an interest equivalent to a fee simple absolute in possession or for

---

[1]    Law of Property Act 1925, s 1(2)(a).

[2]    See para 2.4.

[3]    See para 2.77.

a term of years absolute. Easements equivalent to interests in fee simple absolute in possession or for a term of years may also fall short of being legal easements because of a failure to comply with formalities or for want of registration. An easement which takes effect as an equitable right will enure for the benefit of the dominant tenement.[4] However, the general rule in equity is that an equitable right is binding on all who acquire the servient land but will not bind a *bona fide* purchaser without notice.[5] This general rule is now subject to the requirements of statute.

5.4    In deciding how an easement might benefit or burden successors to the original parties to a grant of a right of light, three codes need to be considered. Their interrelationship with the law of prescription also needs to be considered, as does how they affect deeds dealing with light. Which code operates depends on whether:

(a)   the title to land is unregistered;

(b)   the Land Registration Act 1925 applies; or

(c)   the Land Registration Act 2002 applies.

## UNREGISTERED LAND

5.5    The formalities for the creation of a legal easement are explained above.[6] Whether the benefit of an easement (legal or equitable) has passed to a successor to the owner of the dominant tenement will depend upon the terms of the conveyance of the dominant land.

5.6    Where land is unregistered, *legal* easements will bind successors to the servient tenement. Questions of notice do not enter into it. However, the position is different where the easement is an *equitable* easement.

5.7    An equitable easement over or affecting land created or arising on or after 1 January 1926 and being merely an equitable interest is a

---

[4]   *E R Ives Investment Ltd v High* [1967] 2 QB 379.

[5]   See *Inwards v Baker* [1965] 2 QB 29 at 37; *Voyce v Voyce* (1991) 62 P & CR 290 at 294 and 296; see also *Hervey v Smith* (1855) 1 K & J 389.

[6]   See para 2.4 ff.

class D(iii) land charge under the Land Charges Act 1972.[7] Such an easement is void against a purchaser for money or money's worth of a legal estate charged with it unless the land charge is registered in the appropriate register before the completion of the purchase.[8] An example of such an easement is one granted for life only.

5.8    However, not all easements which take effect in equity are within the scope of these provisions. The Court of Appeal in *E R Ives Investment Ltd v High*[9] considered that an 'equitable easement' for the purposes of the Land Charges Act 1972 was limited to a proprietary interest in land such as would before 1926 have been recognised as capable of being conveyed or created at law, but which since 1926 only took effect as an equitable interest, such as an easement granted for life.[10] Accordingly, these provisions do not apply to easements taking effect by acquiescence or estoppel.[11] An easement taking effect in equity but which did not fall within class D(iii), therefore, would be enforceable against successors to the servient land unless they were *bona fide* purchasers of the servient land without notice of the interest.

5.9    It has also been suggested that a specifically enforceable contract to grant a legal easement over unregistered land is outside class D(iii) because no easement is presently exercisable or because it is an interest which even before 1926 would not have taken effect at law and is thus to be treated as being outside the scope of class D(iii).[12] This suggestion follows from the reasoning in *E R Ives Investment Ltd v High*,[13] mentioned in the previous paragraph, because such an easement is not one which before 1926 could have existed at law.

---

[7]    Land Charges Act 1972, s 2(5).

[8]    Land Charges Act 1972, s 4(6).

[9]    *E R Ives Investment Ltd v High* [1967] 2 QB 379.

[10]   See para 2.4 ff, and Law of Property Act 1925, s 1(2)(a): legal easements will only exist as legal easements if they are for an interest 'equivalent to an estate in fee simple absolute in possession or for a term of years absolute'.

[11]   *E R Ives Investment Ltd v High* [1967] 2 QB 379, approved in *Shiloh Spinners Ltd v Harding* [1973] AC 691 at 721.

[12]   Gaunt, J and Morgan, Mr Justice (eds) (2012), *Gale on Easements* (19th edn), Sweet & Maxwell, at para 2-37.

[13]   *E R Ives Investment Ltd v High* [1967] 2 QB 379.

5.10 Further, such a contract could not be registered as a class C(iv) estate contract which is defined as:

> a contract by an estate owner or by a person entitled at the date of the contract to have a legal estate conveyed to him to convey or create a legal estate, including a contract conferring either expressly or by statutory implication a valid option to purchase a right of pre-emption or any other like right.[14]

An easement is not an estate[15] so a contract to create an easement is not a contract to convey or create an estate.[16]

5.11 A deed affecting rights of light might contain restrictive covenants.[17] If so, they must be registered as a Class D(ii) land charge in the name of the estate owner of the land burdened in order to bind successors to that owner.[18] If unregistered they will not bind a purchaser of the estate for money or money's worth.[19]

## LAND REGISTRATION ACT 1925

### Generally

5.12 Under the Land Registration Act 1925, the benefit of a legal easement could be entered on the register if it was appurtenant to a registered estate.[20]

5.13 Where a servient owner *expressly* granted or reserved an easement over his land, such grant had to be in the prescribed form[21] and had to be

---

[14]  Land Charges Act 1972, s 4(6).

[15]  Law of Property Act 1925, s 1.

[16]  Gaunt, J and Morgan, Mr Justice (eds) (2012), *Gale on Easements* (19th edn), Sweet & Maxwell, at para 2-38.

[17]  See paras 1.5 and 4.11.

[18]  See Land Charges Act 1972, s 2(5).

[19]  Land Charges Act 1972, s 4(6).

[20]  Land Registration Rules 1925 (SR&O 1925/1093), r 257.

[21]  Land Registration Act 1925, ss 18(1), (2) and 21(1).

entered on the register against the registered servient tenement.[22] So, if the easement was to take effect as a legal easement appurtenant to the dominant land, it had to be registered.[23] Until such registration it took effect only as an *equitable* easement.[24]

## Benefit

5.14   On a disposition of the dominant tenement or a charge on the dominant tenement, the benefit of the easement entered on the register accrued on registration to the grantee as part of the legal estate (subject to any express exception or reservation).[25]

5.15   In any event, a registered disposition of the dominant tenement would confer on the transferee or grantee all easements appurtenant to the registered dominant tenement.[26] So, a legal easement did not have to be registered for the benefit of it to pass to successors to the original dominant owner.[27] Indeed, the benefit of equitable easements would also pass in this way upon the transfer of the dominant tenement unless excluded from the transfer.

## Burden

5.16   Legal easements registered against the title to the servient land bind the servient owner. However, under the Land Registration Act 1925 not all legal easements needed to be noted on the register, and such easements bind successors to the servient tenement as legal easements without registration:

(a)   There was no need to register a legal easement granted on the disposition of a registered estate by the implication of general words under section 62 of the Law of Property Act 1925. This is because

---

[22]   Land Registration Act 1925, ss 19(2) and 22(2).

[23]   Land Registration Act 1925, ss 19(2) and 22(2).

[24]   See para 2.4 ff.

[25]   Land Registration Rules 1925 (SR&O 1925/1093), r 256.

[26]   Land Registration Act 1925, ss 20, 23 and 72; Land Registration Rules 1925 (SR&O 1925/1093), r 251.

[27]   Cf *Re Evans' Contract* [1970] 1 WLR 583.

provision was made that on registration of a person as registered proprietor there vested all rights which would pass under that section.[28] It should be noted, however, that there was no analogous provision dealing with other forms of implied easements (under *Wheeldon v Burrows*[29] or otherwise, including easement of necessity[30]) or implied reservations. This will usually make no difference because of the provisions relating to overriding interests.[31]

(b) An easement 'not being an equitable easement required to be protected by notice on the register' was an overriding interest within section 70(1)(a) of the Land Registration Act 1925.[32] Registration of the legal estate of the servient land took effect subject to any such overriding interests.[33] An easement which was created before the land became registered bound the first and subsequent registered proprietors of the servient land. It is important to note that even where at the time of first registration a note of the easement has to be entered on the register, this will not affect the status of the easement as an 'overriding interest' binding on the servient land.[34]

(c) If a legal easement had been acquired by prescription, then the Registrar, if he thought fit, might register it as part of the description of the dominant land,[35] but in any event a legal easement acquired by prescription would take effect and bind successors to the servient owner as an overriding interest.

5.17 On the other hand, on the face of things an 'equitable easement' did require to be protected by notice on the register if it was to bind transferees of the servient land. There are two circumstances in which an equitable

---

[28] Land Registration Act 1925, s 19(3); Land Registration Rules 1925 (SR&O 1925/1093), r 251. See para 2.39 ff for consideration of when Law of Property Act 1925, s 62 applies.

[29] *Wheeldon v Burrows* (1879) 12 ChD 31, see para 2.26 ff.

[30] See para 2.20.

[31] See para 5.16(b).

[32] Land Registration Act 1925, s 70(1)(a).

[33] Land Registration Act 1925, ss 20(1) and 23(1); Land Registration Rules 1925 (SR&O 1925/1093), r 258.

[34] *Re Dances Way, West Town, Hayling Island* [1962] Ch 490 at 507.

[35] Land Registration Rules 1925 (SR&O 1925/1093), r 250(2)(b).

easement could take effect as an overriding interest under the Land Registration Act 1925 capable of binding servient land:

(a) The first was where the right is the right of a person in actual occupation of the land (or in receipt of rent or profits thereof) save where inquiry is made of such persons and the rights are not disclosed.[36] However, it is difficult to see how enjoyment of a right of light can amount to actual occupation of the servient land.[37]

(b) The second was by reason of the operation of section 70(1)(a) when read with the Land Registration Rules 1925.[38]

5.18   As noted above, under section 70(1)(a) of the Land Registration Act 1925, easements 'not being an equitable easement required to be protected by notice on the register' take effect as overriding interests.[39] Therefore, if an equitable easement was *not* required to be protected by notice on the register, then it could take effect as an overriding interest under this section. In *Celsteel Ltd v Alton House Holdings Ltd*,[40] Scott J held the words 'equitable easements' in this section should not be read in the narrow manner in which the Court of Appeal had approached class D(iii) land charges under the Land Charges Act 1972.[41] They extended to all forms of equitable easements. The words 'required to be protected', however, were to be read as 'need to be protected'. Accordingly, Scott J concluded:[42]

> The exception in the paragraph was ... intended to cover all equitable easements other than such as by reason of some other statutory provision or applicable principle of law, could obtain protection otherwise than by notice on the register. The most obvious example would be equitable

---

[36]   Land Registration Act 1925 ss 20, 23 and 70(1)(g).

[37]   Cf *Holaw (470) Ltd v Stockton Estates Ltd* (2000) 81 P & CR 404.

[38]   SR&O 1925/1093.

[39]   See para 5.16.

[40]   *Celsteel Ltd v Alton House Holdings Ltd* [1985] 1 WLR 204 (reversed but not on this point at [1986] 1 WLR 512).

[41]   See para 5.8.

[42]   *Celsteel Ltd v Alton House Holdings Ltd* [1985] 1 WLR 204 at 220. See also *Thatcher v Douglas* [1996] NLJ 282; *Sweet v Sommer* [2004] EWHC 1504 (Ch), [2005] EWCA Civ 227.

easements which qualified for protection under paragraph (g) as part of the rights of a person in actual occupation.

Further, section 144(1) (xxi) of the Land Registration Act 1925 authorised rule 258 of the Land Registration Rules 1925,[43] which provided that rights:

> appertaining or reputed to appertain to land occupied or enjoyed therewith or reputed or known as part or parcel of or appurtenant thereto, which adversely affect registered land, are overriding interests within section 70 of the Act, and shall not be deemed incumbrances for the purposes of the Act.

In other words, the category of rights which were 'overriding interests' had been extended by the rules.[44] Accordingly, Scott J held that an equitable easement within the description of rule 258 took effect as an overriding interest and did not require to be protected by notice on the register. In principle, there is no reason why an equitable right of light enjoyed with dominant land should not bind transferees of the servient land in this way under the 1925 legislation even if not registered against the title to the servient land.

5.19   A deed affecting rights of light which takes effect as a restrictive covenant,[45] however, would need to be registered against the title to the servient land if it is to bind transferees of that land.

## LAND REGISTRATION ACT 2002

5.20   Where land is registered, an 'express grant or reservation' of an easement (other than one which is being registered under the Commons Registration Act 1965) is a disposition which requires to be completed by registration and it does not operate *at law* until the relevant registration requirements are met.[46] However:

---

[43]   SR&O 1925/1093.

[44]   *Sweet v Sommer* [2005] EWCA Civ 227 at [20].

[45]   See paras 1.5 and 4.11.

[46]   Land Registration Act 2002, s 27(1) and (2)(d).

(a) an express grant for these purposes does not include a grant of an easement as a result of the operation of section 62 of the Law of Property Act 1925;[47]

(b) implied easements are not dispositions that are required to be registered (the provision that an 'express grant or reservation' does not operate at law until registration suggests that implied grants[48] or reservations[49] of easements need not be registered to operate at law); and

(c) there is no requirement to perfect an easement acquired by prescription by registration for it to take effect at law.

5.21 Where an easement must be registered, the provisions for the requirement of registration are that:

(a) notice in respect of the interest created must be entered in the register; and

(b) if the interest is created for the benefit of a registered estate, the proprietor must be entered in the register as its proprietor.[50]

5.22 The transfer of registered title to the dominant tenement when completed by registration will vest all the interests (including easements such as right of light) in the registered proprietor. The transferee of the dominant tenement will obtain the benefit of all legal and equitable easements (unless excluded from the transfer).

5.23 On the other hand, on the transfer of the servient tenement for valuable consideration, the disponee will have priority over an easement affecting the servient tenement unless the easement:

(a) is protected by notice in the register relating to the servient tenement; or

(b) takes effect as an overriding interest.[51]

---

[47] Land Registration Act 2002, s 27(7); see generally para 2.39 ff.

[48] See para 2.18 ff for implied grants.

[49] See para 2.35 ff for implied reservations.

[50] Land Registration Act 2002, Sch 2, para 7. See generally Land Registry, *Practice Guide 62: Easements*, updated 24 June 2015.

[51] Land Registration Act 2002, s 29(1),(2)(a).

5.24   A *legal* easement takes effect as an overriding interest and binds successors to the servient tenement unless at the time of the disposition:

(a)   it is not within the actual knowledge of the person to whom the disposition is made;[52] and

(b)   it would not have been obvious on a reasonable inspection of the land over which the easement is exercisable.[53]

However, this exception does not apply if the person entitled to the easement proves that it has been exercised in the period of one year ending on the day of the disposition.[54] If the access of light has not been interrupted in the year before disposition, it would seem that a right of light would be one which was exercised within one year before the disposition. If so, a legal easement of light will usually bind successors in title to the servient tenement.

5.25   There are two important further provisions which qualify this:

(a)   An easement (including an equitable easement) which was an overriding interest in relation to a registered estate immediately before 13 October 2003 but which would not be an overriding interest under the Land Registration Act 2002 if created after that date can take effect as an overriding interest.[55]

(b)   For the period of 3 years beginning with 13 October 2003, 'the exception' (which excludes easements not within the actual knowledge of the person to whom the disposition is made and which would not have been obvious on a reasonable inspection of the land over which the easement was exercisable) was disapplied.[56]

5.26   It follows, therefore, that unless within these last two qualifications mentioned in the previous paragraph equitable easements will *not* be overriding interests as such for the purposes of the Land Registration Act

---

[52]   Land Registration Act 2002, Sch 3, para 3(1)(a).

[53]   Land Registration Act 2002, Sch 3, para 3(1)(b).

[54]   Land Registration Act 2002, Sch 3, para 3(2).

[55]   Land Registration Act 2002, Sch 12, para 9.

[56]   Land Registration Act 2002, Sch 12, para 10.

2002. Except where these qualifications apply, equitable easements must be protected by notice on the register if they are to bind successors to the servient tenement.[57]

5.27　There are other categories of overriding interest. However, these are unlikely to give protection to owners of equitable easements of light. For instance, under paragraph 2 of Schedule 3 to the Land Registration Act 2002, rights of persons in actual occupation of land affected by the right may be overriding interests in certain circumstances. However, *ex hypothesi*, the dominant owner of an equitable right of light will not be in occupation of the servient tenement. Accordingly, he will not be able to claim it is an overriding interest on this ground.[58]

5.28　Deeds affecting rights of light which are enforceable as restrictive covenants need to be registered against the burdened title if they are to bind successors to the servient land.

## Easements in the course of acquisition

5.29　Subject to the question of whether there is a competent grantor or grantee,[59] changes in the ownership of the dominant or of the servient tenement will not preclude the prescription period from running. Further, enjoyment of light by a tenant is enjoyment of his landlord, so successive grants of leases of the dominant tenement will not preclude the acquisition of rights of light by prescription over the servient tenement.[60] This will also be the case where a tenant's interest is assigned from time to time or even where it is surrendered.[61]

---

[57]　Cf para 5.18 for the position under the Land Registration Act 1925; *Celsteel Ltd v Alton House Holding Ltd* [1985] 1 WLR 204 at 220. See also *Thatcher v Douglas* [1996] NLJ 282; *Sweet v Sommer* [2004] EWHC 1504 (Ch), [2005] EWCA Civ 227.

[58]　See *Chaudhary v Yavuz* [2011] EWCA Civ 1314.

[59]　See paras 2.59 and 2.76.

[60]　See para 2.55.

[61]　It is also possible that the benefit of inchoate rights in the course of being acquired are in principle capable of being passed by a grant of the freeholders to tenants either expressly or by the general words implied by Law of Property Act 1925, s 62; *Midtown Ltd v City of London Real Property Co Ltd* [2005] EWHC 33 (Ch) at [15]–[17]. See para 2.40(g). But see para 2.42 (g).

## Pending land actions

5.30   Under the Land Charges Act 1972, 'pending land action' means any action or proceeding pending in court relating to land or any interest in or charge on land.[62] Where land is unregistered, such an action is registrable under the Act.[63]

5.31   Under the Land Registration Act 1925, a caution against dealings may be registered land where in the case of unregistered land a caution against dealings could be registered.[64] In most cases where rights of light are in issue, this would be unnecessary, since any easement of light would take effect as an overriding interest.[65] Further, the court may order a caution to be vacated where the cautioner could be as equally well protected by an injunction or undertakings.[66] Where the only dispute is as to damages and there is no issue over the existence of an easement, then a registration of the dispute as pending action or caution is inappropriate and may be vacated.[67]

5.32   Under the Land Registration Act 2002, notice of a 'pending land action' within the meaning of the Land Charge Act 1972[68] may be subject to entry of notice in the register since it burdens an interest affecting a registered estate or charge.[69]

## Consents and agreements

5.33   The potential difficulties in establishing how 'consent' to the enjoyment of light might endure through title are considered above.[70] If

---

[62]   Land Charges Act 1972, s 17(1).

[63]   Land Charges Act 1972, s 5(1)(a).

[64]   Land Registration Act 1925, s 59(1).

[65]   See above; *Willies-Williams v National Trust* (1993) 65 P & CR 359.

[66]   *Willies-Williams v National Trust* (1993) 65 P & CR 359 at 363. See also *Clearbrook Property Holdings v Verrier* [1974] 1 WLR 243.

[67]   *Regan & Blackburn Ltd v Rogers* [1985] 1 WLR 870.

[68]   Land Registration Act 2002, s 87(1)(a); para 5.30.

[69]   Land Registration Act 2002, ss 32, 33 and 34.

[70]   See para 3.13 ff.

the deed is to be construed as a restrictive covenant, then registration against the burdened land will be required, as described above.[71]

5.34 If an easement enabling the interference with light has been granted,[72] then the extent to which the benefit and burden of such an easement will pass and will require registration will be the same as other easements, as described above.[73]

5.35 Likewise, if an express reservation of a right to build is construed so that it takes effect as an easement over the 'dominant' land enjoying the light,[74] such an easement will need to be registered to take effect at law in accordance with the above principles.[75]

---

[71] See para 5.11 (unregistered land); para 5.19 (Land Registration Act 1925); para 5.28 (Land Registration Act 2002).

[72] See para 3.21.

[73] See this chapter generally.

[74] See para 3.21.

[75] See para 3.22; Land Registration Act 2002, s 27(1).

# Chapter 6

# The Nature and Extent of a Right to Light

## GENERALLY

6.1   As explained above,[1] 'rights of light' as commonly understood are easements. The extent and nature of the right will be determined by how the easement was created. In the case of rights created by express[2] or implied grants,[3] consideration of the deed or other instrument by which the right was created will determine the extent of the right. In the case of a right acquired by prescription, it is necessary to consider the case law which explains the extent of prescriptive rights.

## RIGHTS GRANTED BY DEED OR OTHER INSTRUMENT

6.2   The extent of a right granted by deed will depend upon the construction of the deed.[4] If a deed simply envisages that the dominant owner will have a 'right to light' over the servient land through apertures which can be identified at the date of the grant without any further qualification or explanation, it is likely that the parties will be taken to have agreed that the right granted will be akin to a right which could have been acquired by prescription. As explained above, however, there seems no reason in principle why wider rights (or less rights) cannot be agreed,

---

[1]   See para 1.1 ff.

[2]   See paras 2.16 and 6.2.

[3]   See paras 2.18 ff and 6.2.

[4]   See para 4.2 ff for principles of construction.

provided that they are the sort of rights which are recognised as an easement.[5]

## THE NATURE OF PRESCRIPTIVE RIGHTS TO LIGHT

### A right to receive light through an aperture

6.3    A prescriptive right to light is a right enjoyed by the dominant tenement through a defined aperture whose purpose is to admit light.[6] As explained above, the right to light acquired by prescription under section 3 of the Prescription Act 1832 is an easement of access of light to a building.[7] So, while it is true that the 1832 Act does not refer to a window or aperture,[8] for a building to enjoy light, there must be some aperture through which the light must pass. It is, therefore, necessary to consider the nature of 'apertures' in a little more detail before going on to consider how the aperture defines the right acquired.

### The nature of the aperture through which light passes (or might pass)

6.4    A building may enjoy a right to light passing through an aperture such as a window whose purpose is to admit light. A skylight[9] or glass roof of a greenhouse[10] will suffice. An ordinary doorway will not.[11]

6.5    Provided that an aperture can be identified, in determining the existence or extent of the right acquired, it does not matter how the dominant owner makes use of the aperture. Thus it will not prevent a right to light being acquired that a window is obscured at certain times by blinds or curtains or that a window is obscured by external shutters which are

---

[5]   See para 2.15.

[6]   See paras 2.14, 2.62 and 2.67 ff.

[7]   See para 2.66 ff.

[8]   *National Provincial Plate Glass Insurance Co v Prudential Assurance Co* (1877) 6 ChD 757 at 764, per Fry J.

[9]   *Smith v Evangelization Society (Incorporated) Trust* [1933] Ch 515.

[10]   *Allen v Greenwood* [1980] Ch 119.

[11]   *Levet v Gas Light & Coke Co* [1919] 1 Ch 24.

capable of being opened and closed.[12] Similarly, it will make no difference that a window is partially obscured by the manner in which the interior of the premises is used, for example by the placing of shelves against the aperture.[13]

6.6    In the case of a presumed lost modern grant, unless there is evidence of an intention to abandon the right to light, then the mere fact that the aperture which has already acquired rights has been bricked up may not affect the existence or extent of the right.[14] This, however, would prevent actual enjoyment continuing for the purposes of the Prescription Act 1832.[15]

## Aperture defines the extent of the right

6.7    The aperture in the building on the dominant tenement defines the extent of the right over the servient land, i.e. the envelope which is to be kept free over the servient tenement.[16] While the aperture through which light is able to pass defines the area which is to be kept free on the servient tenement, the dominant owner's right is to enjoyment of the light passing through the aperture. As was said by Bowen LJ in *Scott v Pape*:[17]

> the measure of the enjoyment and the measure of the right acquired are not the windows and apertures themselves, which would involve a continuing structural identity of the windows, but the size and position of the windows, which necessarily limit and define the amount of light that arrives ultimately for the house's use.

The aperture, therefore, can be altered and the light previously enjoyed can continue to be enjoyed within the scope of the easement.[18] Where alterations occur and an aperture through which light passes is reconstructed, then the rights enjoyed by such a new aperture are often referred to in practice as 'transferred rights'.

---

[12]   *Cooper v Straker* (1888) 40 ChD 21.

[13]   See *Smith v Baxter* [1900] 2 Ch 138 at 146. See also para 2.73.

[14]   See *Marine & General Mutual Life Assurance Society v St James' Real Estate Co Ltd* [1991] 2 EGLR 178; see para 7.9 regarding abandonment of rights of light.

[15]   *Smith v Baxter* [1900] 2 Ch 138 at 146; see para 2.66.

[16]   *Scott v Pape* (1886) 31 ChD 554 at 575.

[17]   *Scott v Pape* (1886) 31 ChD 554 at 572.

[18]   See para 6.8 ff.

## Alteration of apertures: 'transferred rights'

6.8    The demolition or alteration of the building on a dominant tenement which enjoys rights of light may in some instances lead to an inference that the right of light has been lost or extinguished. The circumstances in which this inference may be made are considered below.[19] In general, however, the alteration of the windows through which light is enjoyed will not in itself lead to the loss of the right to light where there is complete or partial coincidence between the old and new apertures so that the light can continue to be enjoyed after the alteration.[20] Alterations may be made not only in the size or area of a window but may include its location, provided that the light enjoyed through the aperture is coincident with the light enjoyed by right.[21]

6.9    So, for example, in *Andrews v Waite*,[22] it was held that in cases where the light comes to any window over the roof of higher buildings at an angle, and the dominant building is altered by advancing the wall in which the window is, the right to access of light will be preserved if any window or aperture in the new wall intercepts and gives access to any substantial part of the light which passed through the old window. It makes no difference that the new window or aperture is at a much higher level than the old window.

6.10    Thus, in considering whether the right to light is preserved, one considers not the coincidence between the apertures but whether or not light is received in the same position as when the original window existed.[23] Even the demolition of a building will not bring an end to the rights if there is an intention to use the rights in the reconstructed new building.[24]

---

[19]   See para 7.9.

[20]   See *Tapling v Jones* (1865) 11 HLC 290, considered in detail at para 7.12; see also *Staight v Burn* (1869) LR 5 Ch App 163.

[21]   *National Provincial Plate Glass Insurance Co v Prudential Assurance Co* (1877) 6 ChD 757. See also *Barnes v Loach* (1879) 4 QBD 494; *Bullers v Dickinson* (1885) 29 ChD 155. See also para 7.9 ff (extinction of rights).

[22]   *Andrews v Waite* [1907] 2 Ch 500.

[23]   *National Provincial Plate Glass Insurance Co v Prudential Assurance Co* (1877) 6 ChD 757; see also *Barnes v Loach* (1879) 4 QBD 494; *Bullers v Dickinson* (1885) 29 ChD 155.

[24]   *Ecclesiastical Commissioners v Kino* (1880) 14 ChD 213; see also para 7.9 ff (extinction of rights).

6.11   In principle, therefore, rights of light are 'transferrable' to a new structure if, and to the extent that, the light entering the apertures in the new building coincides with the light entering apertures in the previous building.[25] The principle when applied to section 3 of the Prescription Act 1832 has been held at first instance to mean that no alteration of a building which would not involve the loss of a right to light when indefeasibly acquired will, if made during the currency of the statutory period, prevent the acquisition of the right provided that there is sufficient identity in the apertures through which the light claimed has been admitted to the dominant building.[26] However, to crystallise an inchoate right under section 3, it is necessary for a claimant to prove that (emphasis supplied):

> the access and use of light to and for any … building shall have been actually *enjoyed therewith for the full period of twenty years without interruption.*

6.12   Whether there has been actual enjoyment for a full period of 20 years is a question of fact. In a case where there is a radical alteration of the building (e.g. where walls with apertures are demolished and substantial new structures requiring significant works and time are constructed), it must be doubtful whether it would be possible for the putative dominant owner (regardless of its intentions) to prove actual enjoyment for the full statutory period of 20 years under section 3 of the Prescription Act 1832 (subject to the provisions of section 4). As explained above, section 4 provides that the 20-year period is next before action. It excludes from that period interruptions which have been 'submitted to or acquiesced in' for less than one year. An 'interruption' here is plainly not a voluntary discontinuance of enjoyment by a putative dominant owner himself: it is something which can be 'submitted to or acquiesced in after the party interrupted shall have had or shall have notice thereof'. These words simply do not apply to voluntary discontinuance. The purpose of this provision is to enable a putative dominant owner to commence proceedings after 20 years' actual enjoyment but there are

---

[25]   *Scott v Pape* (1886) 31 Ch D 554 at 569–570.

[26]   *Andrews v Waite* [1907] 2 Ch 500 at 508–509. See para 7.9 for when abandonment will be inferred.

disregarded interruptions by third parties which have not been acquiesced in for a year.[27]

6.13   In any event, the burden on the servient land cannot be increased by the alteration. So, where the reduction in the size of a window in the dominant building would mean that following the erection of buildings on the servient land there was insufficient light for the enjoyment of the dominant building, the owner of the dominant land could not complain (in circumstances where, if there had been no alteration, the dominant owner would have had sufficient light).[28] So, in *News of the World v Allen Fairhead & Sons*,[29] Farwell J said:[30]

> If the plaintiff pulls down the building with ancient light windows and erects a new building totally different in every respect, but having windows to some extent in the same position as the old windows, he cannot require the servient owners to do more than see that the ancient lights, if any, to which he is still entitled are not obstructed to the point of nuisance. He cannot require them not to obstruct non-ancient light merely because a portion of the window through which that non-ancient light enters his premises, also admits a pencil of ancient light. If the obstruction of the pencil itself causes a nuisance the plaintiff is entitled to relief, but if taking the building as it stands the pencil obstruction causes no nuisance at all, the plaintiff is not entitled to relief.

## Right of light for a building not a particular room

6.14   The right is a right for the building and is not attached to a particular room within it. This means that the extent of the right is not to be measured by the internal arrangements of the building.[31] Another way of looking at it is that the use to which the dominant property is – or may be – put

---

[27]   Gaunt, J and Morgan, Mr Justice (eds) (2012), *Gale on Easements* (19th edn), Sweet & Maxwell, para 4-55; cf also *Smith v Baxter* [1900] 2 Ch 138. See also paras 2.66 and 3.25 ff.

[28]   *Ankerson v Connelly* [1906] 2 Ch 55; [1907] 1 Ch 678; *W H Bailey & Son Limited v Holborn & Frascati Limited* [1914] 1 Ch 598; *News of the World Limited v Allen Fairhead & Sons Limited* [1931] 2 Ch 402. See also para 7.15.

[29]   *News of the World v Allen Fairhead & Sons* [1931] 2 Ch 402.

[30]   *News of the World v Allen Fairhead & Sons* [1931] 2 Ch 402 at 406–407.

[31]   *Carr-Saunders v Dick McNeil Associates Ltd* [1986] 1 WLR 922 at 928C–H. See also paras 2.62, 2.67 and 2.73.

determines neither: (a) the aperture through which the dominant property is entitled to receive light; nor (b) the area which is to be kept free over the servient land for the light to continue to be enjoyed through that aperture.

## Right to receive light for reasonable use to which the building may be put

6.15   In the case of all rights to light acquired by prescription (whether at common law, by lost modern grant or under the Prescription Act 1832), the basic principle is that a right is acquired to that measure of light which is required for the beneficial use of the building for any ordinary purpose for which it is adapted. Thus not only current but all potential reasonable uses of the property should be considered.

6.16   Accordingly, the dominant owner's right of light is measured by the reasonable use to which the building may be put and not by a particular arrangement of the building at the date when the existence of the dominant owner's rights happens to be decided.

6.17   So, in *Carr-Saunders v Dick McNeil Associates Ltd*,[32] Millett J stated the law as follows:

> Thus, the dominant owner's right of light is not measured by the particular use to which the dominant tenement has been put in the past: see *Price v. Hilditch*.[33] The extent of the dominant owner's right is neither increased nor diminished by the actual use to which the dominant owner has chosen to put his premises or any of the rooms in them: for he is entitled to such access of light as will leave his premises adequately lit for all ordinary purposes for which they may reasonably be expected to be used. The court must, therefore, take account not only of the present use, but also of other potential uses to which the dominant owner may reasonably be expected to put the premises in the future: see *Moore v. Hall*,[34] where Cockburn C.J. said:[35]

---

[32]   *Carr-Saunders v Dick McNeil Associates Ltd* [1986] 1 WLR 922 at 929.

[33]   *Price v Hilditch* [1930] 1 Ch 500.

[34]   *Moore v Hall* (1878) 3 QBD 178.

[35]   *Moore v Hall* (1878) 3 QBD 178 at 182.

'The matter, in my opinion, to be considered is, whether there is any diminution of light for any purpose for which the dominant tenement may be reasonably considered available.'

In my judgment, an alteration in the internal arrangement of the premises comes within the same principle. In *Colls v. Home and Colonial Stores Ltd*[36] Lord Davey said:[37]

'The easement is for access of light to the building, and if the building retains its substantial identity, or if the ancient lights retain their substantial identity, it does not seem to me to depend on the use which is made of the chambers in it, or to be varied by any alteration which may be made in the internal structure of it.'

And later on the same page:

'But while agreeing that a person does not lose his easement by any change in the internal structure of his building or the use to which it is put, and that regard may be had, not only to the present use, but also to any ordinary uses to which the tenement is adapted, I think it is quite another question whether he is entitled to be protected at the expense of his neighbour in the enjoyment of the light for some special or extraordinary purpose.'

And:[38]

'According to both principle and authority, I am of opinion that the owner or occupier of the dominant tenement is entitled to the uninterrupted access through his ancient windows of a quantity of light, the measure of which is what is required for the ordinary purposes of inhabitancy or business of the tenement according to the ordinary notions of mankind, and that the question for what purpose he has thought fit to use that light, or the mode in which he finds it convenient to arrange the internal structure of his tenement, does not affect the question.'

6.18   In *Ough v King*,[39] it was pointed out that higher standards of light may now be demanded for comfort, and it may well be that in today's

---

36   *Colls v Home and Colonial Stores Ltd* [1904] AC 179.

37   *Colls v Home and Colonial Stores Ltd* [1904] AC 179 at 202.

38   *Colls v Home and Colonial Stores Ltd* [1904] AC 179 at 204.

39   *Ough v King* [1967] 1 WLR 1547.

economic conditions smaller as well as lighter rooms are now accepted as reasonable uses.

6.19   While there have been numerous cases considering what is 'required for ordinary purposes', in essence this is a question of fact. As was stated by Goff LJ in *Allen v Greenwood*:[40]

> It seems that what is ordinary must depend upon the nature of the building and to what it is ordinarily adapted. If, therefore, the building be, as it is in this case, a greenhouse, the normal use of which requires a high degree of light, then it seems to me that that degree is ordinary light.

How light for these purposes is measured is considered at para 8.16 and in detail in Appendix A.

## Artificial light

6.20   The availability of artificial light does not affect the amount of light which is required for these purposes (albeit that this might be relevant to the question of relief). If artificial light were relevant, then it could always be argued that there could be sufficient artificial light to supplement natural light but, in any event, natural light can be better suited to particular tasks.[41] Indeed, there is a body of evidence which supports the conclusion that natural light has material benefits over and above anything that can be provided by artificial light.[42]

---

[40]　*Allen v Greenwood* [1980] Ch 119 at 131.

[41]　*Midtown Ltd v City of London Real Property Co Ltd* [2005] EWHC 33 (Ch) at [61]. See paras 8.13 and 10.46.

[42]　I have been referred by Jerome Webb of GIA to the following publications: Tregenza, P and Wilson, M (2011), *Daylighting: Architecture and Lighting Design*, Routledge; Boyce, PR (2003), *Human Factors in Lighting* (2nd edn), Taylor & Francis; 'Employee Productivity in a Sustainable Building: Pre- and Post-Occupancy Studies in 500 Collins Street', A Study commissioned by Sustainability Victoria and the Kador Group; Edwards, L and Torcellini, P (2002), *A Literature Review of the Effects of Natural Light on Building Occupants*, National Renewable Energy Laboratory, Colorado; Figueiro, MG, Rea, MS, Stevens, RG and Rea, AC (2002), *Daylight and Productivity – A Possible Link to Circadian Regulation*, Lighting Research Center, Rensselaer Polytechnic Institute.

## The extent of the right does not depend on location

6.21 The measure of what is sufficient light is not different in manufacturing and in country districts. The extent of the right depends on how much light the eye needs for ordinary purposes.[43] In *Fishenden v Higgs and Hill Ltd*,[44] the court said:

> It seems to me quite unreasonable to say that, because you find that in some places in Mayfair there is less access of light than would be left here in Chesterfield Gardens, it can be said that the plaintiff has suffered no wrong ... when this building has been set up there will be a diminution of light reaching the windows which will render the premises less comfortable than they had been before ...

## Buildings which are already poorly lit

6.22 As explained above,[45] a right to light is a right to receive that measure of light which is required for the beneficial use of the building for any ordinary purpose for which it is adapted. The question which arises is how this principle is to be applied to a building which is so poorly lit that it might be said that it does not, even with the benefit of the light of the servient land, enjoy enough light for 'ordinary purposes'.

6.23 There is some authority for the proposition that a person cannot complain if his building is badly lit. So, it might appear that one cannot assert a right to light where a building has insufficient light already. In *Colls v Home and Colonial Stores Ltd*,[46] Lord Robertson asked (rhetorically):

> Can a man by making one window where there should be five to give proper light, and living twenty years in this case, prevent his neighbour from building a house which would have done no harm to the light if there had been five windows?

---

[43]   See *Horton's Estate Ltd v James Beattie Ltd* [1927] 1 Ch 75 at 78.

[44]   *Fishenden v Higgs and Hill Ltd* (1935) 153 LT 128 at 137.

[45]   See para 6.15 ff.

[46]   *Colls v Home and Colonial Stores Ltd* [1904] AC 179, 181. See also *Litchfield-Speer v Queen Anne's Gate Syndicate Ltd (No 2)* [1919] 1 Ch 407 at 414 (interference with badly lit kitchen not a nuisance).

6.24   There is, however, another line of authority which suggests that an ill-lit building may still enjoy the benefit of a right of light over the servient land. Thus in *Dent v Auction Mart Ltd*,[47] Sir William Page Wood V-C said:

> it was argued by the Defendants ... that the Plaintiffs might have made their windows larger. I apprehend it is not for the Defendants to tell the Plaintiffs how they are to construct their house, and to say, 'You can avoid this injury by doing something for which you would have no protection'. If the Plaintiffs constructed their new window, it could be immediately obstructed as being a new window. They have a right already acquired by their old existing window; that right they wish to have preserved intact; and I think they are clearly entitled to retain the light as they acquired it, without being compelled to make any alteration in their house to enable other people to deal with their property.

In many circumstances, the little light enjoyed from the servient land by a poorly lit dominant building may be very important for the enjoyment of that building or a particular room within that building. For instance, it might make a room capable of use because there is just enough light to illuminate a desk or work surface even though the rest of the room is gloomy. In such a case, a small interference could have a significant effect. This appears to be the approach taken in Ireland.[48] This has also been the approach in the county court in England and Wales: where a room is already ill-let, every bit of light may be precious.[49] In principle, this approach appears to be correct. Prescription recognises a *status quo* which has prevailed for a long time. If the dominant building has enjoyed light to a poorly lit room over servient land for a period of 20 years or more, there seems no reason in principle why the light so enjoyed should not be protected.

6.25   However, even though an ill-lit room might enjoy a right of light, it will not be every reduction in light that will be actionable. A reduction may in practice be imperceptible even if quantifiable: for instance, in a large room a reduction in light of a strip of 5 mm width might result in a

---

[47]   *Dent v Auction Mart Ltd* (1866) LR 2 Eq 238 at 251.

[48]   *O'Connor v Walsh* (1908) 42 ILTR 20; *McGrath v Munster and Leinster Bank Ltd* [1959] IR 313; *Cannon v Hughes* [1937] IR 284.

[49]   *Deakins v Hookings* [1994] 1 EGLR 190.

large overall reduction of light in terms of floor area, but to a user of a room such loss might be imperceptible. In such circumstances, it is difficult to see how the interference could be regarded as so substantial as to be actionable: see generally para 8.16 ff and Appendix A for the measurement of light.

# Chapter 7

# Extinguishing Rights of Light

## INTRODUCTION

7.1 The extinction of a right of light must be distinguished from the authorisation of an interference with the right. The former ends the right once and for all. The latter simply makes lawful an interference with the right. This chapter deals with how a right of light may be ended. The circumstances in which an interference may be authorised without extinction of the right are considered below.[1] The distinction is conceptually an important one but is sometimes not understood in practice.

7.2 An easement of light may end in a number of ways:

(a) it may expire because it is of limited duration;[2]

(b) it may end because the dominant and servient tenements become united in the same ownership;[3]

(c) it might (possibly) end as a result of merger of dominant and servient tenements;[4]

(d) it may be extinguished by express release;[5]

---

[1] See para 9.1 ff.

[2] See para 7.3.

[3] See para 7.4.

[4] See para 7.7.

[5] See para 7.8.

(e)    it may be extinguished by a release to be implied from the conduct of the dominant owner;[6]

(f)    it may be lost as a result of estoppel arising from a decision of the court;[7]

(g)    it may be ended by statute.[8]

## EXPIRY OF LIMITED RIGHT

7.3    As explained above, an easement may be granted for a term of years.[9] Where the period has expired, then the easement will come to an end.[10] Similarly, a grant of a right might be made for a particular purpose. If that purpose comes to an end, the right may also end.[11]

## UNITY OF OWNERSHIP

7.4    A right of light constituting an easement must benefit a 'dominant' tenement and burden a 'servient' tenement. So, if the dominant and servient tenements come into the same ownership, then the easement will be extinguished because a man cannot have an easement over his own land.[12] In other words, there would no longer be a dominant tenement and a servient tenement. The principle applies where the absolute interests in both the dominant and servient tenements are united in the same person but this principle is qualified in two important ways.

---

[6]    See para 7.9 ff.

[7]    See para 7.17.

[8]    See para 7.18.

[9]    See para 2.4.

[10]   See para 2.16 and, generally, para 4.2 ff for how rights may be construed.

[11]   Cf *National Guaranteed Manure Company Co v Donald* (1859) 4 H & N 8; *Huckvale v Aegean Hotels* (1989) 58 P & CR 163.

[12]   See *Roe v Siddons* (1888) 22 QBD 236; *Metropolitan Railway v Fowler* [1892] 1 QB 164; *Kilgour v Gaddes* [1904] 1 KB 461.

7.5    First, it has been said that no easement of absolute necessity to the dominant tenement is extinguished by unity of ownership.[13] This is not strictly accurate. The better analysis is that if there is unity of ownership, easements are extinguished; but if the tenements are subsequently separated, easements of necessity would be implicit on the separation.[14]

7.6    Secondly, if the dominant and servient owners become vested in the same owner for *different* estates and interests, then the easement is not extinguished.[15] So, in *Richardson v Graham*,[16] the dominant tenement which enjoyed access and use of light over the servient tenement for a period of 20 years without interruption was let to the plaintiffs; subsequently, and during the continuance of the lease, the freehold owner conveyed the freehold reversion to the lease to the freehold owner of the servient tenement. It was held that unity of the estate in fee did not cause the right to be extinguished because there was no unity of possession or enjoyment. The original freehold owner of the dominant tenement could not derogate from his grant and neither could his successor in title. Obviously, in such a case there would be unity of ownership and enjoyment when the lease expired, so at that point the easement would be extinguished.

## MERGER?

7.7    It has been held that easements are treated as being appurtenant to *land* rather than to any particular interest in the land.[17] On that basis, it has been held that if a lessee of the dominant tenement acquires the freehold, he does not thereby lose the benefit of any easement granted by his lease which enured for the term of the original grant as a result of merger of the freehold and leasehold interests.[18] This decision has been criticised: it is inconsistent with previous cases in which it was held that an easement

---

[13]    *Pheysey v Vicary* (1847) 16 M & W 484 at 490; *Margil Pty Ltd v Stegul Pastoral Pty Ltd* [1984] 2 NSWR 1.

[14]    See para 2.20; cf *Holmes v Goring* (1824) 2 Bing 76.

[15]    See *Canham v Fisk* (1831) 2 Cr & J 126; *Thomas v Thomas* (1835) 2 CM&R 34 at 41; *Simper v Foley* (1862) 2 J & H 555 at 563 and 564.

[16]    *Richardson v Graham* [1908] 1 KB 39.

[17]    *Wall v Collins* [2007] EWCA Civ 444.

[18]    *Wall v Collins* [2007] EWCA Civ 444.

granted for the term of the lease expires with the expiry of the tenancy (which as a matter of logic must terminate upon merger).[19]

## EXTINGUISHMENT BY EXPRESS RELEASE

7.8    The dominant owner of a right of light may expressly release an easement. To be effective at law, an express release must be under seal.[20] However, a written instrument not under seal may be evidence to prove cessation of enjoyment[21] or may be enforceable in equity[22] subject to compliance with formalities for enforceable agreements.[23]

## EXTINGUISHMENT BY IMPLIED RELEASE: ABANDONMENT

7.9    If the dominant owner does something or authorises something of a permanent nature the consequence of which will prevent him enjoying the easement, he will not be entitled to assert his right and it is extinguished.[24] The courts, however, will not easily make such an inference, given the

---

[19]    See *Beddington v Atlee* (1887) 35 ChD 317; *MRA Engineering Ltd v Trimster Co Ltd* (1888) 56 P & CR 1. See Gaunt, J and Morgan, Mr Justice (eds) (2012), *Gale on Easements* (19th edn), Sweet & Maxwell, at para 1-32; see also Law Commission (2011), *Making Land Work: Easements, Covenants and Profits à Prendre*, Law Com No. 327, The Stationery Office, at paras 3.232–3.263.

[20]    Co. Litt. 264b; Com. Dig. Release (A.1), (B.1). *Allen v Jones* [2004] EWHC 1119. See *Lovell v Smith* (1857) 3 CB (ns) 127, per Willes J (parol agreement no evidence of abandonment of old way); see e.g. *Poulton v Moore* [1915] 1 KB 400 (deed operating by estoppel effective). Cf *Norbury v Meade* (1821) 3 Bli 241 (release of tithes).

[21]    See para 7.9 ff for cessation of enjoyment.

[22]    *Davies v Marshall* (1861) 10 CB (ns) 697; *Fisher v Moon* (1865) 11 LT 623; *Waterlow v Bacon* (1866) LR 2 Eq 514; cf *Salaman v Glover* (1875) LR 20 Eq 444. Cf also *Allen v Jones* [2004] EWHC 1119 (QB), in which agreement not enforceable where no registration or notice. See also *Robinson Webster (Holdings) Ltd v Agombar* [2002] 1 P & CR 243.

[23]    See Law of Property (Miscellaneous Provisions) Act 1989, s 2.

[24]    *Winter v Brockwell* (1807) 8 East 308; *Liggins v Inge* (1831) 7 Bing 682; *Davies v Marshall* (1861) 10 CB (ns) 697; *Johnson v Wyatt* (1863) 9 Jur (ns) 1333; *Bosomworth v Faber* (1995) 60 P & CR 28; cf *Armstrong v Sheppard & Short Ltd* [1959] 2 QB 384 at 399–401, per Lord Evershed MR (damages appropriate instead of an injunction – as to which, see para 10.19 ff).

proprietary and potentially valuable nature of an easement, and the court will need to find it proven that the dominant owner had a fixed intention never at any time again to assert the right himself or transfer it to someone else.[25]

7.10   So, the reconstruction of a building with a blank wall where there had been windows might, after a considerable period, lead to the inference that there was an intention to abandon the rights (in the absence of evidence to the contrary).[26] On the other hand, the inference is not lightly made. So, in *Marine and General Mutual Life Assurance Society v St James Real Ltd*,[27] where window apertures had been filled in with brick but sills remained and the position of the apertures was clearly visible, an intention to abandon was not inferred.

7.11   As seen above, rights may be enjoyed following rebuilding of a building on the dominant tenement.[28] So, in the context of rights of light, it has been held that the mere alteration of a building[29] and even pulling down a building[30] will not in themselves lead to the inference of an intention to abandon a right of light.

7.12   Accordingly, in *Tapling v Jones*,[31] the plaintiff had altered the size and position of the lower windows in his house (which enjoyed ancient rights of light) so that the new windows coincided with parts only of the

---

[25]   See *Tehidy Minerals v Norman* [1971] 2 QB 528 at 553; *Re Yateley Common, Hampshire* [1977] 1 WLR 840; *Benn v Hardinge* (1993) 66 P & CR 246; *Snell & Prideaux v Dutton* [1995] 1 EGLR 259; *ADM Milling Ltd v Tewkesbury Town Council* [2011] EWHC 595 (Ch).

[26]   See *Moore v Rawson* (1824) 3 B & C 332 at 336; also *Smith v Baxter* [1900] 2 Ch 138. See also *Stokoe v Singers* (1857) 8 E & B 31, in which there are *dicta* suggesting that if the windows are closed up so as to lead the servient owner to alter his position in the reasonable belief that the lights had been permanently abandoned, then rights might be taken to be abandoned.

[27]   *Marine and General Mutual Life Assurance Society v St James Real Ltd* [1991] 2 EGLR 178.

[28]   See para 6.8 ff.

[29]   *Greenwood v Hornsey* (1886) 33 ChD 471.

[30]   *Ecclesiastical Commissioners v Kino* (1880) 14 ChD 213.

[31]   *Tapling v Jones* (1861) 11 CB (ns) 283, affirmed (1862) 12 CB (ns) 286, affirmed (1865) 20 CB (ns) 166, 11 HLC 290.

old apertures; he also opened upper windows in positions which the servient owner could not obstruct without also obstructing the portions of the lower windows which coincided with the ancient lights. The defendant built a wall which obstructed all the plaintiff's windows. The plaintiff restored his lower windows to their original size and blocked up the upper windows. The plaintiff then asked the defendant to pull down his wall. When the defendant refused, the plaintiff commenced an action. The House of Lords held that the wall to the extent that it obstructed the plaintiff's ancient lights was an illegal act from the beginning. The alteration did not result in the plaintiff losing his rights. By enlarging the windows, the plaintiff was not evincing any intention to abandon his entitlement to the rights which he already enjoyed. While the ancient lights were protected in that case, there was no protection for the new lights: the only reason the new lights could not be obstructed was that the obstruction also obstructed the ancient lights.[32] Lord Chelmsford, however, noted:[33]

> It will, of course, be a question in each case, whether the circumstances satisfactorily establish an intention to abandon altogether the future enjoyment and exercise of the right. If such an intention is clearly manifested, the adjoining owner may build as he pleases upon his own land; and should the owner of the previously existing window restore the former state of things, he could not compel the removal of any building which had been placed upon the ground during the interval: for a right once abandoned is abandoned for ever.

7.13    Similarly, a change in the plane of a window (rather than simply its size or area) will not in itself lead to a loss of a right of light unless the changes are such that an inference of abandonment can be made.[34]

7.14    Cotton LJ in *Scott v Pape*[35] summarised the position as follows:

---

[32]  See *Frechette v La Compagnie Manufacturiere de St Hyacinthe* (1883) 9 App Cas 170 at 186.

[33]  *Tapling v Jones* 11 HLC 290 at 319.

[34]  *National Provincial Plate Glass Insurance Co v Prudential Assurance Co* (1877) 6 ChD 757. See also *Barnes v Loach* (1879) 4 QBD 494; *Bullers v Dickinson* (1885) 29 ChD 155.

[35]  *Scott v Pape* (1886) 31 ChD 554 at 569–570.

What alteration, then, will deprive the Plaintiff of his right, this right which can be claimed only in respect of a dwelling-house, workshop, or other building? Will the alteration of the purpose or object for which the building is to be used, as the conversion of a workshop into a house, or of a house into a workshop, have this effect? It will not: that is definitely settled by the case of *Ecclesiastical Commissioners v Kino*.[36] The old building there was a church, and that which was to be built on the site of the church was a warehouse, an entire alteration of the purposes and of the character of the building. Then will moving back the plane of the wall deprive the Plaintiff of his right? In my opinion, no. It is difficult to see how the mere fact of moving back can do so, and in fact there is authority against such a proposition. Then if moving it back will not, will simply moving it forward have this effect? In my opinion both the moving back and the moving forward may destroy the right, because the new building when constructed may, either by being substantially advanced or substantially set back, be so placed that the light which formerly went into the old windows will not go into the new. If a building is set back, say 100 feet, it will not enjoy the same cone of light that was enjoyed before, but will have an entirely different cone, and it may be moved so far forward that it will not enjoy the same light as that enjoyed by the old building. In my opinion the question to be considered is this, whether the alteration is of such a nature as to preclude the Plaintiff from alleging that he is using through the new apertures in the new wall the same cone of light, or a substantial part of that cone of light, which went to the old building. If that is established, although the right must be claimed in respect of a building, it may be claimed in respect of any building which is substantially enjoying a part, or the whole, of the light which went through the old aperture.[37]

7.15 As explained above,[38] however, an alteration to the dominant tenement cannot increase the burden on the servient tenement, and the dominant owner's rights will be judged by reference to the ancient lights of which he has the benefit. So, where the dominant owner alters the dominant tenement, he is not entitled to prevent the obstruction of his lights which, though obstructing light to an altered window, would not

---

[36] *Ecclesiastical Commissioners v Kino* (1880) 14 ChD 213.

[37] While the right extends to the light which 'went through the old aperture', whether or not an obstruction of that light amounts to an actionable interference will depend on whether the interference is so substantial as to amount to a nuisance: see para 8.4 ff.

[38] See para 6.13.

before the alteration have caused a nuisance.[39] In other words, while an alteration of the dominant tenement may not lead to an inference of abandonment, it cannot be used to increase the burden on the servient tenement.[40]

7.16 The above principles apply to easements of light acquired by grant or by prescription at common law or under the doctrine of lost modern grant.[41] However, it should be noted that if an aperture is altered so that there is interruption of enjoyment, then this will preclude the establishment of the existence of an easement of light in reliance on section 3 of the Prescription Act 1832, since the putative dominant owner will not have enjoyed the light for the requisite period prior to commencing proceedings.[42]

## ESTOPPEL PER REM JUDICATAM

7.17 This is not strictly an example of extinguishment of an easement. However, a failure to establish the existence of an easement in litigation may preclude a party from subsequently raising its existence because of the doctrines of cause of action estoppel or issue estoppel.[43]

## BY STATUTE

7.18 Parliament may make express provision for the extinction of easements.[44] It may also implicitly extinguish an easement by authorising

---

[39] *Ankerson v Connelly* [1906] 2 Ch 554, [1907] 1 Ch 678.

[40] *W H Bailey & Sons Ltd v Holborn and Frascati Ltd* [1914] 1 Ch 598 at 602–603; *News of the World v Allen Fairhead & Sons* [1931] 2 Ch 402.

[41] *Marine & General Mutual Life Assurance Society v St James' Real Estate Co Ltd* [1991] 2 EGLR 178.

[42] *Smith v Baxter* [1900] 2 Ch 138 at 146. See also *Lord Battersea v Commissioners of Sewers for the City of London* [1895] 2 Ch 708. See para 2.66.

[43] *Long v Gowlett* [1923] 2 Ch 177; *Price v Nunn* [2013] EWCA Civ 1002.

[44] See e.g. the Inclosure (Consolidation) Act 1801; Inclosure Act 1845, s 68; *A-G v Great Central Railway* [1912] 2 Ch 110 (South Yorkshire Railway (Sheffield and Thorne) Act 1862).

something inconsistent with the continuation of an easement.[45] However, in general, a statute will not be construed as extinguishing a property right unless there is provision for compensation to be paid.[46]

7.19 There are numerous statutes giving bodies performing public functions powers of compulsory purchase. Some statutes, such as section 295 of the Housing Act 1985 (making provision for slum clearance), provide for the extinguishment of easements over land acquired. As explained below, however, in general a person whose land is not acquired but who enjoys an easement over land which is acquired may bring a claim for disturbance to the extent that statute authorises interference with his easement, and there are express provisions for the 'overriding' of easements.[47] In such a case, however, the easement is not strictly extinguished: there is merely authorisation of the interference with the easement subject to the payment of compensation.[48]

---

[45] *Yarmouth Corpn v Simmons* (1878) 10 ChD 518 (the General Pier and Harbour Act 1861 authorised construction of a pier, which was inconsistent with a public right of way).

[46] See *A-G v Horner* (1884) 14 QBD 245 at 257, per Lord Brett MR; *Jones v Cleanthi* [2006] EWCA 1712 at [82], per Parker LJ; see also European Convention for the Protection of Human Rights and Fundamental Freedoms 1950, First Protocol, Article 1.

[47] See New Towns Act 1981, s 19; Town and Country Planning Act 1990, s 237.

[48] See para 9.1 ff.

# Chapter 8

# Interference with Rights of Light

## INTRODUCTION

8.1 Where a right of light is contractual in origin, an interference with the right might amount to a breach of the contractual obligations under which the right was granted.[1] Further, since a right of light constitutes an easement, an interference with such right might constitute a tort, namely a nuisance.[2] In determining whether there is an actionable interference with a right of light it is necessary, first, to consider the *extent* of the right of light. This is considered above,[3] and this chapter must be read in conjunction with Chapter 6.

## INTERFERENCE CONSTITUTING BREACH OF CONTRACTUAL OBLIGATIONS

8.2 Where there is a grant or demise of an easement, then the grantor or lessor is implicitly (if not expressly) obliged to do nothing to derogate from his grant.[4] This is a principle that 'merely embodies in a legal maxim

---

[1]   See para 8.2 ff.

[2]   See para 8.4 ff.

[3]   See para 6.1 ff.

[4]   *Browne v Flower* [1911] 1 Ch 219 at 224–225. See also *Ward v Kirkland* [1967] Ch 194; *Sovmots Investments Ltd v Secretary of State for the Environment* [1979] AC 144 at 175; *Johnston & Sons Ltd v Holland* [1988[ 1 EGLR 264. See also *British Leyland v Armstrong Patents* [1986] AC 577.

a rule of common honesty'.[5] Thus, if the grantor or lessor interferes with the rights granted, then the grantee or lessee with the benefit of the rights may have a claim for breach of covenant. In the absence of something unusual in the nature of the right granted, whether or not an interference with a contractual right is actionable is likely to be judged in the same manner in which a tortious interference is judged.[6]

8.3　　Further, as explained above,[7] access of light may be protected by restrictive covenants. Whether or not an interference with light amounts to a breach of a restrictive covenant will depend upon the construction of the covenant.

## INTERFERENCE WITH EASEMENTS GENERALLY: NUISANCE

8.4　　An action for an interference with a right to light, as with other easements, may constitute a tort. The cause of action is in nuisance. This is because an easement does not entitle the dominant owner to possession of the servient land, such that an interference with his rights would constitute a trespass. The interference being with an incorporeal hereditament, however, it is not necessary for a claimant to plead damage for an action to lie: 'Damage is not the gist of the action'.[8]

8.5　　As in the case of other nuisances interfering with a servitude, a reversioner (e.g. someone whose interest is subject to a tenancy) can sue for acts which tend either to destroy evidence of the existence on adjoining land of a servitude in his favour or to establish against him that his own land is burdened with a servitude in favour of the adjoining land. So a reversioner can sue in respect of the erection of a hoarding which

---

5　　*Harmer v Jumbil (Nigeria) Tin Area Ltd* [1921] 1 Ch 200 at 225.

6　　See para 8.4 ff.

7　　See paras 1.5 and 4.11.

8　　*Nichols v Ely Beet Sugar Factory Ltd* [1936] Ch 343 at 348–349. But see para 10.56 (*Stoke on Trent City Council v W & J Wass Ltd (No 1)* [1988] 1 WLR 1406).

interferes with his ancient lights.[9] Again, 'damage' as such is not the gist of the action – the question is whether or not the acts of which complaint is made tend to destroy evidence of the existence of the reversioner's rights.

8.6    In the context of prescriptive rights to light, the test for whether an interference is actionable is whether the interference affects the comfortable use and enjoyment of the premises for the ordinary purposes to which they might be put.[10] There are a number of points to note.

## Not what is taken but what is left

8.7    First, in determining whether an interference with a prescriptive right of light is actionable, what matters is not how much light is taken but whether sufficient is left. No actionable wrong is committed if the amount of light remaining is sufficient for the comfortable enjoyment of the property by the dominant owner according to the ordinary notions of mankind. However, it should be noted that the wrong consists in the disturbance of the dominant owner in the comfortable enjoyment not of a particular room but of his property as a whole.[11] The question is whether the light left is sufficient for ordinary purposes such as reading;[12] therefore, if a significant part of the property which previously enjoyed sufficient light for comfortable enjoyment of that part would no longer enjoy sufficient light for that purpose, then the interference is substantial and actionable.[13]

---

[9]    *Metropolitan Association v Petch* (1858) 5 CB (ns) 504; see also *Shadwell v Hutchinson* (1831) M & W 350.

[10]   *Colls v Home & Colonial Stores Ltd* [1904] AC 179 at 208, per Lord Lindley.

[11]   *Carr-Saunders v Dick McNeil Associates Ltd* [1986] 1 WLR 922 at 928F, per Millett J. See para 6.14.

[12]   See Appendix A, para A13.

[13]   See Appendix A, para A14.

8.8    Thus, where the skyline of a servient tenement was altered so that part was raised and part was lowered so that overall there remained sufficient light enjoyed by the dominant building, there was no interference.[14]

## Regard to future uses of premises

8.9    Secondly, the extent of the dominant owner's right is tested not only by reference to the present use to which the premises are put.[15] The dominant owner is entitled to such light as is sufficient for all reasonable purposes to which the building may be put.[16] So, an interference with the right will be judged accordingly.[17] For example, it is irrelevant to the question of whether an interference is actionable that windows may, at the date of the interference, be partially obscured by shelving.[18]

## Light from other sources

8.10    Thirdly, the court may have regard to light from other sources than that which has been obstructed, but only so far as this other light is light to which the dominant owner is entitled by grant or prescription to enjoy.[19] Light of which an owner can be deprived because he has no right to receive it will not be taken into account.[20]

8.11    So, if a servient owner places glazed tiles on the servient tenement to reflect light into the dominant tenement to mitigate the impact of an interference with the dominant tenement's right of light, this was not be

---

[14]   *Davis v Marrable* [1913] 2 Ch 421.

[15]   *Carr-Saunders v Dick McNeil Associates Ltd* [1986] 1 WLR 922 at 928G, per Millett J.

[16]   *Yates v Jack* (1866) 1 Ch App 295 at 298, per Lord Carnworth LC; see also *Colls v Home & Colonial Stores Ltd* [1904] AC 179 at 202 and 203. See para 6.15 ff.

[17]   See *Moore v Hall* (1878) 3 QBD 178 at 183; *Aynsley v Glover* (1874) LR 18 Eq 544 at 551; *Dicker v Popham, Radford & Co* (1890) 63 LT 379.

[18]   *Smith v Baxter* [1900] 2 Ch 138 at 146, per Stirling J.

[19]   See *Smith v Evangelization Society (Incorporated) Trust* [1933] Ch 515.

[20]   *Colls v Home and Colonial Stores* [1904] AC 179 at 211; *Kine v Jolly* [1905] 1 Ch 480 at 493 and 497, [1907] AC 7. See also *Price v Hilditch* [1930] 1 Ch 500 at 505 and 506; *Smith v Evangelization Society (Incorporated) Trust* [1933] Ch 515, 523.

taken into account because the dominant owner would have no right to require the maintenance of the tiles in the future.[21]

8.12   As explained below,[22] while this analysis seems ostensibly correct, in practice most buildings will be illuminated by light reflected from sources other than the land over which an easement is claimed. The traditional way of assessing the impact of an interference with light is to ignore this reflected light because there is not necessarily a legal right to it.[23] The practical effect of ignoring such light, however, has meant that interferences have been treated as 'actionable' even though in practice the interference will make no perceptible difference to the enjoyment of the dominant land and never would do because (unless all the surrounding buildings were painted matt black) the dominant land would continue to enjoy reflected light from other sources. This does not appear generally to have been appreciated by legal practitioners and (to date) the consequences have not been explored in the courts.

## Artificial light

8.13   Fourthly, that one may use or be able to use artificial light is irrelevant to whether or not there has been an interference with the natural light enjoyed by the dominant land.[24] This seems to be correct in principle: even in the context of office buildings there is a substantial body of evidence about the importance of the availability of natural light, even if it is often supplemented by artificial light. For instance, research into circadian photobiology suggests that light has a very important role in regulating human behaviour, including sleep–wake cycles and seasonal depression. If the common law's traditional protection of natural light

---

[21]   *Dent v Auction Mart Co* (1866) LR 2 Eq 251 at 252.

[22]   See paras 10.47 and A24 ff.

[23]   See para 8.11.

[24]   *Midtown Ltd v City of London Real Property Co Ltd* [2005] EWHC 33 (Ch) at [56]–[63].

needs scientific support, it exists.[25] If the point were ever seriously put in issue, the question of the important role of light in regulating human behaviour is one which might need to be determined upon evidence from experimental psychologists rather than simply on the submission of lawyers or assertions of surveyors.

## Badly lit premises

8.14   Fifthly, as explained above,[26] there is a conflict of authority over the extent to which poorly lit premises can benefit from a right to light where they are so poorly lit that it might be said that they do not even enjoy enough light for 'ordinary purposes' (i.e. for the measure by which the extent of a prescriptive right to light is usually judged). If it can be established that a poorly lit building has the benefit of a right to the little light which it actually enjoys,[27] then in principle an interference which causes a substantial reduction in that light will be actionable. If, however, the reduction is imperceptible for practical purposes, it is doubtful whether the interference would be sufficiently substantial to constitute an actionable nuisance.

8.15   The test of whether an interference with a right of light is actionable is whether the amount of light remaining is sufficient for the comfortable enjoyment of his property by the dominant owner according to the ordinary notions of mankind. So it seems logical that in the case of ill-lit rooms, the test should be whether there is a practical, perceptible difference in the light which adversely affects the comfortable enjoyment of the property by the dominant owner according to the ordinary notions of mankind.

---

[25]   Tregenza, P and Wilson, M (2011), *Daylighting: Architecture and Lighting Design*, Routledge; Boyce, PR (2003), *Human Factors in Lighting* (2nd edn), Taylor & Francis; 'Employee Productivity in a Sustainable Building: Pre- and Post-Occupancy Studies in 500 Collins Street', A Study commissioned by Sustainability Victoria and the Kador Group; Edwards, L and Torcellini, P (2002), *A Literature Review of the Effects of Natural Light on Building Occupants*, National Renewable Energy Laboratory, Colorado; Figueiro, MG, Rea, MS, Stevens, RG and Rea, AC (2002), *Daylight and Productivity – A Possible Link to Circadian Regulation*, Lighting Research Center, Rensselaer Polytechnic Institute. I am indebted to Jerome Webb of GIA for this research, and for discussing this topic with me over a number of years.

[26]   See para 6.22 ff.

[27]   See para 6.24.

## Measurement and quantification of loss of light

8.16 It is a question for the court whether interference is substantial or not. Technical modelling and analysis, however, provide the most useful objective assessment available for this purpose. The importance of light has long been acknowledged, and technical experts have devised a standard method of measuring the loss of light. A short summary is set out in Appendix A. As explained in that appendix, however, the 'traditional' method of measuring light has a number of potential shortcomings for assessing the practical effects of an interference with light, and is ripe for further technical research and for re-evaluation.

# Chapter 9

# Statutory Authorisation of Interferences with Rights of Light

## INTRODUCTION

9.1    Where interference with light would otherwise be actionable, it may still be lawful if it is authorised by statute. This chapter considers the principles applicable generally and the provisions of section 237 of the Town and Country Planning Act 1990 in particular. It is important to distinguish statutory authorisation of interference with a right of light from the extinction of the right itself. The latter is considered above.[1]

## STATUTORY AUTHORISATION GENERALLY

9.2    Statutes may provide lawful authority for the interference with rights. Where land subject to an easement is acquired compulsorily for statutory purposes and the statutes make provision for the payment of compensation for those injuriously affected by the consequences of the acquisition, then the land acquired may be developed notwithstanding that this interferes with rights of light.[2]

---

[1]    See para 7.1 ff. At the date of writing, Planning and Housing Bill 2015, cl 137 proposes the repeal of s 237 and its replacement with new statutory provisions.

[2]    Under Land Clauses Consolidation Act 1845, s 68: see *Eagle v Charing Cross Railway* (1867) LR 2 CP 638; *Bedford (Duke) v Dawson* (1875) LR 20 Eq 353; *Wigram v Fryer* (1887) 36 ChD 87; *Kirby v Harrogate School Board* [1896] 1 Ch 437. Under Compulsory Purchase Act 1965, s 10: see *Wilson's Brewery Ltd v West Yorkshire MBC* (1977) 34 P & CR 224. See also *Long Eaton Recreation Ground Company Ltd v Midland Railway Co* [1902] 2 KB 574; *Marten v Flight Refuelling* [1982] Ch 115; *Re Elm Avenue* [1984] 1 WLR 1398; *Brown v Heathlands NHS Trust* [1996] 1 All ER 133

9.3    Thus, in *Bedford v Dawson*,[3] where a statute incorporated the Land Clauses Consolidation Act 1845 and a committee was empowered to acquire certain land and to erect buildings on that land for specified statutory purposes, the owners of neighbouring land were not entitled to an injunction to restrain interference with the ancient lights; rather, their remedy was to seek compensation under section 68 of the Land Clauses Consolidation Act 1845. A similar conclusion was reached in the case of *Wigram v Fryer*.[4]

9.4    It should be noted, however, that where land is compulsorily acquired and is subject to an easement which is disturbed, the person whose easement is disturbed is not entitled to serve a notice to treat requiring the purchase of his land. No land as such is acquired. The remedy is a claim for compensation for injurious affection (rather than for compulsory *purchase*). It is important to note that a claim for such compensation cannot be made for harm which could not have been the subject of a common law cause of action.[5]

9.5    While it is not necessary to establish that the value of the property benefitting from the easement has been diminished for a claim for compensation to lie,[6] the measure of compensation under section 68 of the Land Clauses Consolidation Act 1845 and section 10 of the Compulsory Purchase Act 1965 is payable only for damage to the claimant's land or interest in land: he is not entitled to compensation for loss caused to him in his personal capacity.[7] Furthermore, compensation does not include a

---

(for similar cases concerning interference with restrictive covenants); *Manchester Sheffield & Lincolnshire Railway Co v Anderson* [1898] 2 Ch 394 (a case concerning a covenant for quiet enjoyment).

[3]    *Bedford v Dawson* (1875) LR 20 Eq 353.

[4]    *Wigram v Fryer* (1887) 36 ChD 87. See also *Re London, Tilbury and Southend Railway Co and The Trustees of the Gower's Walk Schools* (1889) 24 QBD 326.

[5]    *Wildtree Hotels Ltd v Harrow LBC* [2001] 2 AC 1. For a full treatment of the law relating to compensation for injurious affection, see Barnes, M (2014), *The Law of Compulsory Purchase and Compensation*, Hart Publishing.

[6]    See *Eagle v Charing Cross Railway* (1867) LR 2 CP 638.

[7]    See *Argyle Motors (Birkenhead) Ltd v Birkenhead Corporation* [1975] AC 99; *Wildtree Hotels Ltd v Harrow LBC* [2001] 2 AC 1.

ransom value or take account of the profits made by the developer.[8] The relevant date for assessing loss is likely to be the date when the rights of light are first disturbed.[9]

## TOWN AND COUNTRY PLANNING ACT 1990, SECTION 237

9.6    Under section 237(1) of the Town and Country Planning Act 1990, the erection, construction or carrying out of maintenance of any building or work whether done by the local authority or by a person deriving title under them, on land which has been acquired or appropriated[10] by a local authority for planning purposes if it is done in accordance with planning permission, will be 'authorised', notwithstanding that it involves interference with an interest or right to which this section applies, or a breach of a restriction as to the user of land arising by virtue of a contract. It is important to remember that the function of section 237 is to authorise an interference with rights which would otherwise be a private nuisance.[11] It does not operate by extinguishing private rights.

9.7    The 'interests and rights' to which the section applies are:

> any easement, liberty, privilege, right or advantage annexed to land and adversely affecting other land, including any natural right of support.[12]

Accordingly, the erection of a building within the scope of this section is authorised notwithstanding that it interferes with a right of light. The effect

---

[8]    *Wrotham Park Settled Estates v Hertsmere Borough Council* [1993] 2 EGLR 15 at 16F–18A, per Sir Thomas Bingham MR; see also *Holliday v Breckland DC* [2012] UKUT 193 (LC). See also *Coventry v Lawrence* [2014] UKSC 13 at [128], per Carnwath LJ.

[9]    Cf *Flanagan v Stoke-on-Trent City Council* [1982] 1 EGLR 205; *Puttock v Bexley LBC* [2004] RVR 216.

[10]   See para 9.10.

[11]   *Holliday v Breckland DC* [2012] UKUT 193 (LC) at [14]. At the date of writing there are proposals for the repeal and replacement of Town and Country Planning Act 1990, s 237: see Planning and Housing Bill 2015, cl 137. The final form of this legislation is not yet known.

[12]   Town and Country Planning Act 1990, s 237(2).

of section 237 of the Town and Country Planning Act 1990 is not that rights are acquired by the local authority or developer nor are they extinguished. It is that works are authorised notwithstanding the interference with rights.[13] So, if rights are registered at the Land Registry, they will remain on the register and it is only development which is within the scope of section 237 which is authorised to 'override' those rights.

9.8    This authorisation is subject to the payment of compensation. Compensation is payable by the person carrying out the development, although the local authority retains a residual liability.[14] Compensation is payable under section 63 or section 68 of the Lands Clauses Consolidation Act 1845 or under section 7 or section 10 of the Compulsory Purchase Act 1965 and is assessed in the same manner and subject to the same rules as in the case of other compensation under those sections in respect of injurious affection where:

(a)   the compensation is to be estimated in connection with a purchase under those Acts; or

(b)   the injury arises from the execution of works on land acquired under those Acts.

Section 7 of the 1965 Act (or section 63 of the 1845 Act) deals with compensation where land has been taken in cases of severance or injurious affection. Section 10 of the 1965 Act (or section 68 of the 1845 Act) deals with compensation, whether or not land has been taken, where the land of the claimant has been 'injuriously affected by the execution of works'. As explained above, such compensation is payable only for damage to the claimant's land or interest in land: he is not entitled to compensation for loss caused to him in his personal capacity.[15] Furthermore, it does not include a ransom value or take account of the profits made by the

---

[13]   See para 8.4 ff for what constitutes an actionable interference with rights.

[14]   Town and Country Planning Act 1990, s 237(4) and (5).

[15]   See para 9.5. *Argyle Motors (Birkenhead) Ltd v Birkenhead Corporation* [1975] AC 99; *Wildtree Hotels Ltd v Harrow LBC* [2001] 2 AC 1.

developer.[16] The statute does not expressly provide for a valuation date. However, the relevant date for assessing loss is likely to be the date when the rights of light are first disturbed.[17]

9.9     The purpose of section 237 of the Town and Country Planning Act 1990 is to ensure that, provided work is done in accordance with planning permission and subject to payment of compensation, a local authority (and those deriving title from it) should be permitted to develop its land in the manner in which it, acting *bona fide*, considers will best serve the public interest. To that end, it is recognised that a local authority should be permitted to interfere with third party rights.[18] In principle, therefore, if the local authority acquires or appropriates land needed for a particular development, then section 237 (subject to the payment of compensation) can be used to override the restrictions in the covenant at least in so far as they restrict the erection of the building. The use of powers such as this for 'washing' a title is considered to be unobjectionable.[19] However, such acquisition or appropriation must take place within the powers of the local planning authority and it will be necessary for the statutory preconditions for such acquisition or appropriation to be satisfied.[20]

9.10     On the other hand, while section 237 of the Town and Country Planning Act 1990 was clearly intended to enable a local authority (and its successor) to redevelop or continue to redevelop a site appropriated for planning purposes from time to time, it has been held that it does not enable a developer who is merely a successor to the local authority to

---

[16]     *Wrotham Park Settled Estates v Hertsmere Borough Council* [1993] 2 EGLR 15 at 16F–18A, per Sir Thomas Bingham MR; see also *Holliday v Breckland DC* [2012] UKUT 193 (LC). See also *Coventry v Lawrence* [2014] UKSC 13 at [128], per Carnwath LJ.

[17]     Cf Lockhart-Mummery, C and Elvin, D (eds) (2015), *Encyclopedia of Planning*, Sweet & Maxwell, vol 2, at para P237-06; *Flanagan v Stoke-on-Trent City Council* [1982] 1 EGLR 205; *Puttock v Bexley LBC* [2004] RVR 216.

[18]     *R v City of London Corporation ex parte Mystery of the Barbers* (1997) 73 P & CR 59 at 64, per Dyson J.

[19]     *Ford-Camber Ltd v Deanminster Ltd* [2007] EWCA Civ 458.

[20]     See Town and Country Planning Act 1990, s 226 (acquisition by compulsory purchase); s 227 (acquisition by agreement). See Local Government Act 1972, s 122 (powers of appropriation).

develop the land otherwise than for the specific purposes for which the land was appropriated.[21]

9.11   Similar provisions are found in other statutes, for instance, in section 19 of the New Towns Act 1981. At the date of writing, specific provision for powers for the overriding of covenants is contained in the Planning and Housing Bill 2015, clause 137.

---

[21]   *Midtown Ltd v City of London Real Property Company Ltd* [2005] EWHC 33 (Ch) at [47]; cf *R v City of London Council & another ex parte Master Governors and Commonality of the Mystery of the Barbers of London* [1996] 2 EGLR 128.

# Chapter 10

# Remedies for Interference with Rights of Light

## GENERALLY

10.1    There are four sorts of remedy to consider when rights of light are in issue:

(a)  abatement after the interference has occurred;

(b)  a declaration whether or not an interference has yet occurred;

(c)  an injunction to stop the interference which has occurred or is threatened to occur;

(d)  damages for the interference (including damages in circumstances where they are awarded instead of an injunction).

This chapter considers each sort of remedy in turn.

## ABATEMENT

10.2    A person who suffers a private nuisance is in some circumstances entitled to abate it by taking action on his own land[1] or by entering on to his neighbour's land and taking appropriate action to abate it.[2] However, the law does not favour abatement by private individuals because of the

---

[1]  *Lemmon v Webb* [1895] AC 1; *Butler v Standard Telephones* [1940] 1 KB 399.

[2]  *Baten's Case* (1610) 9 Rep 54b; *R v Rosewell* (1699) 2 Salk 459; *Raikes v Townsend* (1804) 2 Smith 9; *Jones v Williams* (1843) 11 M & W 176; *Perty v Fitzhowe* (1845) 8 QB 757 at 775.

likelihood of a breach of the peace[3] so the remedy of abatement is generally confined to simple cases such as overhanging branches.[4]

10.3    Before the right of abatement is exercised, notice should be given unless the nuisance can be removed without entry onto the wrongdoer's land[5] or (in a case where entry onto the wrongdoer's land is necessary) in cases of emergency where there is a danger to persons or property and there is no reasonable opportunity to give notice.[6] The justification for the remedy of abatement (in more than trivial cases) appears to be that there is a nuisance that requires immediate remedy more speedily than that which proceedings could provide.[7] Further, no more must be done than is necessary to abate the nuisance[8] and there must be no breach of the peace.[9]

10.4    Accordingly, where interference with light is caused by building works, this remedy will in practice not be appropriate. If it has relevance to cases of interference with light, it should be confined simply to situations where there is an interference caused by foliage overhanging the complainant's own land[10] or where (following notice to the wrongdoer) there is agreement to the abatement taking place.

10.5    If a party had abated a nuisance, the old action *quod permittat posternere*, by which abatement was claimed by order of the court, would

---

[3]    Hale, Sir M, *De Portubus Maris*, Pt 2, Ch VII; *Burton v Winters* [1990] 1 WLR 1077.

[4]    *Burton v Winters* [1990] 1 WLR 1077.

[5]    *Lemmon v Webb* [1894] 3 Ch 1, [1895] AC 1.

[6]    *Jones v Williams* (1843) 11 M & W 176 at 182; cf *Lemmon v Webb* [1894] 3 Ch 1 at 13.

[7]    Blackstone, Sir W (1765–1769), *Commentaries on the Laws of England*, Clarendon Press, Bk III, Ch 1; *Moffett v Brewer* (1848) Iowa 1 Greene 348 at 450; *Burton v Winters* [1990] 1 WLR 1077.

[8]    *Penruddock's Case* (1597) 5 Co Rep 100(b); *James v Hayward* (1631) 1 (W) Jones 221 at 222; *Cooper v Marshall* (1757) 1 Burr 268. See also *Cawkwell v Russell* (1856) 26 LJ Ex 34; *Roberts v Rose* (1865) LR 1 Ex 82 at 89.

[9]    Blackstone, Sir W (1765–1769), *Commentaries on the Laws of England*, Clarendon Press, Bk III, Ch 1, s 4; *Colchester Corpn v Brooke* (1845) 7 QB 339 at 377.

[10]    But in such a case, the complainant may not appropriate what he has severed and must return it to the wrongdoer: see *Mills v Brooks* [1919] 1 KB 555.

not lie.[11] It is still law that an action through the court will not lie for the abatement of a nuisance after the claimant has himself abated the nuisance.[12] However, there is probably nothing to prevent a party who has abated a nuisance from bringing an action for damages which he has sustained prior to the abatement.[13] On the other hand, it should be noted that where a claim for an injunction is made but refused, the right to abate is lost.[14]

## DECLARATIONS

10.6    The court has power to make declarations about the parties' respective rights.[15] When considering whether or not to grant a declaration, the court should take into account justice to the claimant, justice to the defendant, whether a declaration would serve a useful purpose and whether there are any other special reasons why the court should grant a declaration or not.[16] Declarations may be made about whether rights exist and also the extent of parties' respective rights (thus, in effect, determining what might constitute an interference with the rights).[17] A declaration may also in appropriate circumstances be sought to determine whether a party would be entitled to an injunction or only damages.[18] In appropriate circumstances, the court may make a declaration but grant liberty to apply for an injunction should it become necessary.[19]

---

[11]    *Baten's Case* (1610) 9 Co Rep 54(b), 5(a); Fitzherbert, Sir A (1534), *La Novelle Natura Brevium*, 183, I(a).

[12]    *Lane v Capsey* [1891] 3 Ch 411 at 416.

[13]    *Kendrick v Bartland* (1679) 2 Mod Rep 253; see also *Lemmon v Webb* [1894] 3 Ch 1 at 24; *Smith v Giddy* [1904] 2 KB 448; *Job Edwards v Birmingham Navigations* [1924] 1 KB 341 at 356. Cf *Lagan Navigation Co v Lambeg Bleaching, Dyeing and Finishing Co* [1927] AC 226 at 244, per Lord Atkinson (whose *dicta* are probably confined to claims for damage subsequent to the abatement).

[14]    *Burton v Winters* [1990] 1 WLR 1077.

[15]    See Senior Courts Act 1981, s 19; Civil Procedure Rules 1998 (SI 1998/3132), rule 40.20; *Financial Services Authority v Rouke* [2002] C P Rep 14.

[16]    *Financial Services Authority v Rourke* [2002] C P Rep 14.

[17]    See *Well Barn Shoot Ltd v Shackleton* [2003] EWCA Civ 2.

[18]    *Greenwich Healthcare NHS Trust v London & Quadrant Housing Trust and others* [1998] 3 All ER 437.

[19]    *Litchfield-Speer v Queen Anne's Gate Syndicate* [1919] 1 Ch 407.

10.7    This remedy is of considerable importance to developers who wish to resolve issues before they commit themselves to the construction of a building which might interfere with neighbouring lights. Conversely, those whose rights may be affected may seek such relief so that the parties may know where they stand. The grant of a declaration, however, is discretionary. Therefore, declarations must serve a useful purpose and the court will not grant one if it is premature.[20]

## INJUNCTIONS

10.8    The court has power to make an order requiring a party to do or not to do something.[21] It has been suggested that in cases of nuisance involving interference with the enjoyment of land, the primary remedy for interference should be regarded as damages rather than an injunction.[22] An easement, however, is a defined or definable property right, the interference with which is recognised as actionable *per se*.[23] Accordingly, unless there is something special in the particular facts of the case, the court will remain astute to protect that right from interference by an injunction to prohibit or remove the interference.[24] As was pointed out by Sir Thomas Bingham MR in *Jaggard v Sawyer*,[25] 'a plaintiff who can show that his legal right will be violated by the defendant's conduct is prima facie entitled to the grant of an injunction'. If this were not so, then those with large pockets could override legal rights simply because of their ability or willingness to pay damages. Even if an injunction may be inappropriate in many commercial contexts, where light to residential property would be perceptibly and substantially diminished, there must remain a formidable case for an injunction to be granted.[26] Similarly, if the

---

[20]   *CIP Property (AIPT) Ltd v Transport for London* [2012] EWHC 259 (Ch).

[21]   See Senior Courts Act 1981, s 37(1).

[22]   See *Coventry v Lawrence* [2014] UKSC 13, per Lord Sumption.

[23]   See para 8.4.

[24]   Cf *Patel v W.H. Smith (Eziot) Ltd* [1987] 1 WLR 853. This too was recognised by Peter Smith J in *Midtown Ltd v City of London Real Property Co Ltd* [2005] EWHC 33 (Ch) at [70]. See also *Jones v Llanrwst Urban District Council* [1911] 1 Ch 393 at 411, per Parker J.

[25]   *Jaggard v Sawyer* [1995] 1 WLR 269 at 282; see also *Coventry v Lawrence* [2014] UKSC 13 at [101], per Lord Neuberger.

[26]   *Coventry v Lawrence* [2014] UKSC 13 at [168], per Lord Mance.

right of light is necessary for a particular commercial purpose,[27] then again it is difficult to see why the starting point should not be that the law will protect the right from infringement by injunction. On the other hand, if the value of the right is (in practice) its use for stopping development unless a ransom is extracted or if the interference does not for practical purposes harm the current or immediately intended enjoyment of the dominant tenement,[28] then it is less easy to see why the right should be protected by injunction as a matter of course. As explained below, when deciding whether to award damages instead of an injunction, the court has significant discretion.

## Prohibitory, mandatory and quia timet injunctions

10.9    The court may grant an injunction prohibiting the doing of specified acts. Therefore, an order may be made to stop a defendant from constructing a building which would interfere with a right to light.

10.10    The court may also grant an injunction which requires positive steps to prevent the continuation of a wrong. For instance, it may order a person to remove a building or part of a building which unlawfully interferes with light. Such an injunction is referred to as a mandatory injunction.

10.11    An injunction may be granted where future harm is feared: this is a *quia timet* injunction. Such an injunction may even be granted before any harm has occurred at all and no cause of action has arisen at common law. However, before the court will grant such an injunction, there must be evidence that the defendant intends to do something which will infringe the claimant's rights.[29] There must be some evidence that harm is 'imminent' in the sense that the remedy sought is not premature.[30] So, a *quia timet* injunction has been refused where there was no threat of an infringement of rights of light for at least 5 years.[31] On the other hand, in appropriate circumstances, the court may grant declarations setting out the

---

[27]    Cf *Allen v Greenwood* [1980] Ch 119; see para 2.15.

[28]    See e.g. *Midtown Ltd v City of London Real Property Co Ltd* [2005] EWHC 33 (Ch).

[29]    See *Lord Cowley v Byas* (1877) 5 ChD 944; *Phillips v Thomas* (1890) 62 LT 793.

[30]    *Hooper v Rogers* [1975] Ch 43 at 49–50.

[31]    *CIP Property (AIPT) Ltd v Transport for London* [2012] EWHC 259.

parties' respective rights instead of an injunction but with liberty to apply for an injunction should it become necessary.[32] Further, where such an injunction is mandatory, i.e. positive steps are required to prevent harm, the court will be far more circumspect in the exercise of its discretion.

10.12   The court's circumspection when a mandatory injunction is sought was made clear in *Redland Bricks Ltd v Morris*[33] by Lord Upjohn, who stated:[34]

> the grant of a mandatory injunction is, of course, entirely discretionary and unlike a negative injunction can never be 'as of course.' Every case must depend essentially upon its own particular circumstances. Any general principles for its application can only be laid down in the most general terms:
>
> 1.   A mandatory injunction can only be granted where the plaintiff shows a very strong probability upon the facts that grave damage will accrue to him in the future. As Lord Dunedin said in 1919 it is not sufficient to say 'timeo.' [*Attorney-General for the Dominion of Canada v Ritchie Contracting and Supply Co* [1919] AC 999 at 1005, PC] It is a jurisdiction to be exercised sparingly and with caution but in the proper case unhesitatingly.
>
> 2.   Damages will not be a sufficient or adequate remedy if such damage does happen. This is only the application of a general principle of equity; it has nothing to do with Lord Cairns' Act or Shelfer's case [1895] 1 Ch. 287.
>
> 3.   Unlike the case where a negative injunction is granted to prevent the continuance or recurrence of a wrongful act the question of the cost to the defendant to do works to prevent or lessen the likelihood of a future apprehended wrong must be an element to be taken into account: (a) where the defendant has acted without regard to his neighbour's rights, or has tried to steal a march on him or has tried to evade the jurisdiction of the court or, to sum it up, has acted wantonly and quite unreasonably in relation to his neighbour he may be ordered to repair his wanton and unreasonable acts by doing positive work to restore the status quo even if the expense to him is

---

[32]   *Litchfield-Speer v Queen Anne's Gate Syndicate* [1919] 1 Ch 407; see above.

[33]   *Redland Bricks Ltd v Morris* [1970] AC 652.

[34]   *Redland Bricks Ltd v Morris* [1970] AC 652 at 665–666.

out of all proportion to the advantage thereby accruing to the plaintiff ...; (b) but where the defendant has acted reasonably, though in the event wrongly, the cost of remedying by positive action his earlier activities is most important for two reasons. First, because no legal wrong has yet occurred (for which he has not been recompensed at law and in equity) and, in spite of gloomy expert opinion, may never occur or possibly only upon a much smaller scale than anticipated. Secondly, because if ultimately heavy damage does occur the plaintiff is in no way prejudiced for he has his action at law and all his consequential remedies in equity. So the amount to be expended under a mandatory order by the defendant must be balanced with these considerations in mind against the anticipated possible damage to the plaintiff and if, on such balance, it seems unreasonable to inflict such expenditure upon one who for this purpose is no more than a potential wrongdoer then the court must exercise its jurisdiction accordingly. Of course, the court does not have to order such works as upon the evidence before it will remedy the wrong but may think it proper to impose upon the defendant the obligation of doing certain works which may upon expert opinion merely lessen the likelihood of any further injury to the plaintiff's land ...

4. If in the exercise of its discretion the court decides that it is a proper case to grant a mandatory injunction, then the court must be careful to see that the defendant knows exactly in fact what he has to do and this means not as a matter of law but as a matter of fact, so that in carrying out an order he can give his contractors the proper instructions.

## Final injunctions

10.13 Where a claimant has established his legal right and the court considers it appropriate to grant injunctive relief, a 'final' injunction will be awarded. It has been doubted whether the court has a residual jurisdiction to vary an order made in absolute terms.[35] Under rule 3.1(7) of the Civil Procedure Rules 1998,[36] however, there is power to vary or revoke an order. It is only in exceptional circumstances that such a power

---

[35] *Co-operative Insurance Society Ltd v Argyll Stores (Holdings) Ltd* [1998] AC 1 at 18A; *Midtown Ltd v City of London Real Property Co Ltd* [2005] EWHC 33 (Ch).

[36] SI 1998/3132.

will be exercised to vary a substantive final injunction.[37] The discretion will only be exercised where:

(a) there has been a material change of circumstances since the making of the order; or

(b) where the facts on which the original decision was made were misstated.[38]

## Interim injunctions

10.14   The court may grant an injunction to stop an interference with light before the parties' rights have been finally determined in an action. The principles which the court applies when determining whether to grant such an interim (or interlocutory) injunction were considered by the House of Lords in *American Cyanamid Co Ltd v Ethicon Ltd*.[39]

10.15   First, the court will consider whether there is a 'serious issue to be tried'.[40] In determining whether there is such a serious issue to be tried, there are no technical rules requiring the chances of success to be evaluated.[41] Where a mandatory interim injunction is sought, however, the court will require a high assurance that at the trial it will appear that the injunction was rightly granted.[42] In appropriate cases, however, mandatory interim injunctions have been granted to stop interferences with light and require buildings to be pulled down: for instance, where a defendant had sought to hurry on with building works after being served with notice of proceedings[43] or evaded service of a writ.[44] As seen below, however, since a claimant will usually be required to provide a cross-undertaking in

---

[37]   See *Lloyds Investment (Scandinavia) Ltd v Christen Ager-Hanssen* [2003] EWHC 1740 (Ch); *Advent Capital plc v G N Ellinas Imports-Exports Ltd* [2005] EWHC 1242 (Comm); *Collier v Williams* [2006] EWCA Civ 20; *Hackney LBC v Findlay* [2011] HLR 15.

[38]   *Rosling v Pinnegar (No 2)* [1998] EWCA Civ 1510.

[39]   *American Cyanamid Co Ltd v Ethicon Ltd* [1975] AC 396.

[40]   *American Cyanamid Co Ltd v Ethicon Ltd* [1975] AC 396 at 407G.

[41]   *American Cyanamid Co Ltd v Ethicon Ltd* [1975] AC 396 at 407G.

[42]   *Locabil International Finance Ltd v Agroexport* [1986] 1 WLR 657.

[43]   *Daniel v Ferguson* [1891] 2 Ch 27; *Mathias v Davies* [1970] EGD 370.

[44]   *Von Joel v Hornsey* [1895] 2 Ch 774.

damages which will be paid in the event that the interim injunction should not have been granted,[45] a mandatory interim injunction in the context of rights of light is rarely sought.

10.16    Secondly, the court will consider whether if the claimant were to succeed at trial in establishing his right to a permanent injunction, he would be adequately compensated by an award of damages for the loss he would have sustained as a result of the defendant's continuing to do what was sought to be enjoined between the time of the application and the time of trial. If damages in the measure recoverable at common law would be an adequate remedy and the defendant would be in a financial position to pay them, then an interim injunction will not normally be granted, however strong the claimant's right appears to be at that stage.[46]

10.17    Thirdly, the court will then consider whether on the contrary hypothesis, i.e. that if the defendant were to succeed at trial in establishing his right to do that which was sought to be enjoined, he would be adequately compensated under the claimant's undertaking as to damages for the loss he would have sustained by being prevented from doing so between the time of the application and the time of the trial. If damages in the measure recoverable under such an undertaking would be an adequate remedy and the claimant would be in a financial position to pay them, there would be no reason upon this ground to refuse an interim injunction.[47] Such an undertaking by the claimant to pay any damages must be given as a condition of the grant of an interim injunction unless the court determines otherwise. In seeking an interim injunction, therefore, it is usual for a claimant to provide evidence of his ability to satisfy his undertaking in damages.[48] In appropriate circumstances, the court may require the claimant to 'fortify' his undertaking by providing appropriate security.[49]

---

[45]    See para 10.17.

[46]    *American Cyanamid Co v Ethicon Ltd* [1975] AC 396 at 408.

[47]    *American Cyanamid Co v Ethicon Ltd* [1975] AC 396 at 408.

[48]    See *Lunn Poly Ltd v Liverpool & Lancashire Properties Ltd* [2006] EWCA Civ 430 at [42]–[44].

[49]    See *Sinclair Investment Holdings SA v Cushnie* [2004] EWHC 218 (Ch) at [18]–[25]; *JSC Mezhdunarodniy Promyshlenniy Bank v Pugachev* [2015] EWCA Civ 139.

10.18   Fourthly, if there is doubt about the adequacy of damages, the court will then consider what is known as 'the balance of convenience'.[50] The underlying question is whether the injustice that would be caused to the defendant if the claimant were granted an injunction but subsequently failed at trial would outweigh the injustice caused to the claimant if the injunction were refused and he succeeded at trial.[51] The court, when deciding whether or not to grant or refuse an interim injunction, will seek to take the course which will cause the least irremediable prejudice to one party or the other.[52] The court, however, will usually only take into account the merits of the case at this stage if it is apparent upon facts disclosed by evidence about which there is no credible dispute that the strength of one party's case is disproportionate to that of the other party.[53] Where other factors appear to be evenly balanced, however, the court will seek to preserve the status quo,[54] i.e. the circumstances as they prevailed in the period immediately preceding the issue of the claim form or (if later) the application.[55]

## Damages instead of an injunction?

### *Jurisdiction*

10.19   Where the court has jurisdiction to grant an injunction, it also has a statutory jurisdiction to award damages in addition to or instead of an injunction.[56]

---

[50]   *American Cyanamid Co v Ethicon Ltd* [1975] AC 396 at 408.

[51]   *Film Rover International Ltd v Cannon Film Sales Ltd* [1987] 1 WLR 670; see also *NWL Ltd v Woods* [1979] 1 WLR 1294 at 1306G, per Lord Diplock.

[52]   *National Commercial Bank Jamaica v Olint Corp Ltd* [2009] 1 WLR 1405 at [17].

[53]   *American Cyanamid Co v Ethicon Ltd* [1975] AC 396 at 409.

[54]   *American Cyanamid Co v Ethicon Ltd* [1975] AC 396 at 408.

[55]   *Garden Cottage Foods Ltd v Milk Marketing Board* [1984] AC 130 at 140.

[56]   Senior Courts Act 1981, s 50; County Courts Act 1984, s 38. The jurisdiction originally derived from Chancery Amendment Act 1858, s 2 ('Lord Cairns' Act'). See *Holland v Worley* (1884) 26 ChD 578.

## *A wide discretion*

10.20   The court's jurisdiction is a wide one. The classic statement of when damages may be awarded in lieu of an injunction is in *Shelfer's* case.[57] An injunction may be refused where:

(a)   there is a small injury;

(b)   that injury is one which is capable of being estimated in money;

(c)   that injury can be adequately compensated by a small money payment; and

(d)   it would be oppressive to grant an injunction.

10.21   The approach of the court is a flexible one and a mechanistic approach to the application of the guidance in *Shelfer's* case is wrong in principle.[58] As was pointed out by Lord Neuberger in *Coventry v Lawrence*:[59]

> The court's power to award damages in lieu of an injunction involves a classic exercise of discretion, which should not, as a matter of principle, be fettered ... And, as a matter of practical fairness, each case is likely to be so fact-sensitive that any firm guidance is likely to do more harm than good.

Lord Neuberger cited with approval the *dicta* of Millett LJ in *Jaggard v Sawyer*:[60]

> Reported cases are merely illustrations of circumstances in which particular judges have exercised their discretion, in some cases by granting an injunction, and in others by awarding damages instead. Since they are all cases on the exercise of a discretion, none of them is a

---

[57]   *Shelfer v Ciy of London Electric Lighting Co* [1895] 1 Ch 287 at 322–323, per AL Smith LJ.

[58]   See *Coventry v Lawrence* [2014] UKSC 13 at [117] and [119], per Lord Neuberger disapproving the mechanistic approach seemingly adopted in cases such as *Slack v Leeds Industrial Co-operative Society Ltd* [1924] 2 Ch 475; *Miller v Jackson* [1977] QB 966; *Kennaway v Thompson* [1981] QB 88; *Regan v Paul Properties DPF No 1 Ltd* [2006] EWCA Civ 1319; *Watson v Croft Promosport Ltd* [2009] EWCA Civ 15.

[59]   *Coventry v Lawrence* [2014] UKSC 13 at [120].

[60]   *Jaggard v Sawyer* [1995] 1 WLR 269 at 288.

binding authority on how the discretion should be exercised. The most that any of them can demonstrate is that in similar circumstances it would not be wrong to exercise the discretion in the same way. But it does not follow that it would be wrong to exercise it differently.

Accordingly, Lord Neuberger in *Coventry v Lawrence*[61] summarised the position as follows:

> First, the application of the four tests [in *Shelfer's* case] must not be such as 'to be a fetter on the exercise of the court's discretion'. Secondly, it would, in the absence of additional relevant circumstances pointing the other way, normally be right to refuse an injunction if those four tests were satisfied. Thirdly, the fact that those tests are not all satisfied does not mean that an injunction should be granted.

A claimant who has established both a legal right and a threat to infringe that right might still properly argue that he is entitled to an injunction and special circumstances are needed to justify withholding the injunction.[62] The underlying question is likely to be whether it is 'oppressive' to grant an injunction (the fourth element emphasised by the *Shelfer* guidance) rather than simply the balance of convenience between the parties. This emphasis on 'oppression' is reflected in *Jaggard v Sawyer*,[63] where Millett LJ said:[64]

> In considering whether the grant of an injunction would be oppressive to the defendant, all the circumstances of the case have to be considered. At one extreme, the defendant may have acted openly and in good faith and in ignorance of the plaintiff's rights, and thereby inadvertently placed himself in a position where the grant of an injunction would either force him to yield to the plaintiff's extortionate demands or expose him to substantial loss. At the other extreme, the defendant may have acted with his eyes open and in full knowledge that he was invading the plaintiff's rights, and hurried on his work in the hope that by presenting

---

[61]   *Coventry v Lawrence* [2014] UKSC 13 at [123].

[62]   *Jaggard v Sawyer* [1995] 1 WLR 269 at 282F and 283C, per Sir Thomas Bingham MR, and at 286H, 287F–G and 288B, per Millett LJ.

[63]   *Jaggard v Sawyer* [1995] 1 WLR 269.

[64]   *Jaggard v Sawyer* [1995] 1 WLR 269 at 288–289.

the court with a fait accompli he could compel the plaintiff to accept monetary compensation. Most cases, like the present, fall somewhere in between.

In the context of rights to light, in *Colls v Home and Colonial Stores Ltd*,[65] Lord Macnaghten said:

> … if there is really a question as to whether the obstruction is legal or not, and if the defendant has acted fairly and not in an unneighbourly spirit, I am disposed to think that the Court ought to incline to damages rather than to an injunction. It is quite true that a man ought not to be compelled to part with his property against his will, or to have the value of his property diminished, without an Act of Parliament. On the other hand, the Court ought to be very careful not to allow an action for the protection of ancient lights to be used as a means of extorting money. Often a person who is engaged in a large building scheme has to pay money right and left in order to avoid litigation, which will put him to even greater expense by delaying his proceedings. As far as my own experience goes, there is quite as much oppression on the part of those who invoke the assistance of the Court to protect some ancient lights, which they have never before considered of any great value, as there is on the part of those who are improving the neighbourhood by the erection of buildings that must necessarily to some extent interfere with the light of adjoining premises.

Lord Macnaghten clearly considered it 'oppressive' to award injunctions in circumstances where ancient lights were being used as a 'means of extorting money'.

10.22   With these points in mind, it is necessary to be cautious about recent cases in which the court has made mandatory orders requiring the partial demolition of buildings which interfered with rights of light. Nevertheless, despite the flexibility which the court has, if a developer presses on with a development in the face of complaint, an injunction may still be granted to require the interference with light to be remedied as it

---

[65]   *Colls v Home and Colonial Stores Ltd* [1904] AC 179 at 193; 'cautiously' approved by Lord Neuberger in *Coventry v Lawrence* [2014] UKSC 13 at [121] – the caution arising from each case necessarily turning on its own facts.

was in *Regan v Paul Properties Ltd*,[66] where the criteria of the *Shelfer* guidance were not met by the developer (albeit that the approach of the court to these criteria has been held to be too inflexible).[67]

10.23   On the other hand, it is unlikely that an injunction would be granted in a case such as *HKRUK II (CHC) v Heaney*.[68] In that case, the judge considered that the injury as a result of the infringement of Mr Heaney's rights to light caused by a neighbouring building was not small, and having reached that conclusion considered that was the end of the matter. In doing this, the judge appears to have shut his eyes to the prejudice which Mr Heaney's considerable delay in bringing the matter before the court had caused to the developer (he sought relief only by counterclaim some months after the infringing building was not only completed but had been let). If the judge had looked at the matter 'in the round' rather than taking a formulaic approach to applying the *Shelfer* guidance, it is highly likely that he would have reached a different conclusion. It should be noted, however, that the developer in that case did not lead evidence to establish that it would be seriously prejudiced by the injunction: the evidence only established that it would not make as much profit as it would otherwise have done. It must be emphasised, therefore, as Lord Neuberger did in *Coventry v Lawrence*,[69] that the exercise of the court's discretion is going to turn on the precise facts of each case.

### *Shelfer guidance and 'small' money payments: a problem*

10.24   As explained above,[70] the *Shelfer* guidance remains relevant. One question which arises in considering the *Shelfer* guidance is what is meant by a 'small' money payment. In principle, in assessing whether or not the injury can be compensated by a small money payment, it is correct to

---

[66]   *Regan v Paul Properties Ltd* [2006] EWCA 1319; see also *Deakins v Hookings* [1994] 1 EGLR 190 (first instance judge granting injunction to require alteration of development which interfered with light to dwelling); *Mortimer v Bailey* [2004] EWCA Civ 1514 (Court of Appeal upheld injunction requiring demolition of dwelling constructed in breach of covenant that seriously interfered with light to adjoining dwelling).

[67]   See per Lord Neuberger in *Coventry v Lawrence* [2014] UKSC 13 at [117] ff.

[68]   *HKRUK II (CHC) v Heaney* [2010] EWHC 2245 (Ch).

[69]   See *Coventry v Lawrence* [2014] UKSC 13 at [120]; see also above.

[70]   See para 10.21.

consider the 'common law' measure of damages, at least to the extent that they comprise damages compensating the claimant for the diminution in value to his property caused by the interference with his rights. The principles by which 'common law' damages are assessed are considered below.[71]

10.25    On the other hand, the Court of Appeal in *Regan v Paul Properties Ltd*[72] and the court in the subsequent first instance decision in *HKRUK II (CHC) v Heaney*[73] appear to have considered that the 'damages in lieu' measure of damages should be taken into account in assessing whether or not the injury could be adequately compensated in damages. This is problematic.

10.26    The problem with the 'damages in lieu measure' is that it has been held to include a 'release fee' (i.e. the price for the claimant giving up the rights which he sought to protect by injunction). This release fee may take into account the profit to the developer.[74] If one gives too much weight to this, it means that the larger and more profitable the development, the larger the damages payable to the claimant and the less chance there is of an injunction being granted. This seems to be wrong in principle. The formulation of the working rule in *Shelfer* that the injury should be one that should be compensatable by a 'small money payment' took place before the 'release fee' measure of damages was considered to be the correct starting point for quantifying damages payable instead of an injunction. It is doubtful whether the judges in *Shelfer's* case had in mind 'release fee' damages when formulating their test.

10.27    Accordingly, limited weight (at best) should be attached to the quantum of 'release fee' damages in deciding whether or not it is appropriate to award damages instead of an injunction.

---

[71]   See para 10.51 ff.

[72]   *Regan v Paul Properties Ltd* [2006] EWCA Civ 1319.

[73]   *HKRUK II (CHC) v Heaney* [2010] EWHC 2245 (Ch).

[74]   See para 10.65 ff.

## *Would it be oppressive to grant an injunction?*

10.28   As explained above, whether or not it would be oppressive to grant
an injunction would be a largely material fact in the exercise of the court's
discretion. Whether or not it would be oppressive to grant an injunction will
depend on all the circumstances. It is possible to identify particular factors
which the courts have considered to make the grant of an injunction
'oppressive' and other factors which have limited weight in considering this
question. The following list is not intended, however, to be exhaustive.

### *Oppressive to grant an injunction: delay in seeking relief*

10.29   It has been held that delay alone, without prejudice caused to the
defendant, is insufficient to disentitle the claimant from injunctive relief.[75]
On the other hand, in *Blue Town Investments Ltd v Higgs and Hill plc*,[76] it
was held that a claim for a final injunction should be struck out unless the
claimant applied for an interim injunction supported by a cross-
undertaking in damages because the claimant had allowed the defendant
to proceed on the basis that it would only be obliged to pay moderate
compensation. *Blue Town* was therefore an exceptional case where the
claimant had encouraged the defendant to proceed.

10.30   In *Mortimer v Bailey*,[77] Peter Gibson LJ said:

> I own to some doubt as to whether it is appropriate to say that a person
> who does not proceed for an interlocutory injunction when he knows that
> a building is being erected in breach of covenant, but who has made clear
> his intention to object to the breach and to bring proceedings for that
> breach, should generally be debarred from obtaining a final injunction to
> pull down the building. There may be many circumstances in which a
> claimant would not be able to take the risk of seeking an interim
> injunction. He would need to satisfy the *American Cyanamid* test, and
> would have to provide an undertaking in damages. It may be entirely
> reasonable for the claimant, having put the defendant on notice, to
> proceed to trial, rather than take the risk of expending money wastefully
> by seeking interim relief. However, I accept that not to seek an interim

---

[75]   *Tottenham Hotspur Football & Athletic Co Ltd v Princegrove Publishers Ltd* [1974] 1
WLR 113 at 122B–C, per Lawson J.

[76]   *Blue Town Investments Ltd v Higgs and Hill plc* [1990] 1 WLR 696.

[77]   *Mortimer v Bailey* [2004] EWCA Civ 1514 at [30].

injunction is a factor which can be taken into account in weighing in the balance whether a final injunction should be granted.

Further, where A with the benefit of a right raises an issue over whether B's intended course of conduct will infringe that right, it is open to B to seek declaratory relief from the court and in pressing on without doing so B takes a risk. In *Mortimer v Bailey*, Jacob LJ said[78] (in the context of a case concerning restrictive covenants):

> Where there is doubt as to whether a restrictive covenant applies or whether consent under a restrictive covenant is being unreasonably withheld, the prudent party will get the matter sorted out before starting building, as could have been done in this case. If he takes a chance, then it will require very strong circumstances where, the chance having been taken and lost, an injunction will be withheld.

## *Oppressive to grant an injunction: mandatory or prohibitory injunctions?*

10.31   Allied to the question of delay is the issue of the nature of the relief sought: if a claimant delays so that a mandatory injunction becomes necessary, it is likely that it would be all the more oppressive to the defendant for an injunction to be granted. The corollary must be that if a claimant acts sufficiently promptly that only a negative injunction is required to give full effect to his rights, such relief is likely to be less oppressive to the defendant than if the claimant had waited until his rights were actually infringed.

10.32   In *Redland Bricks Ltd v Morris*,[79] Lord Upjohn made clear that a mandatory injunction differed from a negative injunction restraining an interference with a property right which would be granted 'as a matter of course'.[80]

10.33   In appropriate cases, however, a mandatory injunction will be granted, as it was in *Deakins v Hookings*[81] (where the first instance judge

---

[78]   *Mortimer v Bailey* [2004] EWCA Civ 1514 at [41].

[79]   *Redland Bricks Ltd v Morris* [1970] AC 652 at 664–667.

[80]   *Redland Bricks Ltd v Morris* [1970] AC 652 at 665. See para 10.12.

[81]   *Deakins v Hookings* [1994] 1 EGLR 190.

granted an injunction to require alteration of development which interfered with light to a dwelling) and *Mortimer v Bailey*[82] (where the Court of Appeal upheld an injunction requiring demolition of a dwelling constructed in breach of covenant that seriously interfered with light to an adjoining dwelling).

### *Oppressive to grant an injunction: claimant's interest in money?*

10.34   If the court concludes on the evidence that the claimant is really interested in protecting its rights to light with a view to securing more substantial monetary compensation from the defendant, then this is a factor which will be weighed in the balance against the grant of injunctive relief. This was an important factor in the court's approach in *Colls v Home and Colonial Stores Ltd*.[83] In *Gafford v Graham*,[84] an injunction was inappropriate because the plaintiff's 'willingness to settle the dispute on payment of a cash sum can properly be reflected by an award of damages'. One can easily see how it is oppressive to a defendant if equity is used merely as a device to advance the claimant's bargaining position rather than with a view to protecting his rights so that they can actually be enjoyed. This factor was also relevant to the judge's decision to refuse an injunction in *Midtown Ltd v City of London Real Property Company Ltd*.[85] In that case, the learned judge found unconvincing the claimant's response to the suggestion in cross-examination that it had put its own development proposals on hold with a view to extracting money from the defendant for the infringement of its rights to light.

10.35   On the other hand, one must be careful about taking this too far. Commercial parties will, on the face of things, primarily be interested in pecuniary advantage, but a distinction must be drawn between an interest in making money by using the rights which the property enjoys to their full advantage, and an interest in extorting a ransom or compensation from an adjoining owner for the infringement of those rights.

---

[82]   *Mortimer v Bailey* [2004] EWCA Civ 1514.

[83]   *Colls v Home and Colonial Stores Ltd* [1904] AC 179 at 193: see para 10.21.

[84]   *Gafford v Graham* [1999] 3 EGLR 75.

[85]   *Midtown Ltd v City of London Real Property Company Ltd* [2005] EWHC 33 (Ch) at [67].

10.36   Property rights are more than mere financial rights: they affect how the property owner may use and develop his property both now and in the future. In principle, the court should not allow a plea by a defendant that a claimant is a commercial entity which can be compensated in money to give rise to compulsory purchase by the back door. A property owner, even a commercial one, should as a matter of principle have the ability to protect his property rights by an injunction so that he can use and develop his property as he so wishes. In the context of residential property, the point may be more forcefully made as it was by Lord Mance in *Coventry v Lawrence*:[86]

> the right to enjoy one's home without disturbance is one which I would believe that many, indeed most, people value for reasons largely if not entirely independent of money.

If the court does not protect those rights, they become mere contingent rights convertible to money if they are interfered with by a defendant rich enough to buy them off with an award of damages.

10.37   While one must be careful about 'overdoing' such points (as was made clear in *Jaggard v Sawyer*[87] when the court considered the discretion to award mandatory injunctions), underpinning the Rule of Law there is a requirement of certainty in property rights (which is reflected in Article 1 of the First Protocol to the European Convention for the Protection of Human Rights and Fundamental Freedoms 1950) and the court should not allow those who seek to override the property rights of those who stand in their way to do so simply because: (a) they are rich enough; and (b) the property owner's interest can be valued in monetary terms.

10.38   The claimant who is interested in protecting his property and promptly acts to commence proceedings before his rights have been interfered with should be distinguished from the claimant who aims to secure a ransom by obtaining an injunction (particularly where the claimant requires a mandatory injunction).

---

[86]   *Coventry v Lawrence* [2014] UKSC 13 at [168].

[87]   *Jaggard v Sawyer* [1995] 1 WLR 269 at 287B.

### *Discretion: public benefit and planning permission*

10.39    Historically, there has been a reluctance to give weight to public benefit in determining the balance between competing private interests and in deciding whether or not an injunction should be granted. Thus, in *Shelfer's* case, Lindley LJ stated that the circumstance that 'the wrongdoer is in some sense a public benefactor' has not 'ever been a sufficient reason for refusing to protect by injunction an individual whose rights are persistently infringed'.[88]

10.40    However, as explained above, the discretion of the court is a wide one and the public interest cannot be excluded as a material factor in determining whether or not injunctive relief is appropriate. In the case of *Miller v Jackson*,[89] Lord Denning MR considered that the public interest should be balanced against the private interest in deciding what should constitute a nuisance where an action was brought by neighbours of a cricket field from which balls regularly escaped, and Cumming-Bruce LJ concluded that the public interest justified refusing an injunction and confining the remedy to damages.

10.41    In *Midtown Ltd v City of London Real Property Co Ltd*,[90] Peter Smith J considered the fact that the developer's development which had obtained planning permission was 'worthwhile and beneficial' to the area to be relevant in deciding whether it would be oppressive to grant an injunction to prevent an interference with light.

10.42    Most recently in *Coventry v Lawrence*,[91] Lord Neuberger made clear that the public benefit and (in some instances) the existence of planning permission can be a relevant factor in deciding whether or not to grant damages instead of an injunction. He said this:[92]

---

[88]    *Shelfer v Ciy of London Electric Lighting Co* [1895] 1 Ch 287 at 316. See also *Kennaway v Thompson* [1981] 1 QB 88; *Elliott v London Borough of Islington* [1991] 10 EG 145.

[89]    *Miller v Jackson* [1977] QB 966.

[90]    *Midtown Ltd v City of London Real Property Co Ltd* [2005] EWHC 33 (Ch) at [76].

[91]    *Coventry v Lawrence* [2014] UKSC 13.

[92]    *Coventry v Lawrence* [2014] UKSC 13 at [124]–[126].

[124] As for … public interest, I find it hard to see how there could be any circumstances in which it arose and could not, as a matter of law, be a relevant factor. Of course, it is very easy to think of circumstances in which it might arise but did not begin to justify the court refusing, or, as the case may be, deciding, to award an injunction if it was otherwise minded to do so. But that is not the point. The fact that a defendant's business may have to shut down if an injunction is granted should, it seems to me, obviously be a relevant fact, and it is hard to see why relevance should not extend to the fact that a number of the defendant's employees would lose their livelihood, although in many cases that may well not be sufficient to justify the refusal of an injunction. Equally, I do not see why the court should not be entitled to have regard to the fact that many other neighbours in addition to the claimant are badly affected by the nuisance as a factor in favour of granting an injunction.

[125] It is also right to mention planning permission in this context. In some cases, the grant of planning permission for a particular activity (whether carried on at the claimant's, or the defendant's, premises) may provide strong support for the contention that the activity is of benefit to the public, which would be relevant to the question of whether or not to grant an injunction. Accordingly, the existence of a planning permission which expressly or inherently authorises carrying on an activity in such a way as to cause a nuisance by noise or the like, can be a factor in favour of refusing an injunction and compensating the claimant in damages. This factor would have real force in cases where it was clear that the planning authority had been reasonably and fairly influenced by the public benefit of the activity, and where the activity cannot be carried out without causing the nuisance complained of. However, even in such cases, the court would have to weigh up all the competing factors.

[126] In some such cases, the court may well be impressed by a defendant's argument that an injunction would involve a loss to the public or a waste of resources on account of what may be a single claimant, or that the financial implications of an injunction for the defendant would be disproportionate to the damage done to the claimant if she was left to her claim in damages. In many such cases, particularly where an injunction would in practice stop the defendant from pursuing the activities, an injunction may well not be the appropriate remedy.

10.43   Each case, however, needs to be viewed on its own merits. It needs to be borne in mind that if private rights are to be overridden for public benefit, Parliament has provided specific statutes for compulsory acquisition in order to regulate how this can be achieved. The Lord Cairns's Act jurisdiction in this context, by contrast, is primarily concerned with the balance of private interests. It must be remembered that the grant of planning permission for a particular development does not mean that that development is lawful. All it means is that a bar to the use imposed by planning law, in the public interest, has been removed.[93] Thus, as Lord Neuberger pointed out, it is primarily where:[94]

> it was clear that the planning authority had been reasonably and fairly influenced by the public benefit of the activity, and where the activity cannot be carried out without causing the nuisance complained of

that the grant of planning permission will be one of the factors to consider in deciding whether damages are appropriate instead of an injunction.

10.44   It will also be relevant to bear in mind that the planning process may serve to put a landowner on notice that a development will interfere with his interests and may be relevant to the question of whether he has delayed in seeking relief. Again, however, one must be cautious in the weight one gives to such points: the mere existence of a planning permission does not signify that a developer intends to implement that permission; therefore, an application for an injunction which is made simply on the basis that planning permission has been granted is likely to be met with a plea that the action is premature.[95]

### Discretion: availability of artificial light?

10.45   Given the breadth of the court's discretion to grant damages in lieu of an injunction, the availability of artificial light can be a material consideration when deciding whether to grant an injunction when there is an actionable interference with a right to light. On the other hand, the right is a right to natural light and, on the face of things, the onus should be on the defendant to show that the availability of artificial light makes it proper

---

[93]   *Coventry v Lawrence* [2014] UKSC 13 at [89]; see also *Barr v Biffa Waste Services Ltd* [2012] EWCA Civ 312 (whether statutory scheme authorised nuisance).

[94]   *Coventry v Lawrence* [2014] UKSC 13 at [125].

[95]   Cf *CIP Property (AIPT) Limited v Transport for London* [2012] EWHC 259 (Ch) (claim premature prior to grant of planning permission).

to allow the infringement of the claimant's legal rights subject to the payment of compensation.

10.46 It should be noted that in *Midtown Ltd v City of London Real Property Co Ltd*,[96] when refusing an injunction partly on the basis of the availability of artificial light,[97] Peter Smith J had no expert evidence to assist him about the importance of natural light and how artificial light was not an equivalent or adequate substitute; indeed, he was troubled by the absence of expert evidence given in relation to the natural light/artificial light argument advanced in that case.[98] The claimant in *Midtown* merely relied on the subjective impressions of various people working in the building affected. The learned judge had to do the best he could on the material before him. There is a body of expert opinion which supports the importance of natural light.[99] With such evidence it is quite possible that the availability of artificial light will be of limited weight in a decision whether or not to grant an injunction in circumstances where the infringement is substantial and the uses to which the dominant building are put or likely to be put are those for which natural light has a genuine benefit.

### *Discretion: availability of reflected light?*

10.47 As mentioned above[100] and in Appendix A,[101] the traditional method of measuring light means that light reflected from buildings

---

[96] *Midtown Ltd v City of London Real Property Co Ltd* [2005] EWHC 33 (Ch).

[97] *Midtown Ltd v City of London Real Property Co Ltd* [2005] EWHC 33 (Ch) at [79].

[98] *Midtown Ltd v City of London Real Property Co Ltd* [2005] EWHC 33 (Ch) at [58]–[62].

[99] I have been referred by Jerome Webb of GIA to the following publications: Tregenza, P and Wilson, M (2011), *Daylighting: Architecture and Lighting Design*, Routledge; Boyce, PR (2003), *Human Factors in Lighting* (2nd edn), Taylor & Francis; 'Employee Productivity in a Sustainable Building: Pre- and Post-Occupancy Studies in 500 Collins Street', A Study commissioned by Sustainability Victoria and the Kador Group; Edwards, L and Torcellini, P (2002), *A Literature Review of the Effects of Natural Light on Building Occupants*, National Renewable Energy Laboratory, Colorado; Figueiro, MG, Rea, MS, Stevens, RG and Rea, AC (2002), *Daylight and Productivity – A Possible Link to Circadian Regulation*, Lighting Research Center, Rensselaer Polytechnic Institute..

[100] See para 8.12.

[101] See para A24 ff.

surrounding the dominant tenement is ignored in deciding whether rights have been infringed. In reality, however, such light will invariably continue to be enjoyed. Indeed, in many instances, such reflected light will render an interference with light from the servient tenement imperceptible. In such cases, even if such interference is still to be regarded as technically actionable, it is difficult to see why the court would grant an injunction to stop such interference which has no practical impact on the enjoyment of the dominant land.

### Quantification of damages instead of an injunction

10.48    The principles for the quantification of damages instead of an injunction are considered at para 10.63 ff.

## DAMAGES

### Contractual damages

10.49    Where a right is the subject of a grant, then an infringement of the right may amount to a breach of the grantor's contractual obligations in making the grant.[102] The wrong which damages for breach of covenant seek to compensate is the *breaking* of the bargain between the parties. Damages, therefore, will seek to put the grantee/claimant in the position he would have been in if the contract had been performed[103] subject to the principles of remoteness[104] and to the duty of the grantee/claimant to take reasonable steps to mitigate his losses.[105] In practice, however, in the context of rights of light there will usually be no significant difference between damages for a derogation from grant and damages for a tortious interference. It should be noted that exemplary damages are not available for claims for breach of contract.[106]

---

[102]  See para 8.2.

[103]  See *Livingstone v Rawyards Coal Co* (1880) 5 App Cas 25 at 29, per Lord Blackburn.

[104]  See *Hadley v Baxendale* (1854) 9 Ex 342 at 355; *Victoria Laundry v Newman* [1949] 2 KB 528, CA; *Czarnikow v Koufos* [1969] 1 AC 350, HL.

[105]  *British Westinghouse Co v Underground Railway* [1912] AC 673 at 689, per Viscount Haldane LC.

[106]  See para 10.62.

## Tortious damages

10.50    Interference with an easement such as a right of light is a tort, namely nuisance. Damages for tort seek to compensate for the wrong done by putting the claimant in the position he would have been in if the wrong had not been done to him. There are a number of points to note about such damages.

10.51    First, the basic measure of damage for a tortious interference with land is the diminution in value of the land caused by the interference.[107] Thus, if the interference with the right of light causes diminution in value to the claimant's property, damages calculated by reference to that loss will be recoverable. The damages are assessed by considering the impact on the dominant tenement as a whole; they are not limited to considering the impact on those parts of the particular building whose windows are affected.[108] Such damages extending to harm beyond the impact on the easement with which the interference takes place are often referred to as 'parasitic damages'. For example, in *Re London Tilbury and Southend Ry Co and Gower's Walk School Trustees*,[109] the owners of buildings which had the benefit of rights of light demolished them and constructed new buildings on the site. The windows of the new buildings in part coincided with the old windows. The court held that the claimants were entitled to compensation under the Railway Clauses Act 1845 in respect of all the windows obstructed, *including* those which did not coincide with those in the old buildings and which did not enjoy rights of light. The reasoning of the court was that at common law, damages would include compensation for 'the whole of the consequence of the wrongful act of obstructing ancient lights' which included the harm to the new lights as much as to the old lights.[110] The practical consequences of this are considered in Appendix B, paragraphs B6–B7.

---

[107]  See e.g. *Hunter v Canary Wharf* [1997] AC 655, HL.

[108]  *Re London Tilbury and Southend Ry Co and Gower's Walk School Trustees* (1889) 24 QBD 326; *Scott v Goulding Properties Ltd* [1973] IR 200; *Grifftih v Richard Clay & Sons Ltd* [1912] 2 Ch 291; *Wills v May* [1923] 1 Ch 317.

[109]  *Re London Tilbury and Southend Ry Co and Gower's Walk School Trustees* (1889) 24 QBD 326.

[110]  *Re London Tilbury and Southend Ry Co and Gower's Walk School Trustees* (1889) 24 QBD 326 at 329, per Lord Esher MR. This case was followed in *Griffith v Richard Clay & Sons Ltd* [1912] 2 Ch 291; *Wills v May* [1923] 1 Ch 317.

10.52    Secondly, where an interference with rights constituting a nuisance is such that it affects the amenity of the person entitled to the benefit of the rights of light, then damages for loss of amenity have been awarded.[111] However, given that such impact on amenity, if appreciable and permanent, is likely to be reflected in the diminution in value of the land, such damages are perhaps likely to be rare and limited only to cases where the interference with land is temporary in nature so that no diminution in value to the property can be made out.

10.53    Thirdly, even if there is no financial loss as a result of an interference with rights or quantifiable loss of amenity, in principle damages might still be awarded. In *Attorney-General v Blake*,[112] Lord Nicholls of Birkenhead stated the principle as follows:[113]

> A trespasser who enters another's land may cause the landowner no financial loss. In such a case damages are measured by the benefit received by the trespasser, namely by his use of the land. The same principle is applied where the wrong consists of use of another's land for depositing waste, or by using a path across the land or using passages in an underground mine. In this type of case the damages recoverable will be, in short, the price a reasonable person would pay for the right of user.

In the case of trespass, damages by reference to the reasonable price payable for the 'use' of the land made by the wrongdoer is well established.[114]

---

[111]    *Bone v Seale* [1975] 1 All ER 787; *Hirose Electrical UK Ltd v Peak Ingredients Ltd* [2011] JPL 429.

[112]    *Attorney-General v Blake* [2001] 1 AC 268.

[113]    *Attorney-General v Blake* [2001] 1 AC 268 at 278, per Lord Nicholls, who restated the principle in *Kuwait Airways Corpn v Iraqi Airways Co (Nos 4 and 5)* [2002] 2 AC 883 at [87]–[90] and in *Sempra Metals Ltd (formerly Metallgesellschaft Ltd) v Inland Revenue Comrs* [2008] AC 561 at [116]; see also Lord Scott of Foscote, at [140], and Lord Mance at [230]. The same principle applies where a landowner is awarded mesne profits, whether or not he would have re-let the property during the relevant period: *Swordheath Properties Ltd v Tabet* [1979] 1 WLR 285, which was applied by the Privy Council in *Inverugie Investments Ltd v Hackett* [1995] 1 WLR 713.

[114]    *Whitwham v Westminster Brymbo Coal and Coke Co* [1896] 2 Ch 538; *Penarth Dock Engineering Co Ltd v Pounds* [1963] 1 Lloyd's Rep 359, QB (Lord Denning MR); *Swordheath Properties Ltd v Tabet* [1979] 1 WLR 285, CA; see also *Lawson v Hartley-Brown* (1995) 71 P & CR 242.

10.55   In principle, there is no logical distinction between an action in the tort of trespass and an action in which there is interference with an easement from which the tortfeasor benefits. As explained above, damages are not the 'gist' of the action.[115] If so, there would be nothing to preclude damages for a temporary interference with a right of light caused (for instance) during the course of construction works being assessed by reference to the price which would be paid for the licence to cause the interference in question.

10.56   However, the suggestion in the previous paragraph must be regarded as tentative. There are two particular authorities which must be noted:

(a)   In *Stoke on Trent City Council v W & J Wass Ltd (No 1)*,[116] the Court of Appeal refused to extend the 'user principle' for assessing damages to the law of nuisance. This case concerned the nuisance caused by the conducting of a market within the area protected by a market franchise. An injunction had been granted to restrain future nuisances. The question was whether damages were payable for the nuisance which occurred prior to the injunction (even though the claimant council could establish no diminution in the value of its interest). In refusing to extend the 'user principle' to enable the claimant council to recover damages to take account of the price which the defendant should reasonably have paid for the right to conduct a market, Nourse LJ said:[117]

> Although I would accept that there may be a logical difficulty in making a distinction between the present case and the way-leave cases, I think that if the user principle were to be applied here there would be an equal difficulty in distinguishing other cases of more common occurrence, particularly in nuisance. Suppose a case where a right to light or a right of way had been obstructed to the profit of the servient owner but at no loss to the dominant owner. It would be difficult, in the application of the user principle, to make a logical distinction between such an obstruction and the

---

[115]   See para 8.4. *Nichols v Ely Beet Sugar Factory Ltd* [1936] Ch 343 at 349, CA, per Lord Wright; *Pennington v Brinsop Hall Co* (1877) LR ChD 769 at 772; *A-G v Conduit Colliery Co* [1895] 1 QB 301 at 312.

[116]   *Stoke on Trent City Council v W & J Wass Ltd (No 1)* [1988] 1 WLR 1406.

[117]   *Stoke on Trent City Council v W & J Wass Ltd (No 1)* [1988] 1 WLR 1406 at 1415.

infringement of a right to hold a market. And yet the application of that principle to such cases would not only give a right to substantial damages where no loss had been suffered but would revolutionise the tort of nuisance by making it unnecessary to prove loss. Moreover, if the principle were to be applied in nuisance, why not in other torts where the defendant's wrong can work to his own profit, for example in defamation? As progenitors of the rule in trespass and some other areas, the way-leave cases have done good service. But just as their genus is peculiar, so ought their procreative powers to be exhausted.

The learned judge appears to have proceeded on the basis that it was necessary to prove loss in all cases of nuisance, including interference with easements such as rights of light. However, it is well established that where there is interference with easements, *profits à prendre* and certain natural rights, it is *not* necessary to prove pecuniary loss for the interference to be actionable as a nuisance.[118] The fact that disturbances to such rights were interferences with rights absolutely protected was recognised to the extent of importing the rule that no proof of damage was required, as explained above.[119]

(b) As explained below, in *Coventry v Lawrence*,[120] Lord Carnwath appears to have suggested that in the context of rights to light where damages were awarded instead of an injunction, they had been and should be limited to the diminution in value caused by the interference. As explained below,[121] there are difficulties with the details of Lord Carnwath's suggestion. Nevertheless, this suggestion certainly supports the conclusion that damages based on the 'user principle' might not be available where there is an interference with a right of light at common law.

[118] *Nichols v Ely Beet Sugar Factory Ltd* [1936] Ch 343 at 349 CA, per Lord Wright; *Pennington v Brinsop Hall Co* (1877) LR ChD 769 at 772; *A-G v Conduit Colliery Co* [1895] 1 QB 301 at 312.

[119] See para 10.88. *Nichols v Ely Beet Sugar Factory Ltd* [1936] Ch 343 at 349, CA, per Lord Wright; *Pennington v Brinsop Hall Co* (1877) LR ChD 769 at 772; *A-G v Conduit Colliery Co* [1895] 1 QB 301 at 312.

[120] *Coventry v Lawrence* [2014] UKSC 13 at [248].

[121] See para 8.4.

## Tortious damages: quantification of diminution in value – 'book value'

10.57    As stated above,[122] the basic measure of damage for a tortious interference with land is the diminution in value of the land caused by the interference. This is a question for valuation and is not strictly a matter of law. In order to assess the diminution in value of premises affected by a right of light, surveyors who specialise in this area of work developed a way of quantifying loss which has become known as 'book value'. Courts have on occasion proceeded on the basis that this is a valid method of calculating loss.[123] This method of assessing damages and the problems with it are considered in Appendix B. It is doubtful whether this methodology would withstand detailed forensic scrutiny.

## Aggravated and exemplary damages

10.58    The general measure of damages is based upon the compensation for the loss caused by the wrongdoer. There are, however, two circumstances at common law where the general principles do not apply: aggravated damages and exemplary damages.

### *Aggravated damages*

10.59    'Aggravated damages' extend the usual compensatory principles. They provide compensation for conduct which is so outrageous that it heightens the injury suffered. Aggravated damages may be awarded in cases of tort where the defendant's conduct has been high-handed, insulting or oppressive.[124] Lord Hailsham in *Cassell v Broome*[125] said:

> In awarding 'aggravated' damages the natural indignation of the court at the injury inflicted on the plaintiff is a perfectly legitimate motive in making a generous rather than a more moderate award to provide an adequate *solatium*. But that is because the injury to the plaintiff is

---

[122]    See para 10.51.

[123]    See e.g. *HKRUK II (CHC) Ltd v Heaney* [2010] EWHC 2245 at [44].

[124]    See *Horsford v Bird* [2006] UKPC 3; *Eaton Mansions (Westminster) Ltd v Stinger Compania De Inversion SA* [2013] EWCA Civ 1308 at [26].

[125]    *Cassell v Broome* [1972] AC 1027, HL, at 1073.

actually greater and, as the result of the conduct exciting the indignation, demands a more generous *solatium*.

10.60    Thus, in *Perlman v Rayden*,[126] aggravated damages were awarded to compensate a claimant for distress caused by the defendant exceeding his rights. Patten LJ said:[127]

> The purpose of aggravated damages is to compensate a claimant for the mental distress he has suffered, when that has been increased by the defendant's conduct either during or after the commission of the tort. The Court can take into account the defendant's motives and conduct in committing the tort and in resisting a claim for compensation for it.

So, the motives of the defendant, the extent to which he had misled the claimant and concealed what was being or had been done and the denial of wrongdoing were all matters which could be taken into account.

10.61    In *Eaton Mansions (Westminster) Ltd v Stinger Compania De Inversion SA*,[128] it was held that aggravated damages are not recoverable by a company: an award of aggravated damages is designed to compensate the successful claimant for distress and injury to feelings caused by the defendant's conduct which, in the case of a company, was not a possibility.[129]

### Exemplary damages

10.62    Exemplary damages, however, are not strictly compensatory. They are punitive and intended to mark the law's disapproval or cynical disregard of the claimant's rights.[130] Broadly, such damages will be awarded where:

---

[126] *Perlman v Rayden* [2004] EWHC 2192 (Ch) at [111]–[117].

[127] *Perlman v Rayden* [2004] EWHC 2192 (Ch) at [111].

[128] *Eaton Mansions (Westminster) Ltd v Stinger Compania De Inversion SA* [2013] EWCA Civ 1308.

[129] *Eaton Mansions (Westminster) Ltd v Stinger Compania De Inversion SA* [2013] EWCA Civ 1308 at [27] and [30].

[130] *Rookes v Barnard* [1964] AC 1129; *Kuddus v Chief Constable of Leicestershire Constabulary* [2001] UKHL 29.

(a) there has been oppressive, arbitrary or unconstitutional action by servants of government;

(b) the defendant's conduct has been calculated to make a profit for himself which may exceed the compensation payable to the innocent party;[131] or

(c) a statute expressly authorises the same.[132]

It is the second category that is most likely to fall for consideration where there has been an interference with rights of light.[133]

## Quantification of damages instead of an injunction: principles

### *Background*

10.63 The common law courts' jurisdiction to award damages was confined to loss or injury from a cause of action which had accrued before the issue of the writ. After Lord Cairns's Act, however, if the court awarded damages instead of an injunction:

> which had the effect in practice of sanctioning the indefinite continuance of a wrong the court could assess damages to include losses likely to follow from the anticipated future continuance of the wrong as well as losses already suffered. The power to give damages in lieu of an injunction imported the power to give an equivalent for what was lost by the refusal of an injunction.[134]

The circumstances in which the court may exercise this jurisdiction are considered above.[135]

---

[131] See *Rookes v Barnard* [1964] AC 1129.

[132] Cf Housing Act 1988, s 27.

[133] See *Ketley v Gooden* (1997) 73 P & CR 305 (trespass by building works – exemplary damages held not appropriate); *Ramzan v Brookwide Ltd* [2012] 1 All ER 903 at [73]–[83] (trespass – exemplary damages awarded but proportionality of sum must be considered).

[134] *Attorney-General v Blake* [2001] 1 AC 268 at 281.

[135] See para 10.19 ff.

10.64   It has consistently been considered that:

> in the same way as damages at common law for violations of a property
> right may be measured by reference to the benefits wrongfully obtained
> by a defendant, so under Lord Cairns' Act damages may include
> damages measured by reference to the benefits likely to be obtained in
> the future by the defendant.[136]

10.65   The starting point for considering the modern law for how these
damages are to be assessed is *Wrotham Park Estate Co Ltd v Parkside
Homes Ltd*.[137] In that case, the plaintiffs had delayed in seeking to enforce
restrictive covenants restricting building so an injunction was refused but
damages awarded instead. Notwithstanding the fact that there had been no
diminution in the value of the plaintiffs' land to which the benefit of the
covenant was annexed, the judge awarded the plaintiffs damages
equivalent to the sum which they might reasonably have demanded 'as a
quid pro quo for relaxing the covenant', had the first defendants applied
to them for relaxation. He founded himself on the trespass (in particular
*Whitwham v Westminster Brymbo Coal and Coke Co*[138] and *Penarth Dock
Engineering Co Ltd v Pounds*[139] – considered above), detinue and patent
infringement cases. In answer to the defendants' submission that no
damages ought to be awarded he said:[140]

> That would seem, on the face of it, a result of questionable fairness on
> the facts of this case. Had the offending development been the erection
> of an advertisement hoarding in defiance of protest and writ, I apprehend
> (assuming my conclusions on other points to be correct) that the court
> would not have hesitated to grant a mandatory injunction for its removal.
> If, for social and economic reasons the court does not see fit in the
> exercise of its discretion to order demolition of the 14 houses, is it just
> that the plaintiffs should receive no compensation and that the
> defendants should be left in undisturbed possession of the fruits of their
> wrongdoing?

---

[136]   *Attorney-General v Blake* [2001] 1 AC 268 at 281.

[137]   *Wrotham Park Estate Co Ltd v Parkside Homes Ltd* [1974] 1 WLR 798.

[138]   *Whitwham v Westminster Brymbo Coal and Coke Co* [1896] 2 Ch 538.

[139]   *Penarth Dock Engineering Co Ltd v Pounds* [1963] 1 Lloyd's Rep 359 (see above).

[140]   *Wrotham Park Estate Co Ltd v Parkside Homes Ltd* [1974] 1 WLR 798 at 812.

Later he said:[141]

> In the present case I am faced with the problem what damages ought to be awarded to the plaintiffs in the place of mandatory injunctions which would have restored the plaintiffs' rights. If the plaintiffs are merely given a nominal sum, or no sum, in substitution for injunctions, it seems to me that justice will manifestly not have been done.

This was a case where the plaintiffs had suffered no pecuniary loss. The proper measure of damages was a sum which the plaintiff might reasonably have required in return for relaxing the covenants, which was held to be 5% of the developers' profits (damages being payable by the developer and house-owners in equal proportions).

10.66    The same approach to the assessment of damages awarded in lieu of a final injunction was adopted by Graham J in *Bracewell v Appleby*[142] (where the burden of an easement was wrongfully increased). It was also the approach of Millett J in *Carr-Saunders v Dick McNeil Associates Ltd*[143] (where a right to light was wrongfully obstructed). In each of those cases, the plaintiff's claim lay in nuisance and there was actual loss, but damages were not limited to diminution in value. Millett J said:[144]

> I am entitled to take account of the servient owner's bargaining position and the amount of profit which the defendants would look to in the development of their site. I have no evidence of the amount of profit which the defendants are expected to make from their development – largely, I think, because the plaintifff was seeking a mandatory injunction and no one recognised that documents which would throw light upon the profit to be made from the development were material and ought to be disclosed on discovery. But I have evidence of the general loss of amenity, given to me by the lay witnesses and corroborated to some extent by the expert witnesses; and it seems to me obvious that any dominant owner, negotiating with a servient owner for monetary compensation for the loss of light, would take into account the general loss of amenity which his premises would suffer. To that extent, it seems

---

[141]  *Wrotham Park Estate Co Ltd v Parkside Homes Ltd* [1974] 1 WLR 798 at 815.

[142]  *Bracewell v Appleby* [1975] Ch 408.

[143]  *Carr-Saunders v Dick McNeil Associates Ltd* [1986] 1 WLR 922.

[144]  *Carr-Saunders v Dick McNeil Associates Ltd* [1986] 1 WLR 922 at 931.

to me that the court is entitled to approach the question on the basis that damages are awarded in lieu of an injunction, and not merely in compensation for the loss of the actual legal right. If a mandatory injunction had been granted, the building would have been pulled down and the plaintiff would have been restored not only to his direct light, but also to sky visibility, a pleasant view of brickwork and a sloping roof, sunlight, and so on.

10.67    This approach was also taken by the Court of Appeal in *Jaggard v Sawyer*.[145] In that case, a house was built in breach of a restrictive covenant and in a manner which trespassed on part of a roadway owned by the plaintiff. The plaintiff sought an injunction. On the facts of the case, it was held to be oppressive to grant an injunction and damages were awarded instead. Damages were awarded on the *Wrotham Park* basis. Sir Thomas Bingham MR made clear that damages on that basis could properly be awarded when a judge 'declines to prevent commission of a future wrong'.[146] Millett LJ considered that the damages in *Wrotham Park* were assessed not as the profit which the defendant *had* made but:[147]

> the amount which [the judge] judged the plaintiff might have obtained as the price for giving his consent. The amount of the profit which the defendant expected to make was a relevant factor in that assessment, but that was all.

10.68    Summarising the position in *Attorney-General v Blake*, Lord Nicholls had said:[148]

> The measure of damages awarded in this type of case is often analysed as damages for loss of a bargaining opportunity or, which comes to the same, the price payable for the compulsory acquisition of a right. This analysis is correct. The court's refusal to grant an injunction means that in practice the defendant is thereby permitted to perpetuate the wrongful state of affairs he has brought about. But this analysis takes the matter now under discussion no further forward. A property right has value to the extent only that the court will enforce it or award damages for its

---

[145]  *Jaggard v Sawyer* [1995] 1 WLR 269.

[146]  *Jaggard v Sawyer* [1995] 1 WLR 269 at 282.

[147]  *Jaggard v Sawyer* [1995] 1 WLR 269 at 291.

[148]  *Attorney-General v Blake* [2001] 1 AC 268 at 281.

infringement. The question under discussion is whether the court will award substantial damages for an infringement when no financial loss flows from the infringement and, moreover, in a suitable case will assess the damages by reference to the defendant's profit obtained from the infringement. The cases mentioned above [*Wrotham Park, Bracewell v Appleby, Jaggard v Sawyer*] show that the courts habitually do that very thing.

## *The habitual practice of the courts pre-Coventry v Lawrence?*

10.69   Not only was this the habitual practice of the courts prior to *Attorney-General v Blake*,[149] it has also been the consistent approach of the courts subsequently in real property cases.

10.70   In *AMEC Development v Jury's Hotel (UK) Ltd*,[150] damages were awarded instead of an injunction to restrain a breach of covenant restricting development beyond a certain specified line. The defendant built a hotel some 3.9 metres beyond the line. The claimants accepted that there was no diminution in value to their property and that it was not otherwise adversely affected. However, the plaintiff claimed damages based on the 'release fee' principle. Anthony Mann QC (sitting as a deputy judge) described the proper approach to such damages as being:

> [11] … to ascertain 'such a sum of money as might reasonably have been demanded by [the claimant] from [the defendant] as a quid pro quo for [permitting the breach of covenant to perpetuate]', to use (and adapt) the formulation of Brightman J in *Wrotham Park Estate Co Ltd v Parkside Homes Ltd.*

> [12] It is also common ground that the way of ascertaining what that sum is, is to consider the sum that would have been arrived at in negotiations between the parties had each been making reasonable use of their respective bargaining positions without holding out for unreasonable amounts. This requires, in turn, that the parties have regard to the cost or detriment to the claimant and the benefits for the defendant of the latter's being allowed to [breach the covenant]. …

---

[149]   *Attorney-General v Blake* [2001] 1 AC 268.

[150]   *AMEC Development v Jury's Hotel (UK) Ltd* (2001) 82 P & CR 22.

[13] The negotiation analysis is not pursued rigorously to its logical end. I do not have to imagine a negotiation in which the parties have to guess at something which events have in fact made certain. In carrying out my exercise, I can take into account the actual events that have happened, and the actual benefits accrued, as at the date of the trial ...

On that basis he assessed damages at £375,000.

10.71    Further guidance was provided in *Harris v Williams-Wynne*,[151] in the context of the relaxation of a covenant:

(a)    Damages should be awarded in such a sum as the claimants might reasonably have demanded as a *quid pro quo* for relaxing the covenant had the defendants applied to them for relaxation. The assessment assumes a hypothetical negotiation on the basis that each party is willing to agree a proper and not a ransom price. The proper price will have regard to the amount of profit which will predictably result to the person bound by the covenant as a consequence of its release.

(b)    The correct date for assessing damages is normally the date before the building works in question are started.

(c)    In a suitable case, damages may be measured by the benefit gained by the wrongdoer from breach: see especially *Attorney-General v Blake*.[152] Awards of this kind will be made when they are 'the just response to a breach of contract'.

10.72    In *Lunn Poly Ltd v Liverpool & Lancashire Properties Ltd*,[153] the Court of Appeal considered the basis on which damages were awarded where a judge had ordered damages should be paid instead of an injunction where landlords had carried out a development which interfered with the claimant's fire door in breach of the terms of a lease. The issue was not whether or not the judge was right to award damages on a 'negotiating basis'. The issue was whether the judge was right to conclude that in the hypothetical negotiations for the release of the right, the parties should not be assumed to take into account the fact that the tenant was in

---

[151]   *Harris v Williams-Wynne* [2005] EWHC 151 (Ch).

[152]   *Attorney-General v Blake* [2001] 1 AC 268.

[153]   *Lunn Poly Ltd v Liverpool & Lancashire Properties Ltd* [2006] EWCA Civ 430.

fact at risk of losing his lease altogether as a result of forfeiture proceedings based on a breach of covenant when the landlords had interfered with the tenant's rights. The breach had been letting to a company which was part of the same group as the tenant.

10.73    The landlords argued that the hypothetical negotiation was to take place at the date of the landlords' breach of obligation. Neuberger LJ was willing to assume that this was indeed the usual date. However, he pointed out that this was not a case such as a contract or statute where one is assessing the price by what hypothetical parties might agree at a certain date where it might be illegitimate to take account of post-valuation date material. However, he went on:[154]

> [21] ... this argument overlooks the point that one is not here concerned with a strict contractually-based or statutorily-based market value assessment (as, for instance, under most rent review clauses or when assessing compensation for compulsory purchase). Damages under the Act are, of course, quasi-equitable in nature: they are awarded in lieu of equitable relief albeit that their direct origin is statutory. Nonetheless, that does not mean that damages can be assessed in any old way. The approach to assessing damages under the Act must not be arbitrary; nor should it be indefensibly consistent with the approach to assessment of damages and valuations in other fields; nor should it be unpredictable and therefore likely to lead to litigation.

> [22] The court is not limited to any specific basis for assessing damages in lieu of an injunction under the Act. However, principle and practice suggest that the normal three bases are (a) traditional compensatory damages – i.e. a sum which compensates the claimant for past present and future losses as a result of the breach but not for the loss of the covenant; (b) negotiating damages – i.e. a sum based on what reasonable people in the position of the parties would negotiate for a release of the right which has been, is being, and will be breached; and (c) an account – i.e. a sum based on an account, that is, on the profit the defendant has made, is making and will make as a result of the breach.
> ...

> [24] ... there are no absolute rules. Thus, as at present advised, I can see no reason why, when applying the Act, the court should not be able to

---

[154] *Lunn Poly Ltd v Liverpool & Lancashire Properties Ltd* [2006] EWCA Civ 430 at [21]–[22] and [24].

order the defendant simply to pay over to the claimant a proportion of a capital sum that it made as a result of selling its interest with the benefit (as it were) of the breach of the claimant's rights. In a sense, that could be characterised as a form of account, but it serves to emphasise that there is no absolute rule that damages in a case such as this cannot be assessed on the basis of events which arise after the breach occurs, or even after the injunction is refused.

Neuberger LJ departing from the *AMEC* approach considered that as a general rule, post-valuation date events should not be taken into account. He said:[155]

[27] It is obviously unwise to try to lay down any firm general guidance as to the circumstances in which, and the degree to which, it is possible to take into account facts and events that have taken place after the date of the hypothetical negotiations, when deciding the figure at which those negotiations would arrive. Quite apart from anything else, it is almost inevitable that each case will turn on its own particular facts. Further, the point before us today was not before Brightman J. or before Lord Nicholls in the cases referred to by Mr Mann.

[28] Accordingly, although I see the force of what Mr Mann said in [13] of his judgment, it should not, in my opinion, be treated as being generally applicable to events after the date of breach where the court decides to award damages in lieu on a negotiating basis as at the date of breach. After all, once the court has decided on a particular valuation date for assessing negotiating damages, consistency, fairness, and principle can be said to suggest that a judge should be careful before agreeing that a factor that existed at that date should be ignored, or that a factor that occurred after that date should be taken into account, as affecting the negotiating stance of the parties when deciding the figure at which they would arrive.

[29] In my view, the proper analysis is as follows. Given that negotiating damages under the Act are meant to be compensatory, and are normally to be assessed or valued at the date of breach, principle and consistency indicate that post-valuation events are normally irrelevant. However, given the quasi-equitable nature of such damages, the judge may, where there are good reasons, direct a departure from the norm, either by

---

[155] *Lunn Poly Ltd v Liverpool & Lancashire Properties Ltd* [2006] EWCA Civ 430 at [27]–[29].

selecting a different valuation date or by directing that a specific post-valuation-date event be taken into account.

The judge at first instance had been correct in his assessment of damages and the judge had not been wrong to assess damages on the basis that the tenant had effectively seen off any risk of forfeiture of the lease. As explained below, damages are *not* strictly a form of account. However, the point to note is that the correct 'price' by reference to which the 'release' of the claimant's rights is to be made can take account of the *actual* profits made by the *actual* defendant.

10.74    The position has been summarised by the Privy Council in *Pell Frischmann Engineering Ltd v Bow Valley Iran Ltd*:[156]

> ... Damages under Lord Cairns's Act are intended to provide compensation for the court's decision not to grant equitable relief in the form of an order for specific performance or an injunction in cases where the court has jurisdiction to entertain an application for such relief ...[157] Most of the recent cases are concerned with the invasion of property rights such as excessive user of a right of way: *Bracewell v Appleby*,[158] *Jaggard*.[159] The breach of a restrictive covenant is also generally regarded as the invasion of a property right[160] since a restrictive covenant is akin to a negative easement ...
>
> Damages under this head (termed 'negotiating damages' by Neuberger LJ in *Lunn Poly*[161] ... ) represent 'such a sum of money as might reasonably have been demanded by [the claimant] from [the defendant] as a *quid pro quo* for [permitting the continuation of the breach of covenant or other invasion of right]'.[162]

---

[156] *Pell Frischmann Engineering Ltd v Bow Valley Iran Ltd* [2009] UKPC 45, [2011] 1 WLR 2370 at [48]; see also *Eaton-Mansions (Westminster) Ltd v Stinger Compania de Inversion SA* [2013] EWCA Civ 1308, [2014] 1 P & CR 5.

[157] *Attorney General v Blake* [2001] 1 AC 268 at 281, per Lord Nicholls of Birkenhead.

[158] *Bracewell v Appleby* [1975] Ch 408.

[159] *Jaggard v Sawyer* [1995] 1 WLR 269.

[160] *Experience Hendrix LLC v PPX Enterprises Inc* [2003] 1 All ER (Comm) 830 at [56].

[161] *Lunn Poly Ltd v Liverpool & Lancashire Properties Ltd* [2006] EWCA Civ 430 at [22].

[162] *Lunn Poly Ltd v Liverpool & Lancashire Properties Ltd* [2006] EWCA Civ 430 at [25].

## *Consistent approach also in rights of light cases*

**10.75**   This approach was not only taken in the case of *Carr-Saunders v Dick McNeil Associates Ltd*,[163] it has also been taken in other rights of light cases.

**10.76**   In the case of *Midtown Ltd v City of London Real Property Company Ltd*,[164] Peter Smith J suggested that damages might be 'based on a sharing of the Defendant's profits' where he awarded damages to be assessed instead of awarding an injunction to restrain an interference with the claimants' rights to light.

**10.77**   In the case of *Tamares (Vincent Square) Ltd v Fairport (Vincent Square) Ltd*,[165] the judge applied the principles of 'negotiating damages' to the context of infringements of rights of light where damages were awarded instead of an injunction. In summary, he held:

(a)   overall, the court had to attempt to find a 'fair' result of a hypothetical negotiation between the parties;

(b)   the context, including the nature and seriousness of the infringement, had to be considered;

(c)   the right to prevent a development, or part, gave the owner of the right a significant bargaining position;

(d)   the owner of the right with such a bargaining position would be expected to receive some part of the likely profit for the development, or relevant part;

(e)   if there was no evidence of the likely size of the profit, the court could do its best by awarding a suitable multiple of the damages for loss of amenity;

(f)   if there was evidence of the likely size of the profit, the court should normally award a sum which took into account a fair percentage of that profit;

---

[163]   *Carr-Saunders v Dick McNeil Associates Ltd* [1986] 1 WLR 922, see para 10.66.

[164]   *Midtown Ltd v City of London Real Property Company Ltd* [2005] EWHC 33 (Ch) at [76].

[165]   *Tamares (Vincent Square) Ltd v Fairport (Vincent Square) Ltd* [2007] EWHC 212 (Ch), [2007] 1 WLR 2167.

(g)  the size of the award should not be so large that the development, or relevant part, would not have taken place had such a sum been payable; and

(h)  after arriving at a figure which took into consideration all the above and any other relevant factors, the court had to consider whether the 'deal feels right'; that a suitable calculation of compensation in a negotiation of that kind involved a one-third split of the profit; that that calculation accorded with common sense which required the proposed share of profit not to be so high as to put the developer off the relevant part of the development.

In that case, damages of £50,000 were awarded, even though a '*Stokes v Cambridge*'[166] split of the profits would have resulted in damages of £174,500.

10.78   That 'negotiating damages' are a proper basis for awarding damages instead of an injunction in rights of light cases was assumed in *Regan v Paul Properties DPF No 1 Ltd*,[167] and at first instance in *HKRUK II (CHC) Ltd v Heaney*[168] (both cases where injunctions were held to be appropriate).

*Damages not an account*

10.79   As was made clear in *Jaggard v Sawyer*,[169] it is important to distinguish damages of this sort from a claim for an account: the level of profit made by the wrongdoer is a relevant factor, but that is all.

10.80   Thus, in the case of *Sinclair v Gavaghan*,[170] the claimant sought an injunction and damages in respect of trespass by the defendant over a

---

[166]  *Stokes v Cambridge Corporation* (1961) 13 P & CR 77.

[167]  *Regan v Paul Properties DPF No 1 Ltd* [2006] EWCA Civ 1319, [2007] Ch 135 at [72]. Further, in assessing the correct 'price', the court might properly consider the prospect of the claimant's rights being overridden by a local planning authority's intervention and the application of Town and Country Planning Act 1990, s 237: see para 9.6, and cf *Bocardo SA v Star Energy UK Onshore Ltd* [2010] UKSC 35.

[168]  *HKRUK II (CHC) Ltd v Heaney* [2010] EWCA Civ 1168.

[169]  *Jaggard v Sawyer* [1995] 1 WLR 269; see para 10.67.

[170]  *Sinclair v Gavaghan* [2007] EWHC 2256 (Ch).

small piece of land which was needed to get access in order to develop the defendant's site. An injunction was granted to prevent further acts of trespass. The claimant sought damages of £125,000 for the temporary acts of trespass, on the basis that this was the profit which the defendant made. Patten J, however, awarded damages on the basis that the licence fee for the temporary infringement would only have been £5,000, and damages should be assessed in that sum. As the judge pointed out,[171] the remedy is:

> not an account or share of profits as such, but the court takes into account the profits earned by the Defendant from acting in breach of the covenant when calculating what he would have been prepared to pay for the release.

He pointed out[172] that the obvious difference between the case with which he was dealing and *Wrotham Park* was that in the latter case, the court was assessing compensation in lieu of an injunction and therefore seeking:

> to compensate the Claimant from a continuing and permanent invasion and loss of its rights. Without a notional relaxation of the covenant, the developer had no right to build at all. In this case, the award of damages is limited in time to the period from when use of the [claimant's land] began until at latest, the grant of the interim injunction ... In principle, however, I can see no reason why the model developed in cases such as *Wrotham Park* should not be adapted and applied to the present case provided that one bears in mind the more limited nature of the exercise and takes into account the considerations which would have been relevant to negotiations for the limited permission being sought.

The judge referred both to the Court of Appeal's judgment in *Ministry of Defence v Ashmore*[173] and to *Attorney General v Blake*[174] as supporting this approach, and went on:[175]

> The purpose of the assessment is to calculate a sum which compensates the Claimants for the financial benefits which the Defendants actually

---

[171] *Sinclair v Gavaghan* [2007] EWHC 2256 (Ch) at [15].

[172] *Sinclair v Gavaghan* [2007] EWHC 2256 (Ch) at [16].

[173] *Ministry of Defence v Ashmore* (1993) 66 P & CR 195, CA.

[174] *Attorney General v Blake* [2001] 1 AC 268.

[175] *Sinclair v Gavaghan* [2007] EWHC 2256 (Ch) at [17].

made from using the [claimants' land]. But the alternative possibilities open to the Defendants are of course highly relevant as factors which would have influenced the hypothetical negotiations. Clearly the Defendants would not have been prepared to pay and the Claimants would not have been able to demand a fee which was disproportionate to the actual financial advantages of using the [claimants' land] as opposed to postponing the works or creating an alternative access point.

On the facts, the judge concluded that the access point made as a result of the trespass was a 'more convenient way of servicing' the development in the pre-contract period, but did not achieve anything more, so a relatively modest sum for the privilege of using the access was justified.

10.81    A similar point was made by Patten J in *Forsyth-Grant v Allen*.[176] In that case, the claimant owned a hotel next to the defendant's land. The defendant implemented a planning permission which interfered with the claimant's rights of light. In the particulars of claim, the claimant originally sought damages for this, but the pleading was then amended to substitute for damages a claim for an account of all the profits which the defendants had made from the infringement of the claimant's rights of light; and, in the alternative, damages including exemplary damages for the nuisance, calculated again by reference to the profit made by the defendants. There was also a claim for an injunction to prevent the nuisance.[177]

10.82    The judge at first instance had held that, in view of the claimant's unreasonable conduct, the court would have refused to grant the claimant an injunction in respect of the infringement of her rights of light, and that an award of damages calculated on the *Carr-Saunders* or *Wrotham Park* basis was therefore inappropriate. It is important to note that the correctness of this finding was not challenged as part of this appeal.[178] This is significant because the court was not considering the correct basis for an award of damages where they were awarded instead of an injunction. Damages were awarded based on the actual loss in the form of capitalised reduced letting values of the rooms namely £1,848.63 rather than the amount that the developer might reasonably have negotiated. The judge

---

[176]    *Forsyth-Grant v Allen* [2008] EWCA Civ 505, [2008] Env LR 41.

[177]    *Forsyth-Grant v Allen* [2008] EWCA Civ 505, [2008] Env LR 41 at [14].

[178]    *Forsyth-Grant v Allen* [2008] EWCA Civ 505, [2008] Env LR 41 at [27].

did go on to do a profit-based calculation but reduced the amount of profit by 85% to achieve the appropriate 'release fee' in that case. It turned out to be less than the diminution in value figure; therefore he awarded damages on the basis of the diminution in value figure.[179] The claimant appealed. The claimant's appeal was on the basis that an *account for profits* should be awarded.[180] The defendant submitted on appeal that the proper approach was that in *Carr-Saunders v Dick McNeill Associates*[181] and *Tamares (Vincent Square) Ltd v Fairport (Vincent Square) Ltd*,[182] i.e. a sum should be awarded representing the Court's assessment of what the developer would have agreed to pay in order to avoid an injunction to restrain the nuisance.[183] Consistently with *Sinclair v Gavaghan*,[184] the court dismissed the appeal. This was not the sort of exceptional case in which an account of profits was appropriate. Having considered the sort of cases where an account of profits was appropriate, Patten J (sitting in the Court of Appeal) said:[185]

> An actionable nuisance does not involve the misappropriation of the claimant's rights in the same way, even as in a case of trespass, let alone as in a case of conversion or copyright or trademark infringement. The essence of the tort is that the claimant's rights to the reasonable enjoyment of her property have been infringed by the use which the defendant makes of his own land. On the face of it, this should not entitle the claimant, in my judgment, to more than compensation for the loss which she has actually suffered; but the highest that it could be put on the authorities is that the claimant can, in appropriate cases, obtain an award calculated by reference to the price, which the defendant might reasonably be required to pay for a relaxation of the claimant's rights so as to avoid an injunction. This, as already explained, falls a long way short of being awarded the whole profit for the development, which is far in excess and completely unrelated to the measure of loss suffered by

---

[179] *Forsyth-Grant v Allen* [2008] EWCA Civ 505, [2008] Env LR 41 at [28].

[180] *Forsyth-Grant v Allen* [2008] EWCA Civ 505, [2008] Env LR 41 at [29].

[181] *Carr-Saunders v Dick McNeil Associates Ltd* [1986] 1 WLR 922.

[182] *Tamares (Vincent Square) Ltd v Fairport (Vincent Square) Ltd* [2007] EWHC 212 (Ch), [2007] 1 WLR 2167.

[183] *Forsyth-Grant v Allen* [2008] EWCA Civ 505, [2008] Env LR 41 at [26].

[184] *Sinclair v Gavaghan* [2007] EWHC 2256 (Ch), see para 10.80.

[185] *Forsyth-Grant v Allen* [2008] EWCA Civ 505, [2008] Env LR 41 at [32].

the claimant. The decision in the Stoke on Trent[186] case supports this approach.

So, while emphasising the common law position that damages for nuisance are awarded on the 'diminution in value' basis, he accepted that in appropriate cases damages instead of an injunction could be awarded on the 'release fee' basis, but that is something different from requiring the defendant to account for all his profits.

10.84    In his judgment, Toulson LJ dealt with the appellant's arguments which had been 'variously expressed in argument as an account of profits and a restitutionary claim'.[187] He went on to consider the common law approach to 'mesne profits' which was based on a 'waiver of the tort': the claimant was entitled to proceed on the fiction that he had consented to the defendant dealing with his land but the defendant had impliedly promised to account to him for the proceeds.[188] He went on:[189]

> [The appellant's counsel] has not cited authority to show that common law courts have developed the waiver of tort doctrine so as to extend to claims in nuisance. There is no precedent for a claim for restitutionary damages on facts directly comparable to the present case. I would reject the argument that this remedy is, or should be, generally available as a matter of course in cases of nuisance. As already mentioned, there is a volume of academic writing on the subject. This is not an appropriate case for seeking to analyse the arguments in depth, but it is perhaps worth noting that Goff and Jones, who are themselves in general terms supporters of the development of restitution in this area, do not suggest that it should be generally available in cases of nuisance. They give an illustration why the subject needs to be approached with caution. They take the case of a factory which belches out smoke and fumes over an area covering thousands of neighbouring households. Suppose that the owner had previously rejected a proposal to install an anti-pollution device on the ground of expense, and is later held liable in nuisance. If there were a generally available restitutionary remedy to those affected, this would give rise, as the authors point out, to a legion of questions.

---

186  See para 10.56.

187  *Forsyth-Grant v Allen* [2008] EWCA Civ 505, [2008] Env LR 41 at [40].

188  *Forsyth-Grant v Allen* [2008] EWCA Civ 505, [2008] Env LR 41 at [44].

189  *Forsyth-Grant v Allen* [2008] EWCA Civ 505, [2008] Env LR 41 at [46].

What is the factory owner's benefit gained at each household's expense?
Is it the sum which the factory owner would have had to pay each owner
for the privilege of polluting his property? Or is it a proportion of the
owner's profits, or a proportion of the sum which he has saved
from *not* installing the anti-pollution device? Does the owner of a nearby
mansion recover more than the owner of a nearby terraced house? They
observe that the difficulties confronting a court in measuring and valuing
the benefit are powerful reasons for not recognising the existence of
some general restitutionary claim. Moreover, legal problems apart, any
judicial enquiry with complex attendant evidence could well be
inefficient in economic terms.

10.85   Points to notice about *Forsyth-Grant v Allen*[190] are:

(a)   The court was *not* considering the basis on which damages should be
awarded instead of an injunction. It was considering whether an
action for an account was appropriate.

(b)   Toulson LJ was *not* considering damages in lieu of an injunction. He
was considering a general restitutionary claim for an unlawful
interference with land by analogy with mesne profits.

(c)   The court did *not* disapprove the 'negotiating damages' approach
of *Carr-Saunders v Dick McNeill Associates* and *Tamares* in
appropriate cases where damages are awarded instead of an
injunction.

## *Coventry v Lawrence: a different approach?*

10.86   In *Coventry v Lawrence*,[191] one of the defendants had constructed
a stadium for motorsports pursuant to planning permissions. The claimants
brought a claim for an injunction to stop the nuisance which the noise
caused. As explained above,[192] the Supreme Court considered that there
should not be a rigid approach to when damages should be awarded
instead of an injunction. Three members of the Supreme Court expressed
*obiter dicta* on how damages instead of an injunction should be calculated.

---

[190]   *Forsyth-Grant v Allen* [2008] EWCA Civ 505, [2008] Env LR 41.

[191]   *Coventry v Lawrence* [2014] UKSC 13.

[192]   See para 10.21 ff.

10.87   While leaving open the question whether in some circumstances it was appropriate to award gain based damages instead of an injunction, Lord Clarke considered that:[193]

> where a claimant is seeking an injunction to restrain the noise which has been held to amount to a nuisance, it is at least arguable that there is no reason in principle why a court considering whether or not to award damages in lieu of an injunction should not be able to award damages on a more generous basis than the diminution in value caused by the nuisance, including, for example, an award which represented a reasonable price for a licence to commit the nuisance. So, for example, ... in *Jaggard v Sawyer* ... the Court of Appeal awarded damages for trespass in lieu of an injunction which in effect gave the defendant a right of way over the plaintiff's land in return for a capital sum. If that can be done in trespass I do not at present see why it should not in principle be done in nuisance in a case like this, where a similar payment would give the respondents the right to commit what would otherwise be a nuisance by noise. Moreover, ... there may be scope for assessing the claimant's loss by reference to the benefit to the defendant of not suffering an injunction.

10.88   Lord Carnwath, however, appears to have taken a different view. While he was not expressing any final view and made clear that he had not heard full argument, he suggested three reasons why he was 'reluctant to open the possibility of assessment of damages on the basis of a share of the benefit of the defendants' in the context of nuisance:[194]

(a)   His lordship suggested that the approach in *Jaggard v Sawyer* 'has hitherto not been extended to interference with right of light: see *Forsyth-Grant v Allen*'. His lordship, however, appears not to have considered the cases of *Carr-Saunders v Dick McNeill Associates* and *Tamares (Vincent Square) Ltd v Fairport (Vincent Square) Ltd*. Further, as explained above, *Forsyth-Grant v Allen* was about common law damages not about damages instead of an injunction. Indeed, in that case both *Carr-Saunders* and *Tamares* were mentioned without disapproval.

---

[193]   *Coventry v Lawrence* [2014] UKSC 13 at [173].

[194]   *Coventry v Lawrence* [2014] UKSC 13 at [248].

(b)    His lordship said:[195]

> In cases relating to clearly defined interference with a specific
> property right, it is not difficult to envisage a hypothetical
> negotiation to establish an appropriate 'price'. The same approach
> cannot in my view be readily transferred to claims for nuisance such
> as the present relating to interference with the enjoyment of land,
> where the injury is less specific, and the appropriate price much less
> easy to assess, particularly in a case where the nuisance affects a
> large number of people.

However, this problem is not apparent in the case of rights of light
where the windows affected can be easily identified and the injury
measured.

(c)    Lord Carnwath said:[196]

> such an approach seems to represent a radical departure from the
> normal basis regarded by Parliament as fair and appropriate in
> relation to injurious affection arising from activities carried out
> under statutory authority.

But this is not really surprising. The court when awarding damages
in lieu of an injunction is not compensating for a lawful act; it is
compensating for an *unlawful* act. If 'release fee' damages are not to
be awarded and if the court takes a less rigorous approach to granting
injunctions to protect property rights, it means in essence that
developers will be able to take a 'commercial view' and unlawfully
infringe property rights without any impact on their profits and with
limited need to negotiate for their release. This is something which
will appear unpalatable to many home owners, as well as others who
have property rights. This unpalatable prospect is precisely what
underpins the approach which the court has historically taken to the
awarding of release fee damages where it refuses an injunction which
might otherwise have been granted.

---

[195]   *Coventry v Lawrence* [2014] UKSC 13 at [248].

[196]   *Coventry v Lawrence* [2014] UKSC 13 at [248].

10.89    Lord Neuberger indicated that:[197]

> It seems to me at least arguable that, where a claimant has a prima facie right to an injunction to restrain a nuisance, and the court decides to award damages instead, those damages should not always be limited to the value of the consequent reduction in the value of the claimant's property. While double counting must be avoided, the damages might well, at least where it was appropriate, also include the loss of the claimant's ability to enforce her rights, which may often be assessed by reference to the benefit to the defendant of not suffering an injunction.

However, he indicated that he saw the force of Lord Carnwath's analysis.[198]

10.90    The matter cannot be taken as settled. However, since the effect of the award of damages instead of an injunction to restrain an interference with an easement is to deprive a property owner of his right to deal with property, then there seems to be a formidable argument by analogy with *Wrotham Park Estate Co Ltd v Parkside Homes Ltd*[199] that, as a *quid pro quo* for his giving up of this entitlement, he should be entitled to a fair 'price'. In principle, in appropriate circumstances, there seems no objection to the profit made by the wrongdoer being brought into play in the assessment of the fair price. It should be noted, however, that the price must be a fair one, and in practice awards have been relatively modest when compared to the total profits made by developers. This is not surprising: the developer commits substantial resources and takes all the risk, so in most cases it is difficult to see how substantial 'ransom' payments could be justified.

---

[197]   *Coventry v Lawrence* [2014] UKSC 13 at [128].

[198]   *Coventry v Lawrence* [2014] UKSC 13 at [131].

[199]   *Wrotham Park Estate Co Ltd v Parkside Homes Ltd* [1974] 1 WLR 798.

# Chapter 11

# Reform

11.1    This book does not suggest possible reforms of the law. Its purpose is to set out the law as it now appears to be. It should be noted, however, that two final reports have been published by the Law Commission. These reports recommend substantial reform of the law of easements and rights to light.

11.2    In May 2011, the Law Commission published its report entitled *Making Land Work: Easements, Covenants and Profits à Prendre.*[1] This made recommendations about the reform of the law of easements generally. Amongst other proposals, the reform of the law concerning the implication of easements[2] and the law of prescription. The simplification of the law is to be welcomed. However, the Commission recommended that the qualifying use must be carried out by and against the freeholder and did not follow the views of Lord Millett in *China Field Ltd v Appeal Tribunal (Buildings).*[3] There were no special rules proposed relating to rights to light.

11.3    In March 2012, however, the Law Commission began an investigation into whether the law by which rights to light are acquired and enforced provided an appropriate balance between the important

---

[1]    Law Commission (2011), *Making Land Work: Easements, Covenants and Profits à Prendre*, Law Com No 327, The Stationery Office.

[2]    E.g. Law Commission (2011), *Making Land Work: Easements, Covenants and Profits à Prendre*, Law Com No 327, The Stationery Office, at paras 3.30, 3.64 and 3.69.

[3]    *China Field Ltd v Appeal Tribunal (Buildings)* [2009] 5 HKC 231; Law Commission (2011), *Making Land Work: Easements, Covenants and Profits à Prendre*, Law Com No 327, The Stationery Office, at paras 3.144–3.149. See para 2.60.

interests of landowners and the need to facilitate the appropriate development of land. It considered how the law might be clarified, and examined whether the remedies available to the courts are reasonable, sufficient and proportionate.

11.4   On 18 February 2013, the Law Commission published a consultation paper in which it considered the law relating to the entire life-cycle of a right to light, from creation to extinguishment. It received over 130 responses.

11.5   At the end of 2014, the Law Commission published its final report, *Rights to Light*.[4] Its 'key' recommendations were:

(a)   a statutory notice procedure which would allow landowners to require their neighbours to tell them within a specified time if they intend to seek an injunction to protect their right to light, or to lose the potential for that remedy to be granted;

(b)   a statutory test to clarify when courts may order damages to be paid rather than halting development or ordering demolition, i.e. a court must not grant an injunction to restrain the infringement of a right to light if doing so would be a disproportionate means of enforcing the dominant owner's right to light taking into account all of the circumstances, including:

   (i)     the claimant's interest in the dominant land;

   (ii)    the loss of amenity attributable to the infringement (taking into account the extent to which artificial light is relied upon);

   (iii)   whether damages would be adequate compensation;

   (iv)   the conduct of the claimant;

   (v)    whether the claimant delayed unreasonably in claiming an injunction;

   (vi)   the conduct of the defendant;

   (vii)  the impact of an injunction on the defendant; and

   (viii) the public interest.

---

[4]   Law Commission (2014), *Rights to Light*, Law Com No 356, The Stationery Office.

(c) an updated version of the procedure that allows landowners to prevent their neighbours from acquiring rights to light by prescription;

(d) amendment of the law governing where an unused right to light is treated as abandoned; and

(e) a power for the Lands Chamber of the Upper Tribunal to discharge or modify obsolete or unused rights to light.

11.6    The Law Commission did not recommend that prescription should be abolished as a means of acquiring rights to light. This represents a different position to that which it advanced as a provisional recommendation in the consultation paper, and was a result of responses that it received during the consultation process.

11.7    Whether these recommendations will be enacted will depend on whether parliamentary time is made available. Indeed, whether the recommendations concerning rights of light are all, in fact, necessary is a moot point. The recommendation that developers might give those affected notice to enable them to seek an injunction or lose their rights will create certainty, and this on the face of things is to be welcomed. An unintended consequence of this, however might be that protective applications to court will increase and litigation will become 'built in' to the development process. Thus, the consensual resolution which results in the vast majority of cases might be supplanted by the expense, posturing and uncertainty which litigation entails. On the other hand, rather than enact substantive legislation, it is possible that a mere change of policy could itself achieve the practical certainty which developers require. For instance, central government could encourage local authorities to engage actively with developers to acquire interests which would enable the procedures under section 237 of the Town and Country Planning Act 1990[5] to be used to override private rights. If it did so, the extent to which rights of light could thwart development would be much reduced and the 'negotiating position' of those seeking to extort ransoms from developers substantially undermined. In practice, even now, the invocation of section 237 usually encourages realism amongst those who stand in the way of development.

---

[5]    See para 9.6 ff.

11.8    The Law Commission's recommendations can, in some respects, be seen as a response to the overblown reaction of the development industry to the unusual first instance decision in *HKRUK II (CHC) Ltd v Heaney*.[6] As explained above,[7] the rigid approach in that case has been disapproved by the Supreme Court in *Coventry v Lawrence*.[8] What is more, even before *Coventry v Lawrence*, it is doubtful whether *Heaney* was correctly decided or, at any rate, whether another court would have reached the same conclusion on the somewhat unusual facts. In any event, it seems that the proposed new statutory test for whether an injunction should be granted would be unnecessary, given the clarification of the law in Lord Neuberger's judgment in *Coventry v Lawrence*.

11.9    The problem with new, substantive legislation is that experience dictates that it is likely to throw up as many problems as it solves. The courts at present seem willing to grapple with the problems as they arise on a case-by-case basis. This is the way the common law has traditionally been developed, and allows for gradual adaptability to varying circumstances. A 'blanket' attempt at reform may fail to take account of the numerous varieties of situation that are encountered in practice.

---

[6]   *HXRUK II (CHC) Ltd v Heaney* [2010] EWHC 2245 (Ch).

[7]   See paras 10.21–10.23.

[8]   *Coventry v Lawrence* [2014] UKSC 13.

# Appendices

# A   Quantification of Light and its Loss

*Liam Dunford, MSc Surv, FRGS, Paul Fletcher, MSc, Dr Martin Howarth, DPhil (Oxon) and Dr Malcolm Macpherson, DPhil (Oxon) of Point 2 Surveyors*

## General

A1   As is apparent from the main text of this book, the law of rights of light was developed by the courts. There is, however, little consideration in the cases of what is meant by 'light' nor a critical assessment of how it may be measured and interference with it assessed. In the early 20th century (long after the principal legal concepts were developed), a method of assessing light was adopted by practitioners and accepted without much analysis by the courts. The adoption of this method of assessment, which we describe below, is largely attributable to the work of Percy Waldram. It is as important, however, to understand what this method is *not* assessing as much as what it *is* assessing. When this is understood, one can see that this method may have practical shortcomings. It is beyond the scope of this appendix to provide a full introduction to the concepts and methods involved in calculations within the rights of light field. We must restrict ourselves to a short discussion of the way that these methods have conventionally been applied, and of how the perceived shortcomings in these methods might be overcome. Before doing this, we need to examine some basic concepts.

## Light

A2   What is light? Many people, if confronted by this question, would immediately turn to a dictionary for an answer. For example, the *Concise Oxford Dictionary* defines it as:

the natural agent (electromagnetic radiation of wavelength between about 390 and 740 mm [sic]) that stimulates sight and makes things visible.

Not a bad first stab, except for an unfortunate typo in this particular volume that gives the wavelength incorrectly in mm (millimetres) – this of course should be nm (nanometres), which are a factor of a million different in size. The main problem, however, with this definition is that it does not really address the question – what physically is light?

A3    There is, in fact, no simple answer to this question, mainly because light is a complicated phenomenon. Light is a form of electromagnetic radiation corresponding to a small portion of the electromagnetic spectrum – the portion referred to above. The electromagnetic spectrum itself ranges from long wavelength radio waves, through microwaves, infrared radiation (which we know as heat radiation), through to the visible spectrum which is of course light. Beyond, at increasingly shorter wavelengths, lie ultraviolet light, X-rays and gamma rays.

A4    Electromagnetic radiation is generally energy given off when the motion of any electrically charged particle is changed. However, from many careful observations, it appears to have a split personality. On the one hand, it shows wavelike (classical) behaviour, such as interference and diffraction. On the other hand, it behaves (quantum mechanically) as if it is a particle – Einstein won a Nobel prize for demonstrating this fact for the photoelectric effect, and we are all familiar with Geiger counters and the discrete clicks produced by the arrival of a gamma ray photon. The fact that light can act in these different ways is known as wave particle duality. Generally, longer wavelength radiation shows more wave-like behaviour (radio waves easily go around corners), whilst the shorter wavelength radiation behaves more like particles. Interestingly, visible light falls in between and so exhibits both behaviours, depending on the situation. The energy given off by our charged particle can therefore be viewed either as being carried off by a wave consisting of a pair of interacting electric and magnetic fields which oscillate at right angles to each other, or by a stream of photons. Either way, the energy given off propagates at the speed of light – 186,000 miles per second or 300,000 km per second – and the amount of energy carried by each photon is inversely related to its wavelength – the shorter the wavelength, the higher the energy.

# Light from the sun

A5    The sun burns by nuclear fusion of hydrogen nuclei to produce helium. When this happens, the excess energy is given off as gamma radiation, which as we have mentioned is a highly energetic form of electromagnetic radiation. As the gamma ray photons make their way through the sun to the surface, they are absorbed and re-emitted, gradually losing energy in the process, and at the same time, heating up the outer reaches of the sun. Interestingly, it is estimated that this process takes between 10,000 and 170,000 years. By the time they reach the sun's surface, the photons have a range of wavelengths (energies) covering a broad range of the electromagnetic spectrum, and the radiation emitted in the visible range of the spectrum is what we perceive to be sunlight (the light takes 8 minutes to reach us). If we examine sunlight therefore, as Sir Isaac Newton famously found, although it appears to us to be white light, it can be split up by a prism into a rainbow spectrum – ranging from red to green through blue to violet. This confirms that sunlight actually consists of a continuous range of visible wavelengths. The spectrum is close to that of a black body (a thermal spectrum) with a typical temperature of around 6,000 K,[1] and for this temperature the peak of the spectrum is in the visible range. It is no coincidence therefore that the human eye has evolved to utilise radiation (light) around this peak.

# What we perceive

A6    For the purposes of assessing light enjoyed by a building and the extent to which there might be an interference with a legal right to that light, we are interested in how light illuminates a surface within that building (or a room within that building) and how bright that surface will appear. From our earlier discussion, we know that light (and all electromagnetic radiation) is in fact (radiant) energy. Energy is measured in joules (it takes 4.2 joules of energy to heat 1 gramme of water by 1 degree). So why do we not measure light in joules? Of course, it depends on exactly what we are interested in. First, we are interested in the amount of light continuously falling on the surface, so that we would need to measure the amount of energy *per second* falling on the surface. We have a familiar unit for that – *a watt* – 1 watt is simply 1 joule per second, and this is actually known as the radiant flux. This is all very well, but we have

---

[1]    Kelvin, the unit of absolute temperature.

not specified how big our surface is. Surely the same amount of light (flux) spread over a small area would appear brighter than that same amount spread over a large area? Indeed, so we need to measure the number of watts *per square metre*. We have a name for this too – the *irradiance* (or sometimes the intensity). There is, however, one final problem. What we have said above takes no account of the wavelength of the light; indeed, ultraviolet 'light' is invisible to us, but it still carries energy in the same way as visible light. So we have to account for the spectral sensitivity of the human eye. In general, the eye has a spectral response curve (known as the *luminosity function*) which can be used to convert radiant energy (measured in watts per square metre) into luminous energy (measured in *lumens per square metre* – or *lux*). The curve peaks around the green wavelength of 555 nm, and gradually drops off towards zero below about 400 nm and above 750 nm. For any particular spectral distribution of light, this results in a constant multiplying factor – known as the *luminous efficacy*. For example, for a 555 nm monochromatic light source, the luminous efficacy is 683 lumens per watt. For the sun, the figure is 93 lumens per watt – this reflects the fact that a large portion of the sun's output is outside of the visible spectrum.

## Light from the sky

A7    After their 100,000-year (plus 8-minute) journey, the photons generated from within the sun finally arrive on earth. Of course, they have to traverse the earth's atmosphere first. If you are lucky enough to live in a part of the world with little cloud cover, you will see the majority of photons directly from the sun. A proportion are, however, scattered by the earth's atmosphere – shorter (blue) wavelengths are scattered more than longer (red) wavelengths, and we therefore perceive the sky as blue.

A8    In the UK, the sky is more likely to be overcast. Under such conditions, there is essentially no direct sunlight, and all sunlight is scattered. The light is scattered by water droplets which tend to scatter different colours of light to a similar extent, resulting in a white sky colour. The resulting lux level on average varies with time of day and time of year. In the UK at Kew, this is around 35,000 lux at midday in June, through 20,000 lux in March/September, to around 10,000 lux in December.

A9    When considering light in the context of 'rights of light', we are interested in calculating the effect a new building (or other potential interruption) has on the light received by a neighbouring building. Clearly, if the light measured is varying with time, date and atmospheric conditions, we cannot make a meaningful comparison between the light levels before and after development. The solution to this is to deal with a quantity which does not vary with overall sky brightness. Any change would then be entirely due to the effect of the new building. If we are calculating (or measuring) a light level at a point in a room, we would expect that level to scale up or down with the overall sky brightness. If the sky is twice as bright, the light level would be twice its previous value, all other things being equal. If we therefore divide our light level by the overall sky brightness, we form a quantity which is independent of the overall sky brightness. This is a *sky factor*.

## Sky factor

A10 A sky factor is simply the amount of light received at a point directly from an overcast sky, divided by the total amount of light available on a horizontal plane at that same point. When making an assessment for the purposes of assessing how much light a building enjoys before or after development which interferes with its light, an overcast sky is assumed and most commonly the sky is assumed to be of uniform distribution (although a different sky distribution may be used, as defined by the Commission Internationale de l'Eclairage, or CIE – see below). The maximum sky factor on a horizontal plane is 100%. In calculating a sky factor, the hemispherical sky (uniform or CIE) is imagined to be split into small sub-areas, and each area provides a small contribution to the illuminance at a point. The contributions, which depend on the angle they subtend and their intensity, are summed at the point where the sky factor is being evaluated. In the presence of buildings, each sub-area must first be tested to establish if it is obstructed by any part of the buildings, and if so these sub-areas do not contribute to the sky factor.

## The Waldram diagram

A11 As an aid to the calculation of sky factors, Waldram diagrams are often used. The axes are arranged so that the contribution to the illumination at a point from an overcast sky is proportional to the corresponding area on the diagram. In the presence of buildings which obstruct light, the buildings can be plotted on the diagram so that the area of unobstructed sky can be found on the diagram. This area, expressed as a fraction of the total diagram area, gives the sky factor at the point under consideration (see Figure A1). There are various types of Waldram diagrams: horizontal or vertical according to the orientation of the plane on which the light is incident, and uniform or CIE depending upon the intensity distribution of the overcast sky.

A12   In the past, Waldram diagrams were plotted by hand. This was a laborious process. These days, the exercise is undertaken using computer models, but the underlying methodology is the same.

## Rights of light contours

A13   The dominant owner of a right of light is entitled to 'sufficient light according to the ordinary notions of mankind'.[2] This concept (deriving from case law) was considered in Waldram's work of the 1920s,[3] and some later work in the 1930s by the CIE.[4] Since then, experts have used Waldram's methods to calculate the area of the room which receives this sufficient level of light. This method treats sufficient light as being 1 foot-candle (1 lumen per square foot), or approximately 10 lux (10 lumen per square metre). This is the illumination provided by a candle 1 foot away from you: this is supposed to be enough light to read a newspaper. Using a total sky illuminance value of 5,000 lux as a value representative of a typical overcast sky, this leads to a threshold value of 0.2% sky factor.

A14   The conventional wisdom here is that if half the area at desk-height within a room has a sky factor of 0.2% or more then the room may be considered to be 'well-lit'. The rights of light practitioner will, therefore, calculate the extent of the area at desk-height which receives a 0.2% sky factor, both before and after the development in question has taken place. If the area is less than 50% with the development in place, a reduction in the well-lit area is interpreted as a material loss of light to the room in question – this is known as the '50/50 rule'. While this has been accepted

---

[2]   See para 6.15 ff.

[3]   Waldram, PJ and Waldram, JM (1923), 'Window Design and the Measurement and Predetermination of Daylight Illumination', *The Illuminating Engineer* (April–May), pp 90–122.

[4]   CIE Commission Internationale de L'Eclairage (1932), *Recueil des Travaux et Compte Rendu des Seances, Huitieme Session, Cambridge, September 1931*, Cambridge University Press.

as a useful guide,[5] it should be emphasised that this is not a rule of law. It is something which practitioners have adopted over the years. Its application will depend on the facts. So, in *Fishenden v Higgs & Hill Ltd*,[6] Maugham J said that while Waldram diagrams were 'of great use', they could not be conclusive:

> they may, I think, often be exceedingly misleading if the so-called 50-50 rule with regard to the amount of light is applied to a room which has any unusual depth in it, or applied to a room where the windows are in any sense unusual, because the light falling at table height from the window at a particular part of the room depends directly upon the depth of the room and the height of the window

A15    In order to assess the impact of a proposed building on light enjoyed by the dominant tenement, the contour areas before and after the development has taken place are then subtracted to produce losses in the four quarter areas of the room, starting with the best-lit quarter and ending with the least well-lit quarter – the so-called front, first, second and makeweight zones (see Figure A2). Weighting of the losses in each of these quarters then produces a figure for the equivalent first zone (EFZ) loss to the room. Such EFZ losses are then used to calculate 'book value' damages to the affected building, which along with some idea of the property's value is used by light surveyors to calculate an appropriate diminution in value due to the reduction in light levels. We deal with 'book value' in Appendix B.

## Shortcomings of the conventional approach

A16    There are several assumptions which have been regularly used by practitioners in the rights of light field, the validity of which have recently been questioned.[7] The most significant of these are as follows:

---

[5]   See e.g. *Ough v King* [1967] 1 WLR 1547; *Carr-Saunders v Dick McNeil Associates Ltd* [1986] 1 WLR 922 at 927B; *Deakins v Hookings* [1994] 1 EGLR 190; *Midtown Ltd v City of London Real Property Co Ltd* [2005] EWHC 33 (Ch) (where the evidence of the expert witnesses was agreed).

[6]   *Fishenden v Higgs & Hill Ltd* (1935) 153 LT 128 at 143–144; see also *Masonic Hall Co v Sheffield Corp* [1932] 2 Ch 17 at 24.

[7]   Chynoweth, P (2004), 'Progressing the Rights to Light Debate Part 2: The Grumble Point Revisited', *Structural Survey*, 23 (4), pp 251–264; Chynoweth, P (2009), 'Progressing the Rights to Light Debate Part 3: Judicial Attitudes to Current Practice',

(a)  The sufficiency of 1 foot-candle of illuminance (approximately 10 lux).

(b)  The use of the '50/50 rule'.

(c)  The assumption that the distribution of daylight within a room can be ignored.

(d)  The assumption that the effects of reflection may be ignored.

(e)  The assumption that the effect of glazing can be ignored.

(f)  The assumption that a particular reduction in the area of the room at desk-height that can receive a sufficient amount of light will be perceptible by the human eye.

We deal with each deficiency in turn before looking at other shortcomings in the conventional approach.

## *Sufficiency of 1 foot-candle of illuminance, or 10 lux*

A17    The question is whether 1 foot-candle of illuminance (10 lux) really is a good enough touchstone in itself for the sufficiency of light according to the 'ordinary notions of mankind'. Several reviews of Waldram's published reports and research[8] have concluded that his methods were sometimes less than wholly objective, and seem to underestimate the minimum levels of light required within a room. As a result, there is a school of thought which has questioned this standard illuminance value, and there have been attempts to use more realistic calculational methods to improve the assessment of whether light is sufficient. Clearly, if a different level of illuminance is considered to represent a 'sufficient' amount, then the 'before' and 'after' calculations must be carried out with a target light level which is different to 1 foot-candle, or 10 lux.

---

27 (1), pp 7–9; Defoe, P (2005), 'The Validity of Daylight Calculations in Rights to Light Cases', 5th International PostGrad Research Conference, Salford University; Defoe, P (2009), 'Waldram was wrong', *Structural Survey*, 27 (3), pp 186–199; Pitts, M (2000), 'The Grumble Point: is it still worth the candle?', *Structural Survey*, 18 (5), pp 255–258.

8    E.g. Defoe, P (2005), 'The Validity of Daylight Calculations in Rights to Light Cases', 5th International PostGrad Research Conference, Salford University; Defoe, P (2009), 'Waldram was wrong', *Structural Survey*, 27 (3), pp 186–199. Pitts, M (2000), 'The Grumble Point: is it still worth the candle?', *Structural Survey*, 18 (5), pp 255–258.

## The '50/50 rule'

A18    In a typical urban environment, natural light will only penetrate a relatively small distance into a building, and beyond that point there will be no meaningful amount of light. Under the 50/50 rule, deep rooms (which usually have a large dark region at the rear) are often less than 50% well-lit even before new development interferes with the light reaching them. In such circumstances, even a modest development would frequently be considered as giving rise to a substantial interference with the light enjoyed. Rooms will often have a well-lit region nearer the window, the extent of which will not be significantly affected by the distance to the back wall. It seems difficult to see why the presence of an existing large poorly-lit area to the rear of a deep room should affect the development potential of a site opposite.

A19    Secondly, it seems counter-intuitive to regard a small decrease in light to a badly-lit room as being actionable, but a much larger decrease to a well-lit room (albeit that 50% of the room may still be well-lit) as not actionable. As explained in the main text, however,[9] where a room is badly-lit the existing light may have a particular value to the room, making a small decrease significant. In any event, one needs to be cautious and consider whether the decrease will make any practical difference to the use of the room – particularly if one has regard to the presence (and likely continued presence) of reflected light.

A20    Even if the 50/50 rule is a useful guide, to apply it without regard to the shape or size of the room leads to anomalous results, as the judge pointed out in *Fishenden v Higgs and Hill*,[10] quoted above.[11] At best, the 50/50 rule can only be a rough and ready guide to the sufficiency of light in any given case.

## Distribution of daylight

A21    The conventional approach might not adequately take account of the distribution of daylight within an affected room, and thus not properly model the practical impact which an interference with light might have. It

---

[9]    See paras 6.22 ff and 8.14 ff.

[10]    *Fishenden v Higgs and Hill* (1935) 153 LT 128 at 143–144.

[11]    See para A14.

is informative to consider the whole range of light levels within the room, rather than simply one particular minimum level. Figure A3 shows a distribution for a normal room with a window located on the facade of a building. It can be seen that there is a bright region close to the window and the intensity drops off quickly further into the room. This could be thought of as having an intense or 'deep' pool of light near the window. This is a normal situation and represents a typical scenario considered by Waldram in the 1920s and the CIE in 1932.

A22    In other situations, the light levels may be much lower and the variations much less – in other words the pools of light are 'shallow'. This is illustrated in Figure A4. It should be noted that a conventional rights of light assessment based on consideration of the 0.2% sky factor contour alone does not consider the overall amount of light within a room, and in certain situations could be misleading. In a room with a very shallow pool of light a small absolute reduction in light levels could create a significant shift in the 0.2% sky factor contour. The effect of changes to the profile of a distribution is analogous to the measurement of the amount of water in a pool of water by its tideline, or area. A shallow puddle may have the same area as a steep-sided deep pool but each contains very different amounts of water. Furthermore, the loss of a small volume of water from a shallow puddle could cause a dramatic reduction in is surface area whereas the same amount lost from the deep pool would cause a negligible change in its surface area. The perception of light levels within a room is more complex than the measurement of water volume in a pool, but the analogy may help visualise the importance of an intensity distribution on plan area coverage of a particular daylight level.

A23    The results of such complex analyses can usefully be assimilated in a graphical way, either by false colour distributions (such as the coloured depiction of mountain heights on a map) or by visualisations. Whilst the latter do not need to be photorealistic to be useful, they do need to be based on a rigorous analysis of the physics behind the problem rather than 'marketing' images or photomontages, which are often 'staged' to create a desired effect.

## Reflected light and glazing transmittance

A24    Reflected light and the transmittance of light by glazing are not usually considered in rights of light assessment. Historically, the complexity of calculating reflected and transmitted light has made analysis of the real light distribution difficult. Further, the owner of the dominant tenement cannot control the colour and reflectivity of either the proposed development or neighbouring property, so it has been considered proper to ignore reflection.

A25   Light reaching a point in a room can be thought of as comprising three components. First, the direct component which, if the sky is visible from the point in question, is the light that arrives directly from the sky. This is called the sky component and is defined above. The second component is that which may be reflected in through the windows from external obstructions such as walls and the ground. This is known as the externally reflected component. This is the component over which the dominant owner would usually have little or no control. The third, the internally reflected component, is light which bounces around the internal surfaces of the room. The magnitude of the reflected components depends on the surface properties – light coloured surfaces reflect substantially more than dark surfaces. The direction of the reflection can also be important and is affected by the surface finish – for example, shiny surfaces reflect much of the light in a particular direction, whereas matt surfaces scatter light in all directions.

A26   The sky component is relatively easy to calculate, but almost impossible to measure in practice because reflected light cannot be avoided. In order to overcome the difficulties caused by reflected light and the fact that the dominant owner has no right to receive reflected light, conventional rights of light assessments based on a sky component effectively assume that every surface both inside and outside the room is matt black. This is clearly an extreme assumption and a significant departure from reality, as in many dense urban situations where the direct component of skylight falling on a window is small, a significant proportion of light can be reflected off neighbouring buildings. This would in many circumstances remain the case even if changes beyond the control of the dominant owner take place. However, nowadays, technology has advanced so that, although assumptions about the reflective characteristics of the surface finishes are necessary, reliable assessments are possible. This means that a more realistic assessment and visualisation of a proposed impact is possible and, arguably, in many instances appropriate. For example, this can be done using the 'Radiance' software package which has been developed to make possible calculations of daylight within a room and of how changes in the massing of neighbouring buildings might affect the light within the room in a more realistic way. Figure A5 shows the distribution with and without reflected light.

A27   As explained in the main text of the book,[12] even if the courts ultimately decide that this is not something to take into account when considering whether an interference is technically a breach of a claimant's rights, it might well be highly relevant to the consideration of whether an injunction should be granted.

## *Perception of change/material loss of light*

A28   As explained above,[13] the conventional approach proceeds on the assumption that a particular reduction in the area of the room at desk-height that can receive a sufficient amount of light will be perceptible by the human eye. Nowadays, as well as allowing for more accurate modelling of reflected light, sophisticated software and analysis techniques allow a simulation of how the human eye would perceive any change in the light levels within a room, so that accurate visualisations of the situation before and after development may be prepared. It is then possible to gauge the impact that a change in lighting levels might have on the inhabitants of an affected neighbouring property (Figure A6). What might appear to be a significant impact using the conventional 'Waldram' approach might in practice have little or no perceptible effect on the user of a room when one allows for reflected light and more accurately simulated lighting conditions.

## Other measures and criteria

A29   If there are deficiencies in the conventional approach, the question is what should replace it. Building Research Establishment (BRE) guidance on the sufficiency of sunlight and daylight already exists (see next section). Further, as mentioned above, new computer modelling techniques may provide a more accurate assessment of actual impact. In principle, there seems to be no good reason why these should not be used to help the court assess the practical impact of an interference with light caused by development. We deal with each in turn.

---

12   See paras 8.12 and 10.47.
13   See para A13.

## BRE daylight guidelines

A30    The impact of development on daylight and sunlight enjoyed by buildings and how they are affected by development is already assessed by local authorities in the planning context.

A31    Local authorities usually assess the daylight and sunlight impact of a proposed development by reference to the guidelines set out in the 2011 BRE report, *Site Layout Planning for Daylight and Sunlight – A Guide to Good Practice*, by Paul Littlefair (BRE guidelines).[14] One of the primary sources for the BRE report is the more detailed guidance contained within the British Standards Institution, *Lighting for buildings. Code of practice for daylighting* (BSI *Code of practice for daylighting*).[15]

A32    The BRE guidelines refer to three measures of diffuse daylight and provide assessment criteria for each of these measures. They are:

(a)    vertical sky component (VSC);

(b)    average daylight factor (ADF); and

(c)    no-sky line (NSL) – sometimes referred to as the 'daylight distribution contour'.

Some criteria relate only to the proposed levels of daylight, and others relate to the reduction compared to the existing baseline condition.

### *Vertical sky component*

A33    VSC is a measure of the skylight reaching a point from an overcast sky. For existing buildings, the BRE guidelines are based on the loss of VSC at a point at the centre of a window, on the outer plane of the wall. The BRE guidelines state that if the VSC at the centre of a window is less than 27%, and it is less than 0.8 times its former value, then the diffuse daylighting of the existing building may be adversely affected.

---

[14]    Littlefair, P (2011), *Site Layout Planning for Daylight and Sunlight – A Guide to Good Practice* (2nd edn), BR209, BRE Press.

[15]    British Standards Institution (2008), *Lighting for buildings. Code of practice for daylighting*, BS 8206-2:2008, British Standards Institution.

## *Daylight factor*

A34    DF is the ratio of illuminance at a point on a reference plane (usually the working plane in a room) to the outdoor illuminance on a horizontal plane under an unobstructed sky. In this context, *average daylight factor* (ADF) is the average of the daylight factors across the working plane. As such, it is a measure of the daylight within a room, and accounts for factors such as the number of windows and their size in relation to the size of the room. Clearly, a small room with a large window will be better illuminated by daylight than a large room with a small window. It also accounts for window transmittance and the reflectance of the internal walls, floor and ceiling. The general idea is that the daylight which reaches each of the windows is first calculated. Then, allowing for the window size, the daylight which then enters the room through the windows is determined. The light is then imagined to bounce around within the room, controlled by the reflectance of the internal surfaces. ADF is detailed in the BSI *Code of practice for daylighting*. As for the BRE report, it provides guidance for acceptable values in the presence of supplementary electric lighting, depending on the room use. These are 1.0% for a bedroom, 1.5% for a living room and 2.0% for a kitchen.

## *No-sky line*

A35    The NSL contour maps out the region within a room to which light can penetrate directly from the sky; it therefore accounts for the size of and number of windows by simple geometry. The BRE guidelines suggest that the area of the working plane – the area of the room at desk height – within a room that can receive direct skylight should not be reduced to less than 0.8 times its former value. Since NSL maps out the limit of zero sky visibility, its contour can be altered radically by small changes to poorly-lit rooms and can sometimes give misleading results.

## Can the BRE guidelines be used for assessing the sufficiency of light within a room for the ordinary notions of mankind? If so, why should they not be adopted?

A36    It is not the purpose of this technical appendix to provide a definitive answer to these questions, but the following points should be considered.

A37   VSC is a measure of light on the outside face of the building and takes no account of the size of, or the indeed the presence of, windows. Therefore, since rights of light are concerned with a right to light entering a building through clearly defined apertures, it is perhaps of limited use. It is, however, informative to note that according to the BRE guidelines a loss of light greater than 20% would be 'noticeable' and daylight levels may be 'adversely affected'. By implication, a loss of less than 20% would not be noticeable and daylight would not be adversely affected. This raises the question of why small losses of light are sometimes considered 'injunctable' by practitioners.

A38   NSL is a measure of zero sky visibility, or zero sky component. There is a question as to whether a 0.2% sky component is sufficient but clearly zero is insufficient. Therefore, it is doubtful that mapping out the region of zero sky component could give a reasonable indication of a useful amount of daylight. Furthermore, the measurement of the extent of a zero level can lead to anomalous results. For example, consider a thin-walled room lit only by the light entering through a keyhole sized window. In the absence of any external obstructions, a tiny amount of sky would be visible from all points within the room and therefore the NSL would cover the whole room. Of course, in reality, the room would be in almost complete darkness. If the keyhole window were to be obstructed, the portion of the room covered by the NSL would reduce from 100% to 0%. Whilst this methodology shows a 100% reduction, in reality, the change in light levels would not be meaningful.

A39   ADF has some merit as a matter to be taken into account when considering the substantiality of an interference with light. This is because it involves analysis of the whole range of light levels across the room. Commonly, ADF values are calculated using the empirical formula provided in the British Standard[16] and the BRE guidelines. However, the empirical formula was derived for a simple window/room combination facing a uniform obstruction and, as stated in the BSI *Code of practice for daylighting*, should not be used where external obstructions cannot be represented by a single angle of elevation. Therefore, in most real urban situations, the empirical formula will not provide an accurate result.

---

[16]   British Standards Institution (2008), *Lighting for buildings. Code of practice for daylighting*, BS 8206-2:2008, British Standards Institution.

A40    In such circumstances, the ADF can be calculated more accurately from first principles by calculating the distribution of DFs across the working plane.

## More detailed assessments and simulations

A41    Both the conventional rights of light calculation methods and the various measures of daylight in the BRE guidelines are simplifications of reality, and we have already discussed the basis of them. The reason these methods have been used in the past, and are still commonly used today, is that the approximations and assumptions involved make the calculations tractable. Armed with the appropriate Waldram diagram or the appropriate BRE protractor, and enough patience, a trained person could produce a rights of light contour, or calculate a VSC by hand.

A42    However, since in rights of light we are dealing with a loss of light, we should aim at least to consider light levels (illuminance levels), how they change, and how we perceive these changes. This type of calculation is generally too complicated to perform 'by hand', but software such as Radiance, which has been available for some considerable time, allows exactly this to be done. Increasingly, therefore, when the conventional approach raises a potential rights of light issue, consideration of light levels and visualisations are being used to augment the analysis. This is important because it enables conclusions to be drawn about the perceptibility of reductions in natural daylight, i.e. whether a neighbouring development will actually cause a noticeable change to the perceived level of light within a room. This approach also provides an opportunity for the result to be evaluated in terms of the British Standard[17] recommendations on required lux levels.

A43    Whilst any software-based approach will carry its own set of simplifications and assumptions, these can be changed, allowing for an increasingly realistic step-by-step approach. How far we choose to go along that path would depend on the detail and issues of the case in hand.

A44    A first step in any such analysis would correspond precisely to a conventional rights of light calculation. A 3D computer model of the site

---

[17]    British Standards Institution (2011), *Light and lighting. Lighting of work places. Indoor work places*, BS EN 12464-1:2011, British Standards Institution.

is created, consisting of the surrounding properties, the existing buildings on the site and the proposed development. The main assumptions involved in this analysis are that only direct light from the sky is considered – all walls internally and externally are effectively matt black. We assume a uniform overcast sky, and we assume all window apertures are unglazed. We calculate 0.2% sky factors and find the areas on the working plane which exceed 0.2% before and after development. Applying the 50/50 rule, this may highlight a number of rooms which by conventional rights of light methods exhibit an injury.

A45     Rather than stop at this point for such rooms, an attempt should be made to answer the question – is there really a noticeable reduction in light? To answer this question, typically illuminance levels (lux levels) would be calculated and visualisations produced. In order to do this, more realistic assumptions would be necessary. An allowance for reflected light would be made by estimating/assuming reflectances for all surfaces – external and internal. An allowance for the window glazing would also be included by using typical glazing transmittances. Further, a typical unobstructed sky horizontal illuminance model would be used – using a CIE overcast sky rather than a uniform sky. This procedure would produce a reasonable first approximation to the illuminance distributions before and after development. Whilst it must be realised that precise reflectance/transmittance properties of all surfaces will not be known, these factors are less important in a comparative assessment between existing and proposed situations. The extent of the influence of reflected light can be quantified by consideration of sky component distribution and the average sky component. The difference between these and the DF and ADF represents the influence of reflected light.

A46     As soon as we depart from a DF-based approach, as mentioned above, we have to assume a sky horizontal illuminance value – a lux level on a horizontal plane provided by the sky. Since the overall sky brightness varies vastly – from 0 lux at midnight to around 35,000 lux at midday midsummer – so the lux levels within the room would vary enormously. Therefore, for example, at a point in a room where the illuminance is 200 lux under a 10,000 lux sky, it would be 0 lux at midnight, and 700 lux at midday midsummer. This fact can be handled in a number of ways:

(a)   Adopt a 'standard' reasonable sky brightness – say 5,000 lux – to provide a basis for comparison.

(b)   Revert to working with DFs by dividing by the overall sky brightness and consider both the distribution, and their average.

(c)   Instead of assuming a constant value, obtain typical meteorological data for the locality and simulate the dynamically changing sky over a chosen time period. This approach is otherwise known as climate-based modelling.[18]

A47   Whichever approach is taken, the entire distribution of light (be it DF or illuminance) throughout a room should be considered. This enables, for example, the effect on deep rooms to be considered more appropriately since a large area of poorly-lit space at the back of a room will significantly reduce the average. It is questionable how deep into a building a right to light should extend, and therefore an average over the whole area may not always be appropriate.

A48   These are no more than suggestions, but if developed further they may provide parties and courts with more material on which they may be able to make a clearer assessment of the practical effect of an interference with light.

---

[18]   Mardaljevic, J (2008), *Climate-Based Daylight Analysis for Residential Buildings – Impact of various window configurations, external obstructions, orientations and location on useful daylight illuminance*, Technical Report, IESD, De Montfort University, Leicester.

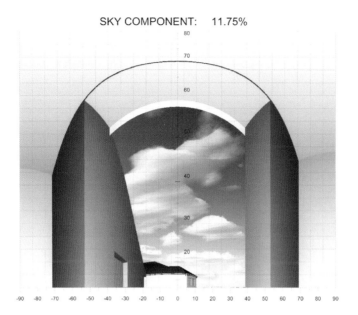

SKY COMPONENT: 11.75%

Figure A1   Waldram Diagram

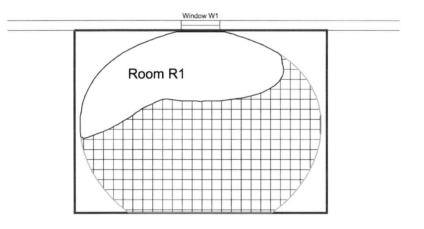

Window W1

Room R1

| | Whole Room sq ft | Existing Well Lit sq ft | % | Proposed Well Lit sq ft | % | Area of Loss sq ft | EFZ ANALYSIS Front sq ft | 1st sq ft | 2nd sq ft | MKWT sq ft | EFZ sq ft |
|---|---|---|---|---|---|---|---|---|---|---|---|
| Room R1 | 465.7 | 367.9 | 79 | 124.4 | 26.71 | 243.5 | 0 | 108.4 | 135.1 | 0 | 176 |

Figure A2   Front, first, second and makeweight zones

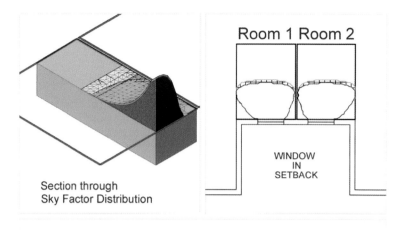

Section through
Sky Factor Distribution

Room 1 Room 2

WINDOW
IN
SETBACK

Section through window head

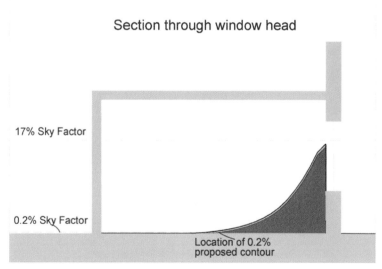

17% Sky Factor

0.2% Sky Factor

Location of 0.2%
proposed contour

Figure A3   Distribution of daylight – normal room

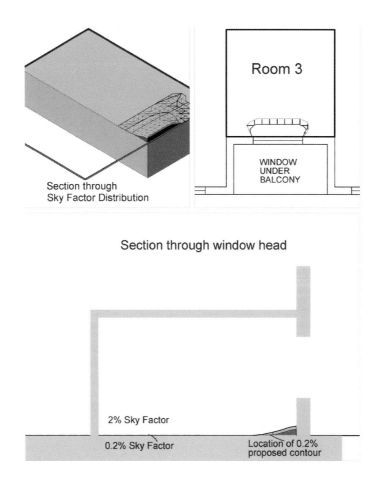

Figure A4   Distribution of daylight – room served by
window under balcony

Daylight Distribution – Sky Component only

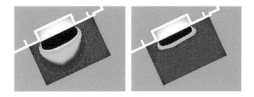

Daylight Distribution – with reflected light

Figure A5   Distribution of daylight – with and without reflected light

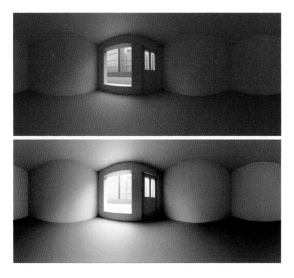

Figure A6   Impact of a change in lighting levels

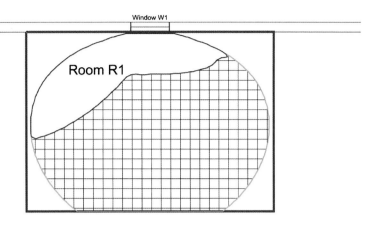

| | Whole Room sq ft | Existing Well Lit sq ft | % | Proposed Well Lit sq ft | % | Area of Loss sq ft | EFZ ANALYSIS | | | | |
|---|---|---|---|---|---|---|---|---|---|---|---|
| | | | | | | | Front sq ft | 1st sq ft | 2nd sq ft | MKWT sq ft | EFZ sq ft |
| Room R1 | 465.7 | 372.4 | 80 | 93.3 | 20 | 279.2 | 23.2 | 116.4 | 139.6 | 0 | 221 |

Figure B1    Contour plot – 'well-lit' scenario with little light

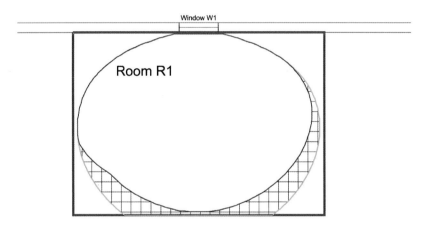

| | Whole Room sq ft | Existing Well Lit sq ft | % | Proposed Well Lit sq ft | % | Area of Loss sq ft | EFZ ANALYSIS | | | | |
|---|---|---|---|---|---|---|---|---|---|---|---|
| | | | | | | | Front sq ft | 1st sq ft | 2nd sq ft | MKWT sq ft | EFZ sq ft |
| Room R1 | 465.7 | 372.4 | 80 | 326 | 70 | 46.4 | 0 | 0 | 0 | 11.6 | 11.6 |

Figure B2    Contour plot – 'well-lit' scenario with some light loss

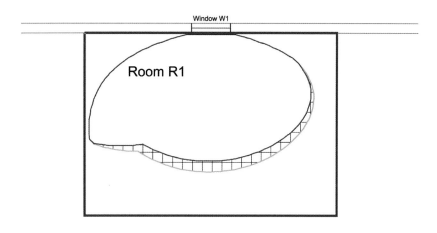

| | Whole Room sq ft | Existing Well Lit sq ft | % | Proposed Well Lit sq ft | % | Area of Loss sq ft | EFZ ANALYSIS | | | | |
|---|---|---|---|---|---|---|---|---|---|---|---|
| | | | | | | | Front sq ft | 1st sq ft | 2nd sq ft | MKWT sq ft | EFZ sq ft |
| Room R1 | 465.7 | 241.4 | 52 | 223.4 | 48 | 18 | 0 | 9.3 | 4.6 | 0 | 13.9 |

Figure B3    Contour plot – 50/50 rule only just breached

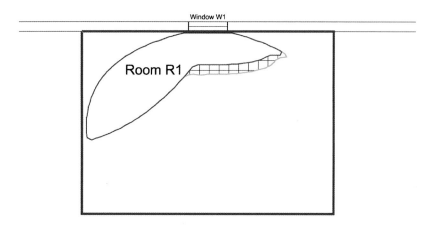

| | Whole Room sq ft | Existing Well Lit sq ft | % | Proposed Well Lit sq ft | % | Area of Loss sq ft | EFZ ANALYSIS | | | | |
|---|---|---|---|---|---|---|---|---|---|---|---|
| | | | | | | | Front sq ft | 1st sq ft | 2nd sq ft | MKWT sq ft | EFZ sq ft |
| Room R1 | 465.7 | 93.3 | 20 | 83.8 | 18 | 9.5 | 14.3 | 0 | 0 | 0 | 14.3 |

Figure B4    Contour plot – poorly-lit scenario with small percentage
reduction in light

# B    Valuation of Light and its Loss

*Liam Dunford, MSc Surv, FRGS, Paul Fletcher, MSc, Dr Martin Howarth, DPhil (Oxon) and Dr Malcolm Macpherson, DPhil (Oxon) of Point 2 Surveyors*

## Introduction

B1    Valuing light and its loss is far from straightforward.

B2    As discussed in the main text, the starting point for the assessment of 'common law' damages is the diminution in value which an interference with light causes to the dominant tenement.[1] The valuation of light enjoyed by a building and how an interference with that light might affect the value of the building is naturally subjective. Attempts to value the effects on the building as a whole are fraught with circular arguments. It can be argued that in a prime city location or an area of regeneration, some light loss as a result of a landmark or new building is unlikely to diminish the value of an adjoining property; indeed, in some cases, there may be arguments that the value of the dominant property could have increased as the result of new neighbouring development despite the light loss. However, such propositions are scuppered if one is to assume a purely hypothetical scenario in which two buildings are identical in every respect, save that one receives a materially inferior level of natural light to the other; clearly, the one that is better lit is more desirable and thus some value has to be attributed to this over the other. These are some of the issues endemic in valuing light: there are too many uniquely different factors to contend with to allow for a logical accepted methodology. To produce consistency and certainty, rights of light practitioners have developed (and, in practice, agree upon) a method of valuation which has become known as 'book value'.

## 'Book value'

B3    In order to understand the basis of this methodology, one must have first digested Appendix A and the conventional approach to the 'test of

---

[1]    See para 10.51.

sufficiency', namely the so-called 50/50 rule. That method of assessing loss in the light involves assessing the loss by 'zoning' the areas affected by the loss, calculating a loss for the areas affected which is equivalent to the first zone (EFZ) loss, and then applying a conventional value (book value) to this loss. This is a convention that has been adopted amongst practitioners. It was one of the methodologies that was presented in valuing light in *Carr-Saunders v Dick McNeil Associates*,[2] and the one on which Millett J appeared to place greater confidence.

B4 The first stage is to calculate the 0.2% contour areas before and after the development. This is explained in more detail at Appendix A, paragraphs A13–A15. These areas are often also expressed as a percentage to aid the identification of an actionable loss. At this stage, any gains in light would also be accounted for and offset against the losses; this would be considered reasonable for the same room, but unlikely to be so if applied from one room to the next, and certainly unlikely to be reasonable if applied to very different parts of the same building.

B5 The next stage is then to 'zone' the room being assessed. The contour areas are subtracted to produce losses in the four quarter areas of the room. This is rather like the zoning used when valuing retail space, but importantly, when valuing loss of light, it is the total quantum that is zoned rather than the specific area from where the light is lost. We start with the best-lit quarter and end with the least well-lit quarter: so-called front, first, second and makeweight zones. The principle behind this is that building on the test of 'sufficiency', the first portion (25%) of light that is lost from the room is regarded as trivial but the loss increases in importance over the four zones to the last portion or 'front zone', in which any light loss is considered serious – the last quarter being that much more precious.

B6 Next, the light loss from each zone is factorised having regard to its importance: the front zone area is multiplied by 1.5, the first zone taken at par, the second zone by 0.5 and the makeweight zone by 0.25. The addition of the weighted losses in each of these quarters then produces a figure for the equivalent first zone (EFZ) loss to the room. It may be that only some rooms within a building are adversely affected and breach the 50/50 rule. It is such rooms which are conventionally considered to have suffered an

---

2   *Carr-Saunders v Dick McNeil Associates* [1986] 1 WLR 922.

'actionable' loss.[3] However, other rooms which remain well-lit may still suffer some loss of light, but not so much that this loss would in itself be actionable. These losses are also taken into account when valuing the consequences of an actionable interference with light: such loss is treated as makeweight and multiplied by 0.25, and is often termed 'parasitic'. This is conventionally taken into account because it is believed that where there has been a wrongful interference with light, damages should take account of the impact on the dominant tenement as a whole.[4]

B7    However, despite this convention amongst practitioners, the fact that the court may properly take into account the impact of an interference with light on the dominant tenement as a whole, does not mean that such impact results in actual quantifiable loss. The practical impact on the remaining rooms may be negligible and it is difficult to see how in many instances the value of the dominant tenement would really be harmed by such impact (indeed, *ex hypothesi* the rooms may remain 'well-lit'). Yet, in practice, value is usually attributed to the 'parasitic' reduction in light. Furthermore, in a large commercial building it may be that only one room experiences an actionable injury, but the 'parasitic loss' inflates the EFZ and ultimately the book value, even though the profit to the developer as a result of the interference is relatively small and a minor change in massing to the proposed interference would restore light to the single room affected.

B8    When applying the 'book value' methodology, regard is also given to ancillary uses within a building, such as staircases, lavatories, store cupboards and garages. Convention considers these as makeweight.

B9    Figures B1–B4 illustrate corresponding contour plots to be read in conjunction with the relevant EFZ table in each case. In the illustrations, all rooms are equal in every respect save for the levels of light loss:

(1)    Figure B1 shows a 'well-lit' scenario that is left with little light and is conventionally considered actionable.

(2)    Figure B2 shows a 'well-lit' scenario with some light loss that is conventionally considered minor and would often (as discussed in

---

[3]    But see Appendix A, para A14.

[4]    Purportedly following the legal analysis set out in at para 10.51.

paragraph B6) fall into the parasitic category, for example if it were within the same demise as the room shown within Figure B1. If, however, it stood on its own, there would be no nuisance.

(3)  Figure B3 shows a scenario where the 50/50 rule is only just breached, and should the 'rule' be applied rigidly, it could by the thoughts of some give rise to nuisance, regardless of the quantum of light being lost.

(4)  Figure B4 shows a small percentage reduction in light in an already poorly-lit situation; the reduction is of some 2% and all in the front zone. Adopting the view that a higher importance should be placed upon small levels of light loss in rooms which are already poorly-lit,[5] this could result in a case for nuisance.

(5)  The scenarios shown in both Figures B3 and B4 are not straightforward and need to be considered in detail; importance should be given to the perception of the light loss and what the appropriate methodology is for establishing the degree of nuisance; see Appendix A, paras A28 and A41 ff.

B10  After the EFZ losses have been ascertained, they are then used to calculate book value damages to the affected building, which along with some idea of the property value, enables a surveyor to attempt to calculate an appropriate diminution in value due to the reduction in light levels.

B11  The conventional book value is arrived at by the following calculation:

EFZ x proportion of rent attributed to light x years' purchase

## Proportion of rent attributed to light

B12  Proportion of rent attributed to light is a convention which was established in the early 1970s by three then leading practitioners (Anstey, McDonald and Arnall),[6] who proposed that the value of light as a proportion of rent varied, and they posited that as rent increases so the proportion of value attributed to light falls. The principle has been

5    See paras 6.22 ff and 8.14 ff.

6    Harris, L and Anstey, J (2006), *Anstey's Rights of Light and How to Deal with Them* (4th edn), RICS Books.

generally adopted by practitioners and in negotiations it does not normal exceed £5 per square foot. The thinking behind this principle is that light as a contributing factor to rent has in recent years been joined by many other additional factors since the 1970s which has not changed the overall value of light. As mentioned above, this convention remains and any discussion outside the courts will generally be met with a 'hold the line' mentality by practitioners, with very little in the way of an apparent justification for it to go up or indeed down. Indeed, it is debatable whether this approach can be suitably applied in a residential context because the amount of light attributed to value in a commercial property is, arguably, different to a residential property. Further, 'book value' does not take a nuanced approach to location. However, there have been attempts to make an adjustment, and a reduced figure in out of town and 'provincial' locations is discussed by John Anstey in his text,[7] and a graph for 'basic provincial rents' is provided.

## *Years' purchase*

B13    Years' purchase (YP) is the amount by which the net income is multiplied to arrive at a capital value and with regard to light is on the basis of freeholder in possession.

B14    Clearly, an appropriate yield (to calculate the YP) requires informed valuation advice, which in city centre locations is often readily available, but elsewhere it may need the input of a local expert. From a rights of light surveyor's perspective the yield used is often taken to the nearest 0.5%, whereas a professional valuer is likely to go into greater deal.

## Apportionment between interests

B15    The right in the first instance belongs to the building and is apportioned between all interests, and in the case of tenants, the unexpired term of the lease. It is common for a landlord to retain rights expressly within the lease. Tenants, however, may also have rights of light as explained in the main text.[8]

---

[7]    Harris, L and Anstey, J (2006), *Anstey's Rights of Light and How to Deal with Them* (4th edn), RICS Books.

[8]    See paras 2.3 and 2.75.

a sum has been agreed, *Parry's Valuation and* s often used to divide it equitably between all relevant g the 'Present Value of a £1 per annum' table relevant the appropriate split can be calculated. The table ount receivable at the expiry of 100 years at the specified yield/YP.

*Example*

Let us assume a compensation sum of £20,000 has been agreed. The yield is agreed at 5%, and a tenant enjoys a 25-year lease, of which 5 years have expired.

The tenant's apportionment is calculated by referring to the 'Present Value of a £1 per annum' table at a 5% yield for 20 years. The appropriate table entry shows a YP of 12.4622. This divided by the total YP in perpetuity (expressed as a percentage) is 62.3%; in this case, it would equate to £12,460 for the tenants and £7,540 for the landlord. Should multiple leases exist over the same building, the principle would be followed on a lease-by-lease basis.

B17    When apportioning damages, regard will be had to break clauses and the duration of the lease before the landlord becomes entitled to possession. If the freehold is subject to a long lease, in many instances, it will be hard to attribute any harm at all to the impact on the reversion. However, if the dominant tenement is subject to a lease which contains a rent review clause, then a reduction in light may cause harm to the landlord if it will affect what he can expect to obtain following a rent review, even though his entitlement to possession is many years hence.

## Damages instead of an injunction: negotiating damages and developer's profit

B18    As explained in the main text, where damages are awarded instead of an injunction, it has become common to award 'negotiating damages'.[10] These do not strictly award damages for diminution in value to the dominant tenement as a result of the loss of light, but seek to compensate the dominant owner for the loss of his ability to assert his right to stop the

---

9    Davidson, AW (2013), *Parry's Valuation and Investment Tables* (13th edn), EG Books.
10   See para 10.65 ff.

development. Accordingly, a 'price' is set which takes account of the profit to the developer. This part of this appendix concerns how the developer's profit is conventionally calculated.

B19   In practice, the calculation of developer's profit starts with the rights to light surveyor producing a cutback to the proposed scheme. The cutback shows how much massing would need to be removed in order to avoid the light loss. There are often several possible iterations to the cutback, and one option maybe more advantageous to the developer than another. The cutback is usually presented in both graphical output and, importantly, a total gross external area[11] of the proposed development. This can then be refined to establish net internal area,[12] as floorplans of the development become known. Care should be taken when calculating or reviewing cutbacks to consider the source parameters that have been or will be used, such as room layouts and room uses.

B20   Once the lost areas attributable to the cutbacks are known, they can be read in conjunction with an appraisal to establish the developer's profit. At this juncture, it is prudent for the dominant owner's professional team to seek specialist advice from a valuer/development surveyor; likewise, any disclosed appraisal from the developer's team needs to be able to withstand scrutiny.

B21   The valuation of developer's profit can become highly contentious in anything other than straightforward scenarios. For example, certain structures/schemes such as places of worship, schools, social housing and civic buildings generate no profit. In the case of social housing provided as part of a section 106 agreement,[13] a blended profit could be considered from across the whole development. Similar difficulties can arise where the cutback solely relates to a parapet, boundary wall or plant space, for example, that generates no apparent profit, but is an integral part of the permitted scheme.

B22   In an urban environment, a cutback that is created for one adjoining owner is likely to have a complex relationship with another. A cutback

---

[11]   GEA.

[12]   NIA.

[13]   Town and Country Planning Act 1990, s 106.

may remove entirely or mitigate light loss being caused to another adjoining building. Naturally, this creates an uneasy position for the developer, who may be subject to a number of competing claims from adjoining owners. The 'last man standing' amongst rival dominant owners would, on the face of things, have the strongest claim to stand in the way of development. Assuming all parties wish to reach a financial settlement or, indeed, damages are being discussed, it seems equitable to apportion the developer's profit between (potential) claimants.

B23    Profit-based settlements will also more than likely follow the same principles of apportionment between landlord and tenant as those discussed in paragraph B16, assuming that both landlord and tenant pursue a joint negotiation/dialogue.

B24    There has been some success, despite the absence of case law, at using the aforementioned EFZ figure for a specific building, to establish a ratio for the amount of light loss it experiences in relation to the total light loss by all buildings that have interacting cutbacks or, indeed, cones of light. The resultant ratio can then be used to apportion any profit.

B25    The approach which the courts take to the level of 'profit' to be taken into account when assessing 'negotiating damages' was considered in the case of *Tamares (Vincent Square) Ltd v Fairport (Vincent Square) Ltd*,[14] and is considered in the main text. The pursuit of high percentages of developer's profit by a dominant owner can often seem unjust and does not take into account the inherent financial risks the developer has taken, nor the capital value of the property being affected. As explained in the main text, however, the courts appear astute to this, and many awards of damages instead of an injunction are relatively modest.[15]

## Comparison of methodologies

B26    Even those with a rudimentary understanding of valuation will appreciate the shortcomings in the book value methodology. On the other hand, the legal or commercial mind which has experience in negotiating

---

[14]    *Tamares (Vincent Square) Ltd v Fairport (Vincent Square) Ltd* [2007] EWHC 212 (Ch), [2007] 1 WLR 2167.

[15]    See para 10.77.

through a restrictive covenant, for example, will see the logic in adopting a developer's profit-based methodology.

B27 In commercial terms, rights of light negotiations between parties are often no more than a 'horse trade', with both the book value and developer's profit calculations acting as a reasoned informative. Indeed, liberties are often taken with the book value methodology, in most scenarios, to attempt to close the gap between it and developer's profit calculations.

B28 Perhaps the first deficiency of the book value methodology was felt by Millett J in *Carr-Saunders v Dick McNeil Associates Ltd*.[16] In that case, the book value was given an uplift to take into account general amenity that would be lost (namely, loss of sky visibility and the proximity of the new massing), and also consideration of the servient owner's bargaining power and the amount of profit the defendants would realise as a result of their development (although it should be noted that no evidence was provided as to the quantum of profits). What seems common between both the book value and developer's profit-based calculations is the underlying principle as to 'what feels right', and the practitioner must be mindful of this when considering both those methodologies.

## REFERENCES

Anstey, J (1971), *Rights to Light and How to Deal with Them*, RICS Books.

British Standards Institution (2008), *Lighting for buildings. Code of practice for daylighting*, BS 8206-2:2008, British Standards Institution.

British Standards Institution (2011), *Light and lighting. Lighting of work places. Indoor work places*, BS EN 12464-1:2011, British Standards Institution.

Chynoweth, P (2004), 'Progressing the Rights to Light Debate Part 2: The Grumble Point Revisited', *Structural Survey*, 23 (4), pp 251–264.

Chynoweth, P (2009), 'Progressing the Rights to Light Debate Part 3: Judicial Attitudes to Current Practice', 27 (1), pp 7–9.

---

[16] *Carr-Saunders v Dick McNeil Associates Ltd* [1986] 1 WLR 922.

Commission Internationale de L'Eclairage (1932), *Recueil des Travaux et Compte Rendue des Seances, Huitieme Session, Cambridge, September 1931*, Cambridge University Press.

Davidson, AW (2013), *Parry's Valuation and Investment Tables* (13th edn), EG Books.

Defoe, P (2005), 'The Validity of Daylight Calculations in Rights to Light Cases', 5th International PostGrad Research Conference, Salford University.

Defoe, P (2009), 'Waldram was wrong', *Structural Survey*, 27 (3), pp 186–199.

Harris, L and Anstey, J (2006), *Anstey's Rights of Light and How to Deal with Them* (4th edn), RICS Books.

Littlefair, P (2011), *Site Layout Planning for Daylight and Sunlight – A Guide to Good Practice* (2nd edn), BR209, BRE Press.

Mardaljevic, J (2008), *Climate-Based Daylight Analysis for Residential Buildings – Impact of various window configurations, external obstructions, orientations and location on useful daylight illuminance*, Technical Report, IESD, De Montfort University, Leicester.

Pitts, M (2000), 'The Grumble Point: is it still worth the candle?', *Structural Survey*, 18 (5), pp 255–258.

Waldram, PJ and Waldram, JM (1923), 'Window Design and the Measurement and Predetermination of Daylight Illumination', *The Illuminating Engineer* (April–May), pp 90–122.

# C1 Prescription Act 1832 (1832 c 71), Extracts

## 2 IN CLAIMS OF RIGHTS OF WAY OR OTHER EASEMENT THE PERIODS TO BE TWENTY YEARS AND FORTY YEARS

... No claim which may be lawfully made at the common law, by custom, prescription, or grant, to any way or other easement, or to any watercourse, or the use of any water, to be enjoyed or derived upon, over, or from any land or water of our said lord the King ... or being parcel of the duchy of Lancaster or of the duchy of Cornwall, or being the property of any ecclesiastical or lay person, or body corporate, when such way or other matter as herein last before mentioned shall have been actually enjoyed by any person claiming right thereto without interruption for the full period of twenty years, shall be defeated or destroyed by showing only that such way or other matter was first enjoyed at any time prior to such period of twenty years, but nevertheless such claim may be defeated in any other way by which the same is now liable to be defeated; and where such way or other matter as herein last before mentioned shall have been so enjoyed as aforesaid for the full period of forty years, the right thereto shall be deemed absolute and indefeasible, unless it shall appear that the same was enjoyed by some consent or agreement expressly given or made for that purpose by deed or writing.

### AMENDMENT
Words omitted repealed by the Statute Law Revision (No 2) Act 1888 and the Statute Law Revision Act 1890.

## 3 RIGHT TO THE USE OF LIGHT ENJOYED FOR TWENTY YEARS, INDEFEASIBLE, UNLESS SHOWN TO HAVE BEEN BY CONSENT

... When the access and use of light to and for any dwelling house, workshop, or other building shall have been actually enjoyed therewith for the full period of twenty years without interruption, the right thereto shall be deemed absolute and indefeasible, any local usage or custom to the contrary notwithstanding, unless it shall appear that the same was enjoyed by some consent or agreement expressly made or given for that purpose by deed or writing.

**AMENDMENT**
Words omitted repealed by the Statute Law Revision (No 2) Act 1888.

## 4 BEFORE MENTIONED PERIODS TO BE DEEMED THOSE NEXT BEFORE SUITS FOR CLAIMING TO WHICH SUCH PERIODS RELATE—WHAT SHALL CONSTITUTE AN INTERRUPTION

. . . Each of the respective periods of years herein-before mentioned shall be deemed and taken to be the period next before some suit or action wherein the claim or matter to which such period may relate shall have been or shall be brought into question; and . . . no act or other matter shall be deemed to be an interruption, within the meaning of this statute, unless the same shall have been or shall be submitted to or acquiesced in for one year after the party interrupted shall have had or shall have notice thereof, and of the person making or authorizing the same to be made.

**AMENDMENT**
Words omitted repealed by the Statute Law Revision (No 2) Act 1888.

## 5 IN ACTIONS ON THE CASE THE CLAIMANT MAY ALLEGE HIS RIGHT GENERALLY, AS AT PRESENT. IN PLEAS TO TRESPASS AND OTHER PLEADINGS, ETC, THE PERIOD MENTIONED IN THIS ACT MAY BE ALLEGED; AND EXCEPTIONS, ETC, TO BE REPLIED TO SPECIALLY

. . . In all actions upon the case and other pleadings, wherein the party claiming may now by law allege his right generally, without averring the existence of such right from time immemorial, such general allegation shall still be deemed sufficient, and if the same shall be denied, all and every the matters in this Act mentioned and provided, which shall be applicable to the case, shall be admissible in evidence to sustain or rebut such allegation; and . . . in all pleadings to actions of trespass, and in all other pleadings wherein before the passing of this Act it would have been necessary to allege the right to have existed from time immemorial, it shall be sufficient to allege the enjoyment thereof as of right by the occupiers of the tenement in respect whereof the same is claimed for and during such of the periods mentioned in this Act as may be applicable to the case, and without claiming in the name or right of the owner of the fee, as is now usually done; and if the other party shall intend to rely on any proviso, exception, incapacity, disability, contract, agreement, or other matter herein-before mentioned, or on any cause or matter of fact or of law not inconsistent with the simple fact of enjoyment, the same shall be specially alleged and set forth in answer to the allegation of the party claiming, and shall not be received in evidence on any general traverse or denial of such allegation.

**AMENDMENT**

Words omitted repealed by the Statute Law Revision (No 2) Act 1888.

## 6 RESTRICTING THE PRESUMPTION TO BE ALLOWED IN SUPPORT OF CLAIMS HEREIN PROVIDED FOR

... In the several cases mentioned in and provided for by this Act, no presumption shall be allowed or made in favour or support of any claim, upon proof of the exercise or enjoyment of the right or matter claimed for any less period of time or number of years than for such period or number mentioned in this Act as may be applicable to the case and to the nature of the claim.

**AMENDMENT**

Words omitted repealed by the Statute Law Revision (No 2) Act 1888.

## 7 PROVISO FOR INFANTS, ETC

Provided also, that the time during which any person otherwise capable of resisting any claim to any of the matters before mentioned shall have been or shall be an infant, idiot, non compos mentis, feme covert, or tenant for life, or during which any action or suit shall have been pending, and which shall have been diligently prosecuted, until abated by the death of any party or parties thereto, shall be excluded in the computation of the periods herein-before mentioned, except only in cases where the right or claim is hereby declared to be absolute and indefeasible.

**AMENDMENT**

Amended in relation to Northern Ireland only by the Mental Health (Northern Ireland) Order 1986, SI 1986/595, art 136(1), Sch 5, Part II.

## 8 WHAT TIME TO BE EXCLUDED IN COMPUTING THE TERM OF FORTY YEARS APPOINTED BY THIS ACT

Provided always, . . . that when any land or water upon, over or from which any such way or other convenient watercourse or use of water shall have been or shall be enjoyed or derived hath been or shall be held under or by virtue of any term of life, or any term of years exceeding three years from the granting thereof, the time of the enjoyment of any such way or other matter as herein last before mentioned, during the continuance of such term, shall be excluded in the computation of the said period of forty years, in case the claim shall within three years next after the end or sooner determination of such term be resisted by any person entitled to any reversion expectant on the determination thereof.

**AMENDMENT**
Words omitted repealed by the Statute Law Revision (No 2) Act 1888.

## 9 EXTENT OF ACT

This Act shall not extend to Scotland ...

**AMENDMENT**
Words omitted repealed by the Statute Law Revision Act 1874.

# C2 Law of Property Act 1925 (1925 c 20), Extracts

## 12 LIMITATION AND PRESCRIPTION ACTS

Nothing in this Part of this Act affects the operation of any statute, or of the general law for the limitation of actions or proceedings relating to land or with reference to the acquisition of easements or rights over or in respect of land.

## 52 CONVEYANCES TO BE BY DEED

(1) All conveyances of land or of any interest therein are void for the purpose of conveying or creating a legal estate unless made by deed.

(2) This section does not apply to—

(a) assents by a personal representative;

(b) disclaimers made in accordance with [sections 178 to 180 or sections 315 to 319 of the Insolvency Act 1986] or not required to be evidenced in writing;

(c) surrenders by operation of law, including surrenders which may, by law, be effected without writing;

(d) leases or tenancies or other assurances not required by law to be made in writing;

[(da)    flexible tenancies;

(db) assured tenancies of dwelling-houses in England that are granted by private registered providers of social housing and are not long tenancies or shared ownership leases;]

(e) receipts [other than those falling within section 115 below];

(f) vesting orders of the court or other competent authority;

(g) conveyances taking effect by operation of law.

[(3) In this section—

"assured tenancy" has the same meaning as in Part 1 of the Housing Act 1988;

"dwelling-house" has the same meaning as in Part 1 of the Housing Act 1988;

"flexible tenancy" has the meaning given by section 107A of the Housing Act 1985;

"long tenancy" means a tenancy granted for a term certain of more than 21 years, whether or not it is (or may become) terminable before the end of that term by notice given by the tenant or by re-entry or forfeiture;

"shared ownership lease" means a lease of a dwelling-house—

(a) granted on payment of a premium calculated by reference to a percentage of the value of the dwelling-house or of the cost of providing it, or

(b) under which the lessee (or the lessee's personal representatives) will or may be entitled to a sum calculated by reference, directly or indirectly, to the value of the dwelling-house.]

**AMENDMENT**

Sub-s (2): in para (b) words "sections 178 to 180 or sections 315 to 319 of the Insolvency Act 1986" in square brackets substituted by the Insolvency Act 1986, s 439(2), Sch 14.

Sub-s (2): paras (da), (db) inserted by the Localism Act 2011, s 156(1).

Sub-s (2): in para (e) words "other than those falling within section 115 below" in square brackets substituted by the Law of Property (Miscellaneous Provisions) Act 1989, s 1, Sch 1, para 2.

Sub-s (3): inserted by the Localism Act 2011, s 156(2).

## 53 INSTRUMENTS REQUIRED TO BE IN WRITING

(1) Subject to the provisions hereinafter contained with respect to the creation of interests in land by parol—

(a) no interest in land can be created or disposed of except by writing signed by the person creating or conveying the same, or by his agent thereunto lawfully authorised in writing, or by will, or by operation of law;

(b) a declaration of trust respecting any land or any interest therein must be manifested and proved by some writing signed by some person who is able to declare such trust or by his will;

(c)  a disposition of an equitable interest or trust subsisting at the time of the disposition, must be in writing signed by the person disposing of the same, or by his agent thereunto lawfully authorised in writing or by will.

(2)  This section does not affect the creation or operation of resulting, implied or constructive trusts.

## 54 CREATION OF INTERESTS IN LAND BY PAROL

(1)  All interests in land created by parol and not put in writing and signed by the persons so creating the same, or by their agents thereunto lawfully authorised in writing, have, notwithstanding any consideration having been given for the same, the force and effect of interests at will only.

(2)  Nothing in the foregoing provisions of this Part of this Act shall affect the creation by parol of leases taking effect in possession for a term not exceeding three years (whether or not the lessee is given power to extend the term) at the best rent which can be reasonably obtained without taking a fine.

## 56 PERSONS TAKING WHO ARE NOT PARTIES AND AS TO INDENTURES

(1)  A person may take an immediate or other interest in land or other property, or the benefit of any condition, right of entry, covenant or agreement over or respecting land or other property, although he may not be named as a party to the conveyance or other instrument.

(2)  A deed between parties, to effect its objects, has the effect of an indenture though not indented or expressed to be an indenture.

## 62 GENERAL WORDS IMPLIED IN CONVEYANCES

(1)  A conveyance of land shall be deemed to include and shall by virtue of this Act operate to convey, with the land, all buildings, erections, fixtures, commons, hedges, ditches, fences, ways, waters, watercourses, liberties, privileges, easements, rights, and advantages whatsoever, appertaining or reputed to appertain to the land, or any part thereof, or, at the time of conveyance, demised, occupied, or

enjoyed with or reputed or known as part or parcel of or appurtenant to the land or any part thereof.

(2) A conveyance of land, having houses or other buildings thereon, shall be deemed to include and shall by virtue of this Act operate to convey, with the land, houses, or other buildings, all outhouses, erections, fixtures, cellars, areas, courts, courtyards, cisterns, sewers, gutters, drains, ways, passages, lights, watercourses, liberties, privileges, easements, rights, and advantages whatsoever, appertaining or reputed to appertain to the land, houses, or other buildings conveyed, or any of them, or any part thereof, or, at the time of conveyance, demised, occupied, or enjoyed with, or reputed or known as part or parcel of or appurtenant to, the land, houses, other buildings conveyed, or any of them, or any part thereof.

(3) A conveyance of a manor shall be deemed to include and shall by virtue of this Act operate to convey, with the manor, all pastures, feedings, wastes, warrens, commons, mines, minerals, quarries, furzes, trees, woods, underwoods, coppices, and the ground and soil thereof, fishings, fisheries, fowlings, courts leet, courts baron, and other courts, view of frankpledge and all that to view of frankpledge doth belong, mills, mulctures, customs, tolls, duties, reliefs, heriots, fines, sums of money, amerciaments, waifs, estrays, chief-rents, quitrents, rentscharge, rents seck, rents of assize, fee farm rents, services, royalties, jurisdictions, franchises, liberties, privileges, easements, profits, advantages, rights, emoluments, and hereditaments whatsoever, to the manor appertaining or reputed to appertain, or, at the time of conveyance, demised, occupied, or enjoyed with the same, or reputed or known as part, parcel, or member thereof.
For the purposes of this subsection the right to compensation for manorial incidents on the extinguishment thereof shall be deemed to be a right appertaining to the manor.

(4) This section applies only if and as far as a contrary intention is not expressed in the conveyance, and has effect subject to the terms of the conveyance and to the provisions therein contained.

(5) This section shall not be construed as giving to any person a better title to any property, right, or thing in this section mentioned than the title which the conveyance gives to him to the land or manor expressed to be conveyed, or as conveying to him any property, right,

or thing in this section mentioned, further or otherwise than as the same could have been conveyed to him by the conveying parties.

(6) This section applies to conveyances made after the thirty-first day of December, eighteen hundred and eighty-one.

## 78 BENEFIT OF COVENANTS RELATING TO LAND

(1) A covenant relating to any land of the covenantee shall be deemed to be made with the covenantee and his successors in title and the persons deriving title under him or them, and shall have effect as if such successors and other persons were expressed.
For the purposes of this subsection in connexion with covenants restrictive of the user of land "successors in title" shall be deemed to include the owners and occupiers for the time being of the land of the covenantee intended to be benefited.

(2) This section applies to covenants made after the commencement of this Act, but the repeal of section fifty-eight of the Conveyancing Act 1881 does not affect the operation of covenants to which that section applied.

## 79 BURDEN OF COVENANTS RELATING TO LAND

(1) A covenant relating to any land of a covenantor or capable of being bound by him, shall, unless a contrary intention is expressed, be deemed to be made by the covenantor on behalf of himself his successors in title and the persons deriving title under him or them, and, subject as aforesaid, shall have effect as if such successors and other persons were expressed.
This subsection extends to a covenant to do some act relating to the land, notwithstanding that the subject-matter may not be in existence when the covenant is made.

(2) For the purposes of this section in connexion with covenants restrictive of the user of land "successors in title" shall be deemed to include the owners and occupiers for the time being of such land.

(3) This section applies only to covenants made after the commencement of this Act.

## 187 LEGAL EASEMENTS

(1) Where an easement, right or privilege for a legal estate is created, it shall enure for the benefit of the land to which it is intended to be annexed.

(2) Nothing in this Act affects the right of a person to acquire, hold or exercise an easement, right or privilege over or in relation to land for a legal estate in common with any other person, or the power of creating or conveying such an easement, right or privilege.

# C3  Rights of Light Act 1959 (1959 c 56)

**1 . . .**

AMENDMENT
Repealed by the Statute Law (Repeals) Act 1974.

## 2 REGISTRATION OF NOTICE IN LIEU OF OBSTRUCTION OF ACCESS OF LIGHT

(1) For the purpose of preventing the access and use of light from being taken to be enjoyed without interruption, any person who is an owner of land (in this and the next following section referred to as the "servient land") over which light passes to a dwelling-house, workshop or other building (in this and the next following section referred to as "the dominant building") may apply to the [Chief Land Registrar] for the registration of a notice under this section.

(2) An application for the registration of a notice under this section shall . . .—

  (a) identify the servient land and the dominant building in the prescribed manner, and

  (b) state that the registration of a notice in pursuance of the application is intended to be equivalent to the obstruction of the access of light to the dominant building across the servient land which would be caused by the erection, in such position on the servient land as may be specified in the application, of an opaque structure of such dimensions (including, if the application so states, unlimited height) as may be so specified.

(3) Any such application shall be accompanied by [a copy of] one or other of the following certificates issued by the [Upper Tribunal], that is to say,—

  (a) a certificate certifying that adequate notice of the proposed application has been given to all persons who, in the circumstances existing at the time when the certificate is issued, appear to the [Upper Tribunal] to be persons likely to be affected by the registration of a notice in pursuance of the application;

    (b)  a certificate certifying that, in the opinion of the [Upper Tribunal], the case is one of exceptional urgency, and that accordingly a notice should be registered forthwith as a temporary notice for such period as may be specified in the certificate.

(4)  Where application is duly made to [the Chief Land Registrar] for the registration of a notice under this section, it shall be the duty of [[the Chief Land Registrar] to register the notice in the . . . local land charges register, and—

    (a)  any notice so registered under this section shall be a local land charge; but

    (b)  section [5(2)] and section 10 of the Local Land Charges Act 1975 shall not apply in relation thereto].

(5)  Provision [may be made by Tribunal Procedure Rules] with respect to the issue of certificates for the purposes of this section, and, subject to the approval of the Treasury, the fees chargeable in respect of those proceedings; and, without prejudice to the generality of subsection (6) of that section, any such rules made for the purposes of this section shall include provision—

    (a)  for requiring applicants for certificates under paragraph (a) of subsection (3) of this section to give such notices, whether by way of advertisement or otherwise, and to produce such documents and provide such information, as may be determined by or under the rules;

    (b)  for determining the period to be specified in a certificate issued under paragraph (b) of subsection (3) of this section; and

    (c)  in connection with any certificate issued under the said paragraph (b), for enabling a further certificate to be issued in accordance (subject to the necessary modifications) with paragraph (a) of subsection (3) of this section.

**AMENDMENT**

Sub-s (1): words "Chief Land Registrar" in square brackets substituted by the Infrastructure Act 2015, s 34(1), (2)(c), Sch 5, Pt 3, paras 27, 28(1), (2).

Sub-s (2): words omitted repealed by the Infrastructure Act 2015, s 34(1), (2)(c), Sch 5, Pt 3, paras 27, 28(1), (3).

Sub-s (3): words "a copy of" in square brackets inserted by the Infrastructure Act 2015, s 34(1), (2)(c), Sch 5, Pt 3, paras 27, 28(1), (4).

Sub-s (3): words "Upper Tribunal" in square brackets in each place they occur substituted by SI 2009/1307, art 5(1), (2), Sch 1, para 35(a).

Sub-s (4): first words "the Chief Land Registrar" in square brackets substituted by the Infrastructure Act 2015, s 34(1), (2)(c), Sch 5, Pt 3, paras 27, 28(1), (5)(a).

Sub-s (4): second words "the Chief Land Registrar" in square brackets substituted by the Infrastructure Act 2015, s 34(1), (2)(c), Sch 5, Pt 3, paras 27, 28(1), (5)(b).

Sub-s (4): words in square brackets ending with the words "in relation thereto" substituted by the Local Land Charges Act 1975, s 17(2), Sch 1.

Sub-s (4): word omitted repealed by the Infrastructure Act 2015, s 34(1), (2)(c), Sch 5, Pt 3, paras 27, 28(1), (5)(c).

Sub-s (4): reference to "5(2)" in square brackets substituted by the Infrastructure Act 2015, s 34(1), (2)(c), Sch 5, Pt 3, paras 27, 28(1), (5)(d).

Sub-s (5): words "may be made by Tribunal Procedure Rules" in square brackets substituted by SI 2009/1307, art 5(1), (2), Sch 1, para 35(b).

## 3 EFFECT OF REGISTERED NOTICE AND PROCEEDINGS RELATING THERETO

(1) Where, in pursuance of an application made in accordance with the last preceding section, a notice is registered thereunder, then, for the purpose of determining whether any person is entitled (by virtue of the Prescription Act 1832, or otherwise) to a right to the access of light to the dominant building across the servient land, the access of light to that building across that land shall be treated as obstructed to the same extent, and with the like consequences, as if an opaque structure, of the dimensions specified in the application,—

   (a) had, on the date of registration of the notice, been erected in the position on the servient land specified in the application, and had been so erected by the person who made the application, and

   (b) had remained in that position during the period for which the notice has effect and had been removed at the end of that period.

(2) For the purposes of this section a notice registered under the last preceding section shall be taken to have effect until either—

  (a) the registration is cancelled, or

  (b) the period of one year beginning with the date of registration of the notice expires, or

  (c) in the case of a notice registered in pursuance of an application accompanied by a certificate issued under paragraph (b) of subsection (3) of the last preceding section, the period specified in the certificate expires without [a copy of] such a further certificate as is mentioned in paragraph (c) of subsection (5) of that section having before the end of that period been lodged with the [Chief Land Registrar],

  and shall cease to have effect on the occurrence of any one of those events.

(3) Subject to the following provisions of this section, any person who, if such a structure as is mentioned in subsection (1) of this section had been erected as therein mentioned, would have had a right of action in any court in respect of that structure, on the grounds that he was entitled to a right to the access of light to the dominant building across the servient land, and that the said right was infringed by that structure, shall have the like right of action in that court in respect of the registration of a notice under the last preceding section.
Provided that an action shall not be begun by virtue of this subsection after the notice in question has ceased to have effect.

(4) Where, at any time during the period for which a notice registered under the last preceding section has effect, the circumstances are such that, if the access of light to the dominant building had been enjoyed continuously from a date one year earlier than the date on which the enjoyment thereof in fact began, a person would have had a right of action in any court by virtue of the last preceding subsection in respect of the registration of the notice, that person shall have the like right of action in that court by virtue of this subsection in respect of the registration of the notice.

(5) The remedies available to the plaintiff in an action brought by virtue of subsection (3) or subsection (4) of this section (apart from any order as to costs) shall be such declaration as the court may consider appropriate in the circumstances, and an order directing the

registration of the notice to be cancelled or varied, as the court may determine.

(6) For the purposes of section four of the Prescription Act 1832 (under which a period of enjoyment of any of the rights to which that Act applies is not to be treated as interrupted except by a matter submitted to or acquiesced in for one year after notice thereof)—

(a) as from the date of registration of a notice under the last preceding section, all persons interested in the dominant building or any part thereof shall be deemed to have notice of the registration thereof and of the person on whose application it was registered;

(b) until such time as an action is brought by virtue of subsection (3) or subsection (4) of this section in respect of the registration of a notice under the last preceding section, all persons interested in the dominant building or any part thereof shall be deemed to acquiesce in the obstruction which, in accordance with subsection (1) of this section, is to be treated as resulting from the registration of the notice;

(c) as from the date on which such an action is brought, no person shall be treated as submitting to or acquiescing in that obstruction:

Provided that, if in any such action, the court decides against the claim of the plaintiff, the court may direct that the preceding provisions of this subsection shall apply in relation to the notice as if that action had not been brought.

**AMENDMENT**
Sub-s (2): in para (c) words "a copy of" in square brackets inserted by the Infrastructure Act 2015, s 34(1), (2)(c), Sch 5, Pt 3, paras 27, 29(a).
Sub-s (2): in para (c) words "Chief Land Registrar" in square brackets substituted by the Infrastructure Act 2015, s 34(1), (2)(c), Sch 5, Pt 3, paras 27, 29(b).

## 4 APPLICATION TO CROWN LAND

(1) Subject to the next following subsection, this Act shall apply in relation to land in which there is a Crown or Duchy interest as it applies in relation to land in which there is no such interest.

(2) Section three of the Prescription Act 1832, as modified by the preceding provisions of this Act, shall not by virtue of this section be construed as applying to any land to which (by reason that there is a Crown or Duchy interest therein) that section would not apply apart from this Act.

(3) In this section "Crown or Duchy interest" means an interest belonging to Her Majesty in right of the Crown or of the Duchy of Lancaster, or belonging to the Duchy of Cornwall, or belonging to a government department, or held in trust for Her Majesty for the purposes of a government department.

## 5 POWER TO MAKE RULES

(1) . . .

(2) Any rules made [under section 14 of the Local Land Charges Act 1975 for the purposes of section 2 of this Act] shall (without prejudice to the inclusion therein of other provisions as to cancelling or varying the registration of notices or agreements) include provision for giving effect to any order of the court under subsection (5) of section three of this Act.

AMENDMENT
Sub-s (1): repealed by the Local Land Charges Act 1975, s 19, Sch 2.
Sub-s (2): words in square brackets substituted by the Local Land Charges Act 1975, s 17(2), Sch 1.

**6 . . .**

. . .

AMENDMENT
Repealed by the Northern Ireland Constitution Act 1973, s 41(1), Sch 6, Pt I.

## 7 INTERPRETATION

(1) In this Act, except in so far as the context otherwise requires, the following expressions have the meanings hereby assigned to them respectively, that is to say:—

"action" includes a counterclaim, and any reference to the plaintiff in an action shall be construed accordingly;

[. . .]

"owner", in relation to any land, means a person who is the estate owner in respect of the fee simple thereof, or is entitled to a tenancy thereof (within the meaning of the Landlord and Tenant Act 1954) for a term of years certain of which, at the time in question, not less than seven years remain unexpired, or is a mortgagee in possession (within the meaning of the Law of Property Act 1925) where the interest mortgaged is either the fee simple of the land or such a tenancy thereof;

["prescribed" means prescribed by rules under section 14 of the Local Land Charges Act 1975].

(2) References in this Act to any enactment shall, except where the context otherwise requires, be construed as references to that enactment as amended by or under any other enactment.

**AMENDMENT**

Sub-s (1): definition "local authority" (omitted) substituted by the Local Land Charges Act 1975, s 17(2), Sch 1.

Sub-s (1): definition "local authority" (omitted) repealed by the Infrastructure Act 2015, s 34(1), (2)(c), Sch 5, Pt 3, paras 27, 30(b).

Sub-s (1): definition "prescribed" substituted by the Infrastructure Act 2015, s 34(1), (2)(c), Sch 5, Pt 3, paras 27, 30(a).

## 8 SHORT TITLE, COMMENCEMENT AND EXTENT

(1) This Act may be cited as the Rights of Light Act 1959.

(2) This Act, except sections one and six thereof, shall come into operation at the end of the period of three months beginning with the day on which it is passed.

(3) This Act shall not extend to Scotland.

(4) This Act, . . . , shall not extend to Northern Ireland.

**AMENDMENT**

Sub-s (4): words omitted repealed by the Northern Ireland Constitution Act 1973, s 41(1), Sch 6.

# C4   Local Land Charges Act 1975 (1975 c 76), Extracts

## DEFINITION OF LOCAL LAND CHARGES

### 1 LOCAL LAND CHARGES

(1)   A charge or other matter affecting land is a local land charge if it falls within any of the following descriptions and is not one of the matters set out in section 2 below:—

   (a)   any charge acquired either before or after the commencement of this Act by a local authority [or National Park authority], water authority [sewerage undertaker] or new town development corporation under the Public Health Acts 1936 and 1937, . . . the Public Health Act 1961 or [the Highways Act 1980 (or any Act repealed by that Act)] [or the Building Act 1984], or any similar charge acquired by a local authority [or National Park authority] under any other Act, whether passed before or after this Act, being a charge that is binding on successive owners of the land affected;

   (b)   any prohibition of or restriction on the use of land—

      (i)   imposed by a local authority [or National Park authority] on or after 1st January 1926 (including any prohibition or restriction embodied in any condition attached to a consent, approval or licence granted by a local authority on or after that date), or

      (ii)   enforceable by a local authority [or National Park authority] under any covenant or agreement made with them on or after that date,

   being a prohibition or restriction binding on successive owners of the land affected;

   (c)   any prohibition of or restriction on the use of land—

      (i)   imposed by a Minister of the Crown or government department on or after the date of the commencement of this Act (including any prohibition or restriction embodied in any condition attached to a consent, approval or licence granted by such a Minister or department on or after that date), or

(ii) enforceable by such a Minister or department under any covenant or agreement made with him or them on or after that date, being a prohibition or restriction binding on successive owners of the land affected;

(d) any positive obligation affecting land enforceable by a Minister of the Crown, government department or local authority [or National Park authority] under any covenant or agreement made with him or them on or after the date of the commencement of this Act and binding on successive owners of the land affected;

(e) any charge or other matter which is expressly made a local land charge by any statutory provision not contained in this section.

**AMENDMENT**
Sub-s (1): words "or National Park authority" wherever they occur inserted by the Environment Act 1995, s 78, Sch 10, para 14; second words in square brackets inserted by the Water Act 1989, s 190, Sch 25, para 52; words omitted repealed and third words in square brackets substituted by the Highways Act 1980, s 343(2), Sch 24, para 26; fourth words in square brackets inserted by the Building Act 1984, s 133(1), Sch 6, para 16.

## [3 THE LOCAL LAND CHARGES REGISTER]

[(1) The Chief Land Registrar must keep the local land charges register.

(2) The local land charges register is a register of—

(a) each local land charge registered in a local land charges register for a local authority's area immediately before this section first had effect in relation to that area, and

(b) each local land charge subsequently registered under section 5 or 6 or another relevant enactment in respect of land which is wholly or partly within that area.

(3) Subsection (2) is subject to any later variation or cancellation of the registration of the local land charge.

(4) The local land charges register may be kept in electronic form.

(5)  In this section—

"local authority" means—

    (a)  a district council,

    (b)  a county council in England for an area for which there is no district council,

    (c)  a county council in Wales,

    (d)  a county borough council,

    (e)  a London borough council,

    (f)  the Common Council of the City of London, or

    (g)  the Council of the Isles of Scilly;

"relevant enactment" means a provision which is made by or under an Act and which provides for the registration of a charge or other matter as a local land charge.

(6)  For the purposes of this section the area of the Common Council of the City of London includes the Inner Temple and the Middle Temple.]

**AMENDMENT**
Substituted by the Infrastructure Act 2015, s 34(1), (2)(a), Sch 5, Pt 1, paras 1, 3.
Sub-s (1): paras (aa), (ab) inserted by the Local Government (Wales) Act 1994, s 66(6), Sch 16, para 49.
Sub-s (3): substituted by the Local Government (Miscellaneous Provisions) Act 1982, s 34(a).


**4 . . .**

. . .


**AMENDMENT**
Repealed by the Infrastructure Act 2015, s 34(1), (2)(a), Sch 5, Pt 1, paras 2, 4.

## 5 REGISTRATION

(1) ...

[(2) Subject to subsection (6) below, the originating authority as respects a local land charge must apply to the Chief Land Registrar for its registration in the local land charges register; and on the application being made the Chief Land Registrar must register the charge accordingly.

(3) The registration in the local land charges register of a local land charge, or of any matter which when registered becomes a local land charge, must be carried out by reference to the land affected.]

(4) In this Act, "the originating authority", as respects a local land charge, means the Minister of the Crown, government department, local authority or other person by whom the charge is brought into existence or by whom, on its coming into existence, the charge is enforceable; and for this purpose—

    (a) where a matter that is a local land charge consists of or is embodied in, or is otherwise given effect by, an order, scheme or other instrument made or confirmed by a Minister of the Crown or government department on the application of another authority the charge shall be treated as brought into existence by that other authority; and

    (b) a local land charge brought into existence by a Minister of the Crown or government department on an appeal from a decision or determination of another authority or in the exercise of powers ordinarily exercisable by another authority shall be treated as brought into existence by that other authority.

(5) The registration of a local land charge may be cancelled pursuant to an order of the court.

(6) Where a charge or other matter is registrable in [the local land charges register] and before the commencement of this Act was also registrable in a register kept under the Land Charges Act 1972, then, if before the commencement of this Act it was registered in a register kept under that Act, there shall be no duty to register it, or to apply for its registration, under this Act and section 10 below shall not apply in relation to it.

**AMENDMENT**

Sub-s (1): repealed by the Infrastructure Act 2015, s 34(1), (2)(a), Sch 5, Pt 1, paras 1, 5(1), (2).

Sub-ss (2), (3): substituted by the Infrastructure Act 2015, s 34(1), (2)(a), Sch 5, Pt 1, paras 1, 5(1), (3).

Sub-s (6): words "the local land charges register" in square brackets substituted by the Infrastructure Act 2015, s 34(1), (2)(a), Sch 5, Pt 1, paras 1, 5(1), (4).

## SEARCHES

### 8 PERSONAL SEARCHES

(1)   Any person may search in [the local land charges register] on paying the prescribed fee [(if any)].

[(1A)   If [the local land charges register is kept in electronic] form, the entitlement of a person to search in it is satisfied if the [Chief Land Registrar] makes the portion of it which he wishes to examine available for inspection in visible and legible form.]

(2)   Without prejudice to [subsections (1) and (1A)] above, [the Chief Land Registrar] may provide facilities for enabling persons entitled to search in the . . . local land charges register to see photographic or other images or copies of any portion of the register which they may wish to examine.

**AMENDMENT**

Sub-s (1): words "the local land charges register" in square brackets substituted by the Infrastructure Act 2015, s 34(1), (2)(a), Sch 5, Pt 1, paras 1, 7(1), (2)(a).

Sub-s (1): words "(if any)" in square brackets inserted by the Infrastructure Act 2015, s 34(1), (2)(a), Sch 5, Pt 1, paras 1, 7(1), (2)(b).

Sub-s (1A): inserted by the Local Government (Miscellaneous Provisions) Act 1982, s 34(b).

Sub-s (1A): words "the local land charges register is kept in electronic" in square brackets substituted by the Infrastructure Act 2015, s 34(1), (2)(a), Sch 5, Pt 1, paras 1, 7(1), (3)(a).

Sub-s (1A): words "Chief Land Registrar" in square brackets substituted by the Infrastructure Act 2015, s 34(1), (2)(a), Sch 5, Pt 1, paras 1, 7(1), (3)(b).

Sub-s (2): words in square brackets substituted by the Local Government (Miscellaneous Provisions) Act 1982, s 34(c).

Sub-s (2): words "the Chief Land Registrar" in square brackets substituted by the Infrastructure Act 2015, s 34(1), (2)(a), Sch 5, Pt 1, paras 1, 7(1), (4)(a).

Sub-s (2): word omitted repealed by the Infrastructure Act 2015, s 34(1), (2)(a), Sch 5, Pt 1, paras 1, 7(1), (4)(b).

## 9 OFFICIAL SEARCHES

(1) Where any person requires an official search of the . . . local land charges register to be made in respect of any land, he may make a requisition in that behalf to the [Chief Land Registrar].

(2) . . .

[(3) The prescribed fee (if any) shall be payable in the prescribed manner in respect of any requisition made under this section.]

(4) Where a requisition is made to [the Chief Land Registrar] under this section and the fee [(if any)] payable in respect of it is paid in accordance with subsection (3) [. . .] above, [the Chief Land Registrar] shall thereupon make the search required and shall issue an official certificate setting out the result of the search.

### AMENDMENT

Sub-s (1): word omitted repealed by the Infrastructure Act 2015, s 34(1), (2)(a), Sch 5, Pt 1, paras 1, 8(1), (2)(a).

Sub-s (1): words "Chief Land Registrar" in square brackets substituted by the Infrastructure Act 2015, s 34(1), (2)(a), Sch 5, Pt 1, paras 1, 8(1), (2)(b).

Sub-s (2): repealed by the Infrastructure Act 2015, s 34(1), (2)(a), Sch 5, Pt 1, paras 1, 8(1), (3).

Sub-s (3): substituted, for sub-ss (3), (3A), by the Infrastructure Act 2015, s 34(1), (2)(a), Sch 5, Pt 1, paras 1, 8(1), (4).

Sub-s (4): words "the Chief Land Registrar" in square brackets substituted by the Infrastructure Act 2015, s 34(1), (2)(a), Sch 5, Pt 1, paras 1, 8(1), (5)(a).

Sub-s (4): words "(if any)" in square brackets inserted by the Constitutional Reform Act 2005, s 15(1), Sch 4, Pt 1, paras 82, 84(1), (3)(a).

Sub-s (4): words omitted in square brackets inserted by the Constitutional Reform Act 2005, s 15(1), Sch 4, Pt 1, paras 82, 84(1), (3)(b).

Sub-s (4): words omitted repealed by the Infrastructure Act 2015, s 34(1), (2)(a), Sch 5, Pt 1, paras 1, 8(1), (5)(b).

Sub-s (4): words "the Chief Land Registrar" in square brackets substituted by the Infrastructure Act 2015, s 34(1), (2)(a), Sch 5, Pt 1, paras 1, 8(1), (5)(c).

## COMPENSATION FOR NON-REGISTRATION OR DEFECTIVE OFFICIAL SEARCH CERTIFICATE

### 10 COMPENSATION FOR NON-REGISTRATION OR DEFECTIVE OFFICIAL SEARCH CERTIFICATE

(1)  Failure to register a local land charge in the . . . local land charges register shall not affect the enforceability of the charge but where a person has purchased any land affected by a local land charge, then—

(a)  in a case where a material personal search of the . . . local land charges register was made in respect of the land in question before the relevant time, if at the time of the search the charge was in existence but not registered in that register; or

[(aa) [if] the . . . local land charges register kept [in electronic] form and a material personal search of that register was made in respect of the land in question before the relevant time, if the entitlement to search in that register conferred by section 8 above was not satisfied as mentioned in subsection (1A) of that section; or]

(b)  in a case where a material official search of the . . . local land charges register was made in respect of the land in question before the relevant time, if the charge was in existence at the time of the search but (whether registered or not) was not shown by the official search certificate as registered in that register,

the purchaser shall (subject to section 11(1) below) be entitled to compensation for any loss suffered by him [in consequence].

(2)  . . .

(3)  For the purposes of this section—

    (a)  a person purchases land where, for valuable consideration, he acquires any interest in land or the proceeds of sale of land, and this includes cases where he acquires as lessee or mortgagee and shall be treated as including cases where an interest is conveyed or assigned at his direction to another person;

    (b)  the relevant time—

        (i)  where the acquisition of the interest in question was preceded by a contract for its acquisition, other than a qualified liability contract, is the time when that contract was made;

        (ii)  in any other case, is the time when the purchaser acquired the interest in question or, if he acquired it under a disposition which took effect only when registered [in the register of title kept under the Land Registration Act 2002], the time when that disposition was made; and for the purposes of sub-paragraph (i) above, a qualified liability contract is a contract containing a term the effect of which is to make the liability of the purchaser dependent upon, or avoidable by reference to, the outcome of a search for local land charges affecting the land to be purchased;

    (c)  a personal search is material if, but only if—

        (i)  it is made after the commencement of this Act, and

        (ii)  it is made by or on behalf of the purchaser or, before the relevant time, the purchaser or his agent has knowledge of the result of it;

    (d)  an official search is material if, but only if—

        (i)  it is made after the commencement of this Act, and

        (ii)  it is requisitioned by or on behalf of the purchaser or, before the relevant time, the purchaser or his agent has knowledge of the contents of the official search certificate.

(4)  Any compensation for loss under this section shall be paid by the [Chief Land Registrar]; and where the purchaser has incurred expenditure for the purpose of obtaining compensation under this section, the amount of the compensation shall include the amount of

the expenditure reasonably incurred by him for that purpose (so far as that expenditure would not otherwise fall to be treated as loss for which he is entitled to compensation under this section).

(5) Where any compensation for loss under this section is paid by [the Chief Land Registrar], then, unless an application for registration of the charge was made to [the Chief Land Registrar] by the originating authority in time for it to be practicable for [the Chief Land Registrar] to avoid incurring liability to pay that compensation, an amount equal thereto shall be recoverable from the originating authority by [the Chief Land Registrar].

[(5A) An amount equal to any compensation paid under this section by the Chief Land Registrar in respect of a local land charge is also recoverable from the originating authority in a case where the matter within subsection (1) giving rise to the Chief Land Registrar's liability is a consequence of—

(a) an error made by the originating authority in applying to register the local land charge, or

(b) an error made by the originating authority in applying for the registration of the local land charge to be varied or cancelled.]

(6) Where any compensation for loss under this section is paid by [the Chief Land Registrar], no part of the amount paid, or of any corresponding amount paid to [the Chief Land Registrar] by the originating authority under subsection (5) [or (5A)] above, shall be recoverable by [the Chief Land Registrar] or the originating authority from any other person except as provided by subsection (5) [or (5A)] above or under a policy of insurance or on grounds of fraud.

[(6A) The Chief Land Registrar may insure against the risk of liability to pay compensation under this section.]

(7) In the case of an action to recover compensation under this section the cause of action shall be deemed for the purposes of the [Limitation Act 1980] to accrue at the time when the local land charge comes to the notice of the purchaser; and for the purposes of this subsection the question when the charge came to his notice shall be determined without regard to the provisions of section 198 of the Law of Property Act 1925 (under which registration under certain enactments is deemed to constitute actual notice).

[(8) Where the amount claimed by way of compensation under this section does not exceed £5,000, proceedings for the recovery of such compensation may be begun in [the county court].]

(9) If in any proceedings for the recovery of compensation under this section the court dismisses a claim to compensation, it shall not order the purchaser to pay the [Chief Land Registrar's] costs unless it considers that it was unreasonable for the purchaser to commence the proceedings.

**AMENDMENT**

Sub-s (1): word omitted in each place it occurs repealed by the Infrastructure Act 2015, s 34(1), (2)(a), Sch 5, Pt 1, paras 1, 9(1), (2)(a).

Sub-s (1): para (aa) inserted and other words in square brackets substituted by the Local Government (Miscellaneous Provisions) Act 1982, s 34(d).

Sub-s (1): in para (aa) word "if" in square brackets substituted by the Infrastructure Act 2015, s 34(1), (2)(a), Sch 5, Pt 1, paras 1, 9(1), (2)(b).

Sub-s (1): in para (aa) words "in electronic" in square brackets substituted by the Infrastructure Act 2015, s 34(1), (2)(a), Sch 5, Pt 1, paras 1, 9(1), (2)(c).

Sub-s (2): repealed by the Infrastructure Act 2015, s 34(1), (2)(a), Sch 5, Pt 1, paras 1, 9(1), (3).

Sub-s (3): in para (b)(ii) words "in the register of title kept under the Land Registration Act 2002" in square brackets substituted by the Land Registration Act 2002, s 133, Sch 11, para 13.

Sub-s (4): words "Chief Land Registrar" in square brackets substituted by the Infrastructure Act 2015, s 34(1), (2)(a), Sch 5, Pt 1, paras 1, 9(1), (4).

Sub-s (5): first words "the Chief Land Registrar" in square brackets substituted by the Infrastructure Act 2015, s 34(1), (2)(a), Sch 5, Pt 1, paras 1, 9(1), (5)(a).

Sub-s (5): second, third and final words "the Chief Land Registrar" in square brackets in each place they occur substituted by the Infrastructure Act 2015, s 34(1), (2)(a), Sch 5, Pt 1, paras 1, 9(1), (5)(b).

Sub-s (5A): inserted by the Infrastructure Act 2015, s 34(1), (2)(a), Sch 5, Pt 1, paras 1, 9(1), (6).

Sub-s (6): first words "the Chief Land Registrar" in square brackets substituted by the Infrastructure Act 2015, s 34(1), (2)(a), Sch 5, Pt 1, paras 1, 9(1), (7)(a).

Sub-s (6): second words "the Chief Land Registrar" in square brackets substituted by the Infrastructure Act 2015, s 34(1), (2)(a), Sch 5, Pt 1, paras 1, 9(1), (7)(b).

Sub-s (6): words "or (5A)" in square brackets in each place they occur inserted by the Infrastructure Act 2015, s 34(1), (2)(a), Sch 5, Pt 1, paras 1, 9(1), (7)(c).

Sub-s (6): final words "the Chief Land Registrar" in square brackets substituted by the Infrastructure Act 2015, s 34(1), (2)(a), Sch 5, Pt 1, paras 1, 9(1), (7)(d).

Sub-s (6A): inserted by the Infrastructure Act 2015, s 34(1), (2)(a), Sch 5, Pt 1, paras 1, 9(1), (8).

Sub-s (7): words "Limitation Act 1980" in square brackets substituted by the Infrastructure Act 2015, s 34(1), (2)(a), Sch 5, Pt 1, paras 1, 9(1), (9).

Sub-s (8): substituted for existing sub-ss (8), (8A), by SI 1991/724, art 2(2)(a), (8), Schedule, Part I.

Sub-s (8): words "the county court" in square brackets substituted by the Crime and Courts Act 2013, s 17(5), Sch 9, Pt 3, para 52(1)(b), (2).

Sub-s (9): words "Chief Land Registrar's" in square brackets substituted by the Infrastructure Act 2015, s 34(1), (2)(a), Sch 5, Pt 1, paras 1, 9(1), (10).

## 11 MORTGAGES, TRUSTS FOR SALE AND SETTLED LAND

(1) Where there appear to be grounds for a claim under section 10 above in respect of an interest that is subject to a mortgage—

   (a) the claim may be made by any mortgagee of the interest as if he were the person entitled to that interest but without prejudice to the making of a claim by that person;

   (b) no compensation shall be payable under that section in respect of the interest of the mortgagee (as distinct from the interest which is subject to the mortgage);

   (c) any compensation payable under that section in respect of the interest that is subject to the mortgage shall be paid to the mortgagee or, if there is more than one mortgagee, to the first mortgagee and shall in either case be applied by him as if it were proceeds of sale.

(2) Where an interest is [subject to a trust of land] any compensation payable in respect of it under section 10 above shall be dealt with as if it were proceeds of sale arising under the trust.

(3) Where an interest is settled land for the purposes of the Settled Land Act 1925 any compensation payable in respect of it under section 10 above shall be treated as capital money arising under that Act.

**AMENDMENT**
Sub-s (2): words in square brackets substituted by the Trusts of Land and Appointment of Trustees Act 1996, s 25(1), Sch 3, para 14; for savings in relation to entailed interests created before the commencement of that Act, and savings consequential upon the abolition of the doctrine of conversion, see s 25(4), (5) thereof.

# C5  Senior Courts Act 1981 (1981 c 54), Extracts

## AMENDMENT

Act: The Supreme Court Act 1981 (c 54) may be cited as the Senior Courts
   Act 1981 (1.10.2009) by virtue of the Constitutional Reform Act 2005
   (c 4), ss 59, 148, Sch 11 para 1(1); Constitutional Reform Act 2005
   (Commencement No 11) Order 2009, SI 2009/1604, art 2(d).

## 37 POWERS OF HIGH COURT WITH RESPECT TO INJUNCTIONS AND RECEIVERS

(1)  The High Court may by order (whether interlocutory or final) grant
     an injunction or appoint a receiver in all cases in which it appears to
     the court to be just and convenient to do so.

(2)  Any such order may be made either unconditionally or on such terms
     and conditions as the court thinks just.

(3)  The power of the High Court under subsection (1) to grant an
     interlocutory injunction restraining a party to any proceedings from
     removing from the jurisdiction of the High Court, or otherwise
     dealing with, assets located within that jurisdiction shall be
     exercisable in cases where that party is, as well as in cases where he
     is not, domiciled, resident or present within that jurisdiction.

(4)  The power of the High Court to appoint a receiver by way of equitable
     execution shall operate in relation to all legal estates and interests in
     land; and that power—

     (a)  may be exercised in relation to an estate or interest in land
          whether or not a charge has been imposed on that land under
          section 1 of the Charging Orders Act 1979 for the purpose of
          enforcing the judgment, order or award in question; and

     (b)  shall be in addition to, and not in derogation of, any power of
          any court to appoint a receiver in proceedings for enforcing such
          a charge.

(5)  Where an order under the said section 1 imposing a charge for the
     purpose of enforcing a judgment, order or award has been, or has
     effect as if, registered under section 6 of the Land Charges Act 1972,
     subsection (4) of the said section 6 (effect of non-registration of writs

and orders registrable under that section) shall not apply to an order appointing a receiver made either—

(a) in proceedings for enforcing the charge; or

(b) by way of equitable execution of the judgment, order or award or, as the case may be, of so much of it as requires payment of moneys secured by the charge.

[(6) This section applies in relation to the family court as it applies in relation to the High Court.]

**AMENDMENT**
Sub-s (6): inserted by the Crime and Courts Act 2013, s 17(6), Sch 10, Pt 2, paras 54, 58.

## 50 POWER TO AWARD DAMAGES AS WELL AS, OR IN SUBSTITUTION FOR, INJUNCTION OR SPECIFIC PERFORMANCE

Where the Court of Appeal or the High Court has jurisdiction to entertain an application for an injunction or specific performance, it may award damages in addition to, or in substitution for, an injunction or specific performance.

# C6 Town and Country Planning Act 1990 (1990 c 8), Extract

### 237 POWER TO OVERRIDE EASEMENTS AND OTHER RIGHTS

(1) Subject to subsection (3), the erection, construction or carrying out or maintenance of any building or work on land which has been acquired or appropriated by a local authority for planning purposes (whether done by the local authority or by a person deriving title under them) is authorised by virtue of this section if it is done in accordance with planning permission, notwithstanding that it involves—

 (a) interference with an interest or right to which this section applies, or

 (b) a breach of a restriction as to the user of land arising by virtue of a contract.

[(1A) Subject to subsection (3), the use of any land in England which has been acquired or appropriated by a local authority for planning purposes (whether the use is by the local authority or by a person deriving title under them) is authorised by virtue of this section if it is in accordance with planning permission even if the use involves—

 (a) interference with an interest or right to which this section applies, or

 (b) a breach of a restriction as to the user of land arising by virtue of a contract.]

(2) Subject to subsection (3), the interests and rights to which this section applies are any easement, liberty, privilege, right or advantage annexed to land and adversely affecting other land, including any natural right to support.

(3) Nothing in this section shall authorise interference with any right of way or right of laying down, erecting, continuing or maintaining apparatus on, under or over land which is—

 (a) a right vested in or belonging to statutory undertakers for the purpose of the carrying on of their undertaking, or

(b) a right conferred by or in accordance with the [electronic communications code] on the operator of [an electronic communications code network].

(4) In respect of any interference or breach in pursuance of subsection (1) [or (1A)], compensation—

(a) shall be payable under section 63 or 68 of the Lands Clauses Consolidation Act 1845 or under section 7 or 10 of the Compulsory Purchase Act 1965, and

(b) shall be assessed in the same manner and subject to the same rules as in the case of other compensation under those sections in respect of injurious affection where—

(i) the compensation is to be estimated in connection with a purchase under those Acts, or

(ii) the injury arises from the execution of works on[, or use of,] land acquired under those Acts.

(5) Where a person deriving title under the local authority by whom the land in question was acquired or appropriated—

(a) is liable to pay compensation by virtue of subsection (4), and

(b) fails to discharge that liability,

the liability shall be enforceable against the local authority.

(6) Nothing in subsection (5) shall be construed as affecting any agreement between the local authority and any other person for indemnifying the local authority against any liability under that subsection.

(7) Nothing in this section shall be construed as authorising any act or omission on the part of any person which is actionable at the suit of any person on any grounds other than such an interference or breach as is mentioned in subsection (1) [or (1A)].

**AMENDMENT**

Sub-s (1A): inserted by the Planning Act 2008, s 194(1), Sch 9, para 4(1), (2).

Sub-s (3): in para (b) words "electronic communications code" in square brackets substituted by the Communications Act 2003, s 406(1), Sch 17, para 103(1)(b), (2)(a).

Sub-s (3): in para (b) words "an electronic communications code network" in square brackets substituted by the Communications Act 2003, s 406(1), Sch 17, para 103(1)(b), (2)(b).

Sub-s (4): words "or (1A)" in square brackets inserted by the Planning Act 2008, s 194(1), Sch 9, para 4(1), (3)(a).

Sub-s (4): in para (b)(ii) words ", or use of," in square brackets inserted by the Planning Act 2008, s 194(1), Sch 9, para 4(1), (3)(b).

Sub-s (7): words "or (1A)" in square brackets inserted by the Planning Act 2008, s 194(1), Sch 9, para 4(1), (4).

# C7  Party Wall etc Act 1996 (1996 c 40), Extract

## 9 EASEMENTS

Nothing in this Act shall—

(a) authorise any interference with an easement of light or other easements in or relating to a party wall; or

(b) prejudicially affect any right of any person to preserve or restore any right or other thing in or connected with a party wall in case of the party wall being pulled down or rebuilt.

# C8 Land Registration Act 2002 (2002 c 9), Extracts

## EFFECT OF FIRST REGISTRATION

### 11 FREEHOLD ESTATES

(1) This section is concerned with the registration of a person under this Chapter as the proprietor of a freehold estate.

(2) Registration with absolute title has the effect described in subsections (3) to (5).

(3) The estate is vested in the proprietor together with all interests subsisting for the benefit of the estate.

(4) The estate is vested in the proprietor subject only to the following interests affecting the estate at the time of registration—

(a) interests which are the subject of an entry in the register in relation to the estate,

(b) unregistered interests which fall within any of the paragraphs of Schedule 1, and

(c) interests acquired under the Limitation Act 1980 (c 58) of which the proprietor has notice.

(5) If the proprietor is not entitled to the estate for his own benefit, or not entitled solely for his own benefit, then, as between himself and the persons beneficially entitled to the estate, the estate is vested in him subject to such of their interests as he has notice of.

(6) Registration with qualified title has the same effect as registration with absolute title, except that it does not affect the enforcement of any estate, right or interest which appears from the register to be excepted from the effect of registration.

(7) Registration with possessory title has the same effect as registration with absolute title, except that it does not affect the enforcement of any estate, right or interest adverse to, or in derogation of, the proprietor's title subsisting at the time of registration or then capable of arising.

**MODIFICATION**

Sub-s (4) modified, in relation to incorporeal hereditaments, by the Land Registration Rules 2003, SI 2003/1417, r 196B.

## 12 LEASEHOLD ESTATES

(1) This section is concerned with the registration of a person under this Chapter as the proprietor of a leasehold estate.

(2) Registration with absolute title has the effect described in subsections (3) to (5).

(3) The estate is vested in the proprietor together with all interests subsisting for the benefit of the estate.

(4) The estate is vested subject only to the following interests affecting the estate at the time of registration—

    (a) implied and express covenants, obligations and liabilities incident to the estate,

    (b) interests which are the subject of an entry in the register in relation to the estate,

    (c) unregistered interests which fall within any of the paragraphs of Schedule 1, and

    (d) interests acquired under the Limitation Act 1980 (c 58) of which the proprietor has notice.

(5) If the proprietor is not entitled to the estate for his own benefit, or not entitled solely for his own benefit, then, as between himself and the persons beneficially entitled to the estate, the estate is vested in him subject to such of their interests as he has notice of.

(6) Registration with good leasehold title has the same effect as registration with absolute title, except that it does not affect the enforcement of any estate, right or interest affecting, or in derogation of, the title of the lessor to grant the lease.

(7) Registration with qualified title has the same effect as registration with absolute title except that it does not affect the enforcement of any estate, right or interest which appears from the register to be excepted from the effect of registration.

(8) Registration with possessory title has the same effect as registration with absolute title, except that it does not affect the enforcement of any estate, right or interest adverse to, or in derogation of, the proprietor's title subsisting at the time of registration or then capable of arising.

**MODIFICATION**
Sub-s (4) modified, in relation to incorporeal hereditaments, by the Land Registration Rules 2003, SI 2003/1417, r 196B.

## REGISTRABLE DISPOSITIONS

## 27 DISPOSITIONS REQUIRED TO BE REGISTERED

(1) If a disposition of a registered estate or registered charge is required to be completed by registration, it does not operate at law until the relevant registration requirements are met.

(2) In the case of a registered estate, the following are the dispositions which are required to be completed by registration—

(a) a transfer,

(b) where the registered estate is an estate in land, the grant of a term of years absolute—

(i) for a term of more than seven years from the date of the grant,

(ii) to take effect in possession after the end of the period of three months beginning with the date of the grant,

(iii) under which the right to possession is discontinuous,

(iv) in pursuance of Part 5 of the Housing Act 1985 (c 68) (the right to buy), or

(v) in circumstances where section 171A of that Act applies (disposal by landlord which leads to a person no longer being a secure tenant),

(c) where the registered estate is a franchise or manor, the grant of a lease,

(d) the express grant or reservation of an interest of a kind falling within section 1(2)(a) of the Law of Property Act 1925 (c 20), other than one which is capable of being registered under the Commons Registration Act 1965 (c 64) [Part 1 of the Commons Act 2006],

(e) the express grant or reservation of an interest of a kind falling within section 1(2)(b) or (e) of the Law of Property Act 1925, and

(f) the grant of a legal charge.

(3) In the case of a registered charge, the following are the dispositions which are required to be completed by registration—

(a) a transfer, and

(b) the grant of a sub-charge.

(4) Schedule 2 to this Act (which deals with the relevant registration requirements) has effect.

(5) This section applies to dispositions by operation of law as it applies to other dispositions, but with the exception of the following—

(a) a transfer on the death or bankruptcy of an individual proprietor,

(b) a transfer on the dissolution of a corporate proprietor, and

(c) the creation of a legal charge which is a local land charge.

[(5A) This section does not apply to—

(a) the grant of a term of years absolute under a relevant social housing tenancy, or

(b) the express grant of an interest falling within section 1(2) of the Law of Property Act 1925, where the interest is created for the benefit of a leasehold estate in land under a relevant social housing tenancy.]

(6) Rules may make provision about applications to the registrar for the purpose of meeting registration requirements under this section.

(7) In subsection (2)(d), the reference to express grant does not include grant as a result of the operation of section 62 of the Law of Property Act 1925 (c 20).

**AMENDMENT**
Sub-s (2): in para (d) words "the Commons Registration Act 1965 (c 64)"
  in italics repealed and subsequent words in square brackets substituted
  by the Commons Act 2006, s 52, Sch 5, para 8(1), (2).
Sub-s (5A): inserted by the Localism Act 2011, s 157(1), (4).

## PART 4 NOTICES AND RESTRICTIONS
### NOTICES

## 32 NATURE AND EFFECT

(1)  A notice is an entry in the register in respect of the burden of an
     interest affecting a registered estate or charge.

(2)  The entry of a notice is to be made in relation to the registered estate
     or charge affected by the interest concerned.

(3)  The fact that an interest is the subject of a notice does not necessarily
     mean that the interest is valid, but does mean that the priority of the
     interest, if valid, is protected for the purposes of sections 29 and 30.

## 34 ENTRY ON APPLICATION

(1)  A person who claims to be entitled to the benefit of an interest
     affecting a registered estate or charge may, if the interest is not
     excluded by section 33, apply to the registrar for the entry in the
     register of a notice in respect of the interest.

(2)  Subject to rules, an application under this section may be for—

     (a)  an agreed notice, or

     (b)  a unilateral notice.

(3)  The registrar may only approve an application for an agreed notice
     if—

     (a)  the applicant is the relevant registered proprietor, or a person
          entitled to be registered as such proprietor,

     (b)  the relevant registered proprietor, or a person entitled to be
          registered as such proprietor, consents to the entry of the notice,
          or

     (c)  the registrar is satisfied as to the validity of the applicant's claim.

(4)  In subsection (3), references to the relevant registered proprietor are to the proprietor of the registered estate or charge affected by the interest to which the application relates.

## 35 UNILATERAL NOTICES

(1)  If the registrar enters a notice in the register in pursuance of an application under section 34(2)(b) ("a unilateral notice"), he must give notice of the entry to—

  (a)  the proprietor of the registered estate or charge to which it relates, and

  (b)  such other persons as rules may provide.

(2)  A unilateral notice must—

  (a)  indicate that it is such a notice, and

  (b)  identify who is the beneficiary of the notice.

(3)  The person shown in the register as the beneficiary of a unilateral notice, or such other person as rules may provide, may apply to the registrar for the removal of the notice from the register.

## 36 CANCELLATION OF UNILATERAL NOTICES

(1)  A person may apply to the registrar for the cancellation of a unilateral notice if he is—

  (a)  the registered proprietor of the estate or charge to which the notice relates, or

  (b)  a person entitled to be registered as the proprietor of that estate or charge.

(2)  Where an application is made under subsection (1), the registrar must give the beneficiary of the notice notice of the application and of the effect of subsection (3).

(3)  If the beneficiary of the notice does not exercise his right to object to the application before the end of such period as rules may provide, the registrar must cancel the notice.

(4) In this section—

"beneficiary", in relation to a unilateral notice, means the person shown in the register as the beneficiary of the notice, or such other person as rules may provide;

"unilateral notice" means a notice entered in the register in pursuance of an application under section 34(2)(b).

## 38 REGISTRABLE DISPOSITIONS

Where a person is entered in the register as the proprietor of an interest under a disposition falling within section 27(2)(b) to (e), the registrar must also enter a notice in the register in respect of that interest.

## SCHEDULE 1
## UNREGISTERED INTERESTS WHICH OVERRIDE FIRST REGISTRATION

Sections 11 and 12

## 3
## EASEMENTS AND PROFITS A PRENDRE

A legal easement or profit a prendre.

## 6
## LOCAL LAND CHARGES

A local land charge.

## SCHEDULE 3
## UNREGISTERED INTERESTS WHICH OVERRIDE REGISTERED DISPOSITIONS

Sections 29 and 30

### LEASEHOLD ESTATES IN LAND

**1**

A leasehold estate in land granted for a term not exceeding seven years from the date of the grant, except for—

(a)  a lease the grant of which falls within section 4(1)(d), (e) or (f);

(b)  a lease the grant of which constitutes a registrable disposition.

**3**

(1)  A legal easement or profit a prendre, except for an easement, or a profit a prendre which is not registered under the Commons Registration Act 1965 (c 64) [Part 1 of the Commons Act 2006], which at the time of the disposition—

(a)  is not within the actual knowledge of the person to whom the disposition is made, and

(b)  would not have been obvious on a reasonably careful inspection of the land over which the easement or profit is exercisable.

(2)  The exception in sub-paragraph (1) does not apply if the person entitled to the easement or profit proves that it has been exercised in the period of one year ending with the day of the disposition.

**AMENDMENT**
Para 3: in sub-para (1) words "the Commons Registration Act 1965 (c 64)" in italics repealed and subsequent words in square brackets substituted by the Commons Act 2006, s 52, Sch 5, para 8(1), (4).

SCHEDULE 12
TRANSITION

Section 134

**8**

Schedule 3 has effect with the insertion after paragraph 2 of—

**"2A**

(1) An interest which, immediately before the coming into force of this Schedule, was an overriding interest under section 70(1)(g) of the Land Registration Act 1925 by virtue of a person's receipt of rents and profits, except for an interest of a person of whom inquiry was made before the disposition and who failed to disclose the right when he could reasonably have been expected to do so.

(2) Sub-paragraph (1) does not apply to an interest if at any time since the coming into force of this Schedule it has been an interest which, had the Land Registration Act 1925 (c 21) continued in force, would not have been an overriding interest under section 70(1)(g) of that Act by virtue of a person's receipt of rents and profits."

**9**

(1) This paragraph applies to an easement or profit a prendre which was an overriding interest in relation to a registered estate immediately before the coming into force of Schedule 3, but which would not fall within paragraph 3 of that Schedule if created after the coming into force of that Schedule.

(2) In relation to an interest to which this paragraph applies, Schedule 3 has effect as if the interest were not excluded from paragraph 3.

**10**

For the period of three years beginning with the day on which Schedule 3 comes into force, paragraph 3 of the Schedule has effect with the omission of the exception.

# C9 Anti-social Behaviour Act 2003 (2003 c 38), Extracts

PART 8
HIGH HEDGES
INTRODUCTORY

## 65 COMPLAINTS TO WHICH THIS PART APPLIES

(1) This Part applies to a complaint which—

    (a) is made for the purposes of this Part by an owner or occupier of a domestic property; and

    (b) alleges that his reasonable enjoyment of that property is being adversely affected by the height of a high hedge situated on land owned or occupied by another person.

(2) This Part also applies to a complaint which—

    (a) is made for the purposes of this Part by an owner of a domestic property that is for the time being unoccupied, and

    (b) alleges that the reasonable enjoyment of that property by a prospective occupier of that property would be adversely affected by the height of a high hedge situated on land owned or occupied by another person,

as it applies to a complaint falling within subsection (1).

(3) In relation to a complaint falling within subsection (2), references in sections 68 and 69 to the effect of the height of a high hedge on the complainant's reasonable enjoyment of a domestic property shall be read as references to the effect that it would have on the reasonable enjoyment of that property by a prospective occupier of the property.

(4) This Part does not apply to complaints about the effect of the roots of a high hedge.

(5) In this Part, in relation to a complaint—

"complainant" means—

    (a) a person by whom the complaint is made; or

(b)  if every person who made the complaint ceases to be an owner or occupier of the domestic property specified in the complaint, any other person who is for the time being an owner or occupier of that property;

and references to the complainant include references to one or more of the complainants;

"the neighbouring land" means the land on which the high hedge is situated; and

"the relevant authority" means the local authority in whose area that land is situated.

## 66 HIGH HEDGES

(1)  In this Part "high hedge" means so much of a barrier to light or access as—

(a)  is formed wholly or predominantly by a line of two or more evergreens; and

(b)  rises to a height of more than two metres above ground level.

(2)  For the purposes of subsection (1) a line of evergreens is not to be regarded as forming a barrier to light or access if the existence of gaps significantly affects its overall effect as such a barrier at heights of more than two metres above ground level.

(3)  In this section "evergreen" means an evergreen tree or shrub or a semi-evergreen tree or shrub.

## 67 DOMESTIC PROPERTY

(1)  In this Part "domestic property" means—

(a)  a dwelling; or

(b)  a garden or yard which is used and enjoyed wholly or mainly in connection with a dwelling.

(2)  In subsection (1) "dwelling" means any building or part of a building occupied, or intended to be occupied, as a separate dwelling.

(3) A reference in this Part to a person's reasonable enjoyment of domestic property includes a reference to his reasonable enjoyment of a part of the property.

## COMPLAINTS PROCEDURE

## 68 PROCEDURE FOR DEALING WITH COMPLAINTS

(1) This section has effect where a complaint to which this Part applies—

    (a) is made to the relevant authority; and

    (b) is accompanied by such fee (if any) as the authority may determine.

(2) If the authority consider—

    (a) that the complainant has not taken all reasonable steps to resolve the matters complained of without proceeding by way of such a complaint to the authority, or

    (b) that the complaint is frivolous or vexatious,

the authority may decide that the complaint should not be proceeded with.

(3) If the authority do not so decide, they must decide—

    (a) whether the height of the high hedge specified in the complaint is adversely affecting the complainant's reasonable enjoyment of the domestic property so specified; and

    (b) if so, what action (if any) should be taken in relation to that hedge, in pursuance of a remedial notice under section 69, with a view to remedying the adverse effect or preventing its recurrence.

(4) If the authority decide under subsection (3) that action should be taken as mentioned in paragraph (b) of that subsection, they must as soon as is reasonably practicable—

    (a) issue a remedial notice under section 69 implementing their decision;

    (b) send a copy of that notice to the following persons, namely—

        (i) every complainant; and

> (ii)   every owner and every occupier of the neighbouring land; and

(c)   notify each of those persons of the reasons for their decision.

(5)   If the authority—

(a)   decide that the complaint should not be proceeded with, or

(b)   decide either or both of the issues specified in subsection (3) otherwise than in the complainant's favour,

they must as soon as is reasonably practicable notify the appropriate person or persons of any such decision and of their reasons for it.

(6)   For the purposes of subsection (5)—

(a)   every complainant is an appropriate person in relation to a decision falling within paragraph (a) or (b) of that subsection; and

(b)   every owner and every occupier of the neighbouring land is an appropriate person in relation to a decision falling within paragraph (b) of that subsection.

(7)   A fee determined under subsection (1)(b) must not exceed the amount prescribed in regulations made—

(a)   in relation to complaints relating to hedges situated in England, by the Secretary of State; and

(b)   in relation to complaints relating to hedges situated in Wales, by the National Assembly for Wales.

(8)   A fee received by a local authority by virtue of subsection (1)(b) may be refunded by them in such circumstances and to such extent as they may determine.

## 69 REMEDIAL NOTICES

(1)   For the purposes of this Part a remedial notice is a notice—

(a)   issued by the relevant authority in respect of a complaint to which this Part applies; and

(b)   stating the matters mentioned in subsection (2).

(2)   Those matters are—

    (a) that a complaint has been made to the authority under this Part about a high hedge specified in the notice which is situated on land so specified;

    (b) that the authority have decided that the height of that hedge is adversely affecting the complainant's reasonable enjoyment of the domestic property specified in the notice;

    (c) the initial action that must be taken in relation to that hedge before the end of the compliance period;

    (d) any preventative action that they consider must be taken in relation to that hedge at times following the end of that period while the hedge remains on the land; and

    (e) the consequences under sections 75 and 77 of a failure to comply with the notice.

(3) The action specified in a remedial notice is not to require or involve—

    (a) a reduction in the height of the hedge to less than two metres above ground level; or

    (b) the removal of the hedge.

(4) A remedial notice shall take effect on its operative date.

(5) "The operative date" of a remedial notice is such date (falling at least 28 days after that on which the notice is issued) as is specified in the notice as the date on which it is to take effect.

(6) "The compliance period" in the case of a remedial notice is such reasonable period as is specified in the notice for the purposes of subsection (2)(c) as the period within which the action so specified is to be taken; and that period shall begin with the operative date of the notice.

(7) Subsections (4) to (6) have effect in relation to a remedial notice subject to—

    (a) the exercise of any power of the relevant authority under section 70; and

    (b) the operation of sections 71 to 73 in relation to the notice.

(8) While a remedial notice has effect, the notice—

    (a) shall be a local land charge; and

(b)   shall be binding on every person who is for the time being an owner or occupier of the land specified in the notice as the land where the hedge in question is situated.

(9)   In this Part—

"initial action" means remedial action or preventative action, or both;

"remedial action" means action to remedy the adverse effect of the height of the hedge on the complainant's reasonable enjoyment of the domestic property in respect of which the complaint was made; and

"preventative action" means action to prevent the recurrence of the adverse effect.

## 70 WITHDRAWAL OR RELAXATION OF REQUIREMENTS OF REMEDIAL NOTICES

(1)   The relevant authority may—

(a)   withdraw a remedial notice issued by them; or

(b)   waive or relax a requirement of a remedial notice so issued.

(2)   The powers conferred by this section are exercisable both before and after a remedial notice has taken effect.

(3)   Where the relevant authority exercise the powers conferred by this section, they must give notice of what they have done to—

(a)   every complainant; and

(b)   every owner and every occupier of the neighbouring land.

(4)   The withdrawal of a remedial notice does not affect the power of the relevant authority to issue a further remedial notice in respect of the same hedge.

## APPEALS

## 71 APPEALS AGAINST REMEDIAL NOTICES AND OTHER DECISIONS OF RELEVANT AUTHORITIES

(1)   Where the relevant authority—

(a) issue a remedial notice,

(b) withdraw such a notice, or

(c) waive or relax the requirements of such a notice,

each of the persons falling within subsection (2) may appeal to the appeal authority against the issue or withdrawal of the notice or (as the case may be) the waiver or relaxation of its requirements.

(2) Those persons are—

    (a) every person who is a complainant in relation to the complaint by reference to which the notice was given; and

    (b) every person who is an owner or occupier of the neighbouring land.

(3) Where the relevant authority decide either or both of the issues specified in section 68(3) otherwise than in the complainant's favour, the complainant may appeal to the appeal authority against the decision.

(4) An appeal under this section must be made before—

    (a) the end of the period of 28 days beginning with the relevant date; or

    (b) such later time as the appeal authority may allow.

(5) In subsection (4) "the relevant date"—

    (a) in the case of an appeal against the issue of a remedial notice, means the date on which the notice was issued; and

    (b) in the case of any other appeal under this section, means the date of the notification given by the relevant authority under section 68 or 70 of the decision in question.

(6) Where an appeal is duly made under subsection (1), the notice or (as the case may be) withdrawal, waiver or relaxation in question shall not have effect pending the final determination or withdrawal of the appeal.

(7) In this Part "the appeal authority" means—

    (a) in relation to appeals relating to hedges situated in England, the Secretary of State; and

(b)  in relation to appeals relating to hedges situated in Wales, the National Assembly for Wales.

## 72 APPEALS PROCEDURE

(1)  The appeal authority may by regulations make provision with respect to—

  (a)  the procedure which is to be followed in connection with appeals to that authority under section 71; and

  (b)  other matters consequential on or connected with such appeals.

(2)  Regulations under this section may, in particular, make provision—

  (a)  specifying the grounds on which appeals may be made;

  (b)  prescribing the manner in which appeals are to be made;

  (c)  requiring persons making appeals to send copies of such documents as may be prescribed to such persons as may be prescribed;

  (d)  requiring local authorities against whose decisions appeals are made to send to the appeal authority such documents as may be prescribed;

  (e)  specifying, where a local authority are required by virtue of paragraph (d) to send the appeal authority a statement indicating the submissions which they propose to put forward on the appeal, the matters to be included in such a statement;

  (f)  prescribing the period within which a requirement imposed by the regulations is to be complied with;

  (g)  enabling such a period to be extended by the appeal authority;

  (h)  for a decision on an appeal to be binding on persons falling within section 71(2) in addition to the person by whom the appeal was made;

  (i)  for incidental or ancillary matters, including the awarding of costs.

(3)  Where an appeal is made to the appeal authority under section 71 the appeal authority may appoint a person to hear and determine the appeal on its behalf.

(4) The appeal authority may require such a person to exercise on its behalf any functions which—

    (a) are conferred on the appeal authority in connection with such an appeal by section 71 or 73 or by regulations under this section; and

    (b) are specified in that person's appointment;

and references to the appeal authority in section 71 or 73 or in any regulations under this section shall be construed accordingly.

(5) The appeal authority may pay a person appointed under subsection (3) such remuneration as it may determine.

(6) Regulations under this section may provide for any provision of Schedule 20 to the Environment Act 1995 (c 25) (delegation of appellate functions) to apply in relation to a person appointed under subsection (3) with such modifications (if any) as may be prescribed.

(7) In this section, "prescribed" means prescribed by regulations made by the appeal authority.

## 73 DETERMINATION OR WITHDRAWAL OF APPEALS

(1) On an appeal under section 71 the appeal authority may allow or dismiss the appeal, either in whole or in part.

(2) Where the appeal authority decides to allow such an appeal to any extent, it may do such of the following as it considers appropriate—

    (a) quash a remedial notice or decision to which the appeal relates;

    (b) vary the requirements of such a notice; or

    (c) in a case where no remedial notice has been issued, issue on behalf of the relevant authority a remedial notice that could have been issued by the relevant authority on the complaint in question.

(3) On an appeal under section 71 relating to a remedial notice, the appeal authority may also correct any defect, error or misdescription in the notice if it is satisfied that the correction will not cause injustice to any person falling within section 71(2).

(4) Once the appeal authority has made its decision on an appeal under section 71, it must, as soon as is reasonably practicable—

(a) give a notification of the decision, and

(b) if the decision is to issue a remedial notice or to vary or correct the requirements of such a notice, send copies of the notice as issued, varied or corrected,

to every person falling within section 71(2) and to the relevant authority.

(5) Where, in consequence of the appeal authority's decision on an appeal, a remedial notice is upheld or varied or corrected, the operative date of the notice shall be—

(a) the date of the appeal authority's decision; or

(b) such later date as may be specified in its decision.

(6) Where the person making an appeal under section 71 against a remedial notice withdraws his appeal, the operative date of the notice shall be the date on which the appeal is withdrawn.

(7) In any case falling within subsection (5) or (6), the compliance period for the notice shall accordingly run from the date which is its operative date by virtue of that subsection (and any period which may have started to run from a date preceding that on which the appeal was made shall accordingly be disregarded).

POWERS OF ENTRY

## 74 POWERS OF ENTRY FOR THE PURPOSES OF COMPLAINTS AND APPEALS

(1) Where, under this Part, a complaint has been made or a remedial notice has been issued, a person authorised by the relevant authority may enter the neighbouring land in order to obtain information required by the relevant authority for the purpose of determining—

(a) whether this Part applies to the complaint;

(b) whether to issue or withdraw a remedial notice;

(c) whether to waive or relax a requirement of a remedial notice;

(d) whether a requirement of a remedial notice has been complied with.

(2) Where an appeal has been made under section 71, a person authorised—

    (a) by the appeal authority, or

    (b) by a person appointed to determine appeals on its behalf,

may enter the neighbouring land in order to obtain information required by the appeal authority, or by the person so appointed, for the purpose of determining an appeal under this Part.

(3) A person shall not enter land in the exercise of a power conferred by this section unless at least 24 hours' notice of the intended entry has been given to every occupier of the land.

(4) A person authorised under this section to enter land—

    (a) shall, if so required, produce evidence of his authority before entering; and

    (b) shall produce such evidence if required to do so at any time while he remains on the land.

(5) A person who enters land in the exercise of a power conferred by this section may—

    (a) take with him such other persons as may be necessary;

    (b) take with him equipment and materials needed in order to obtain the information required;

    (c) take samples of any trees or shrubs that appear to him to form part of a high hedge.

(6) If, in the exercise of a power conferred by this section, a person enters land which is unoccupied or from which all of the persons occupying the land are temporarily absent, he must on his departure leave it as effectively secured against unauthorised entry as he found it.

(7) A person who intentionally obstructs a person acting in the exercise of the powers under this section is guilty of an offence and shall be liable, on summary conviction, to a fine not exceeding level 3 on the standard scale.

ENFORCEMENT POWERS ETC

## 75 OFFENCES

(1) Where—

   (a) a remedial notice requires the taking of any action, and

   (b) that action is not taken in accordance with that notice within the compliance period or (as the case may be) by the subsequent time by which it is required to be taken,

   every person who, at a relevant time, is an owner or occupier of the neighbouring land is guilty of an offence and shall be liable, on summary conviction, to a fine not exceeding level 3 on the standard scale.

(2) In subsection (1) "relevant time"—

   (a) in relation to action required to be taken before the end of the compliance period, means a time after the end of that period and before the action is taken; and

   (b) in relation to any preventative action which is required to be taken after the end of that period, means a time after that at which the action is required to be taken but before it is taken.

(3) In proceedings against a person for an offence under subsection (1) it shall be a defence for him to show that he did everything he could be expected to do to secure compliance with the notice.

(4) In any such proceedings against a person, it shall also be a defence for him to show, in a case in which he—

   (a) is not a person to whom a copy of the remedial notice was sent in accordance with a provision of this Part, and

   (b) is not assumed under subsection (5) to have had knowledge of the notice at the time of the alleged offence,

   that he was not aware of the existence of the notice at that time.

(5) A person shall be assumed to have had knowledge of a remedial notice at any time if at that time—

   (a) he was an owner of the neighbouring land; and

   (b) the notice was at that time registered as a local land charge.

(6) Section 198 of the Law of Property Act 1925 (c 20) (constructive notice) shall be disregarded for the purposes of this section.

(7) Where a person is convicted of an offence under subsection (1) and it appears to the court—

    (a) that a failure to comply with the remedial notice is continuing, and

    (b) that it is within that person's power to secure compliance with the notice,

the court may, in addition to or instead of imposing a punishment, order him to take the steps specified in the order for securing compliance with the notice.

(8) An order under subsection (7) must require those steps to be taken within such reasonable period as may be fixed by the order.

(9) Where a person fails without reasonable excuse to comply with an order under subsection (7) he is guilty of an offence and shall be liable, on summary conviction, to a fine not exceeding level 3 on the standard scale.

(10) Where a person continues after conviction of an offence under subsection (9) (or of an offence under this subsection) to fail, without reasonable excuse, to take steps which he has been ordered to take under subsection (7), he is guilty of a further offence and shall be liable, on summary conviction, to a fine not exceeding one-twentieth of that level for each day on which the failure has so continued.

## 76 POWER TO REQUIRE OCCUPIER TO PERMIT ACTION TO BE TAKEN BY OWNER

Section 289 of the Public Health Act 1936 (c 49) (power of court to require occupier to permit work to be done by owner) shall apply with any necessary modifications for the purpose of giving an owner of land to which a remedial notice relates the right, as against all other persons interested in the land, to comply with the notice.

## 77 ACTION BY RELEVANT AUTHORITY

(1) This section applies where—

    (a) a remedial notice requires the taking of any action; and

(b)  that action is not taken in accordance with that notice within the compliance period or (as the case may be) after the end of that period when it is required to be taken by the notice.

(2)  Where this section applies—

(a)  a person authorised by the relevant authority may enter the neighbouring land and take the required action; and

(b)  the relevant authority may recover any expenses reasonably incurred by that person in doing so from any person who is an owner or occupier of the land.

(3)  Expenses recoverable under this section shall be a local land charge and binding on successive owners of the land and on successive occupiers of it.

(4)  Where expenses are recoverable under this section from two or more persons, those persons shall be jointly and severally liable for the expenses.

(5)  A person shall not enter land in the exercise of a power conferred by this section unless at least 7 days' notice of the intended entry has been given to every occupier of the land.

(6)  A person authorised under this section to enter land—

(a)  shall, if so required, produce evidence of his authority before entering; and

(b)  shall produce such evidence if required to do so at any time while he remains on the land.

(7)  A person who enters land in the exercise of a power conferred by this section may—

(a)  use a vehicle to enter the land;

(b)  take with him such other persons as may be necessary;

(c)  take with him equipment and materials needed for the purpose of taking the required action.

(8)  If, in the exercise of a power conferred by this section, a person enters land which is unoccupied or from which all of the persons occupying the land are temporarily absent, he must on his departure leave it as effectively secured against unauthorised entry as he found it.

(9)  A person who wilfully obstructs a person acting in the exercise of powers under this section to enter land and take action on that land is guilty of an offence and shall be liable, on summary conviction, to a fine not exceeding level 3 on the standard scale.

## 78 OFFENCES COMMITTED BY BODIES CORPORATE

(1)  Where an offence under this Part committed by a body corporate is proved to have been committed with the consent or connivance of, or to be attributable to any neglect on the part of—

    (a)  a director, manager, secretary or other similar officer of the body corporate, or

    (b)  any person who was purporting to act in any such capacity,

he, as well as the body corporate, shall be guilty of that offence and be liable to be proceeded against and punished accordingly.

(2)  Where the affairs of a body corporate are managed by its members, subsection (1) applies in relation to the acts and defaults of a member in connection with his functions of management as if he were a director of the body corporate.

## SUPPLEMENTARY

## 79 SERVICE OF DOCUMENTS

(1)  A notification or other document required to be given or sent to a person by virtue of this Part shall be taken to be duly given or sent to him if served in accordance with the following provisions of this section.

(2)  Such a document may be served—

    (a)  by delivering it to the person in question;

    (b)  by leaving it at his proper address; or

    (c)  by sending it by post to him at that address.

(3)  Such a document may—

    (a)  in the case of a body corporate, be served on the secretary or clerk of that body;

(b) in the case of a partnership, be served on a partner or a person having the control or management of the partnership business.

(4) For the purposes of this section and of section 7 of the Interpretation Act 1978 (c 30) (service of documents by post) in its application to this section, a person's proper address shall be his last known address, except that—

(a) in the case of a body corporate or their secretary or clerk, it shall be the address of the registered or principal office of that body; and

(b) in the case of a partnership or person having the control or the management of the partnership business, it shall be the principal office of the partnership.

(5) For the purposes of subsection (4) the principal office of—

(a) a company registered outside the United Kingdom, or

(b) a partnership carrying on business outside the United Kingdom,

shall be their principal office within the United Kingdom.

(6) If a person has specified an address in the United Kingdom other than his proper address within the meaning of subsection (4) as the one at which he or someone on his behalf will accept documents of a particular description, that address shall also be treated for the purposes of this section and section 7 of the Interpretation Act 1978 as his proper address in connection with the service on him of a document of that description.

(7) Where—

(a) by virtue of this Part a document is required to be given or sent to a person who is an owner or occupier of any land, and

(b) the name or address of that person cannot be ascertained after reasonable inquiry,

the document may be served either by leaving it in the hands of a person who is or appears to be resident or employed on the land or by leaving it conspicuously affixed to some building or object on the land.

## 80 DOCUMENTS IN ELECTRONIC FORM

(1)  A requirement of this Part—

    (a)  to send a copy of a remedial notice to a person, or

    (b)  to notify a person under section 68(4) of the reasons for the issue of a remedial notice,

is not capable of being satisfied by transmitting the copy or notification electronically or by making it available on a web-site.

(2)  The delivery of any other document to a person (the "recipient") may be effected for the purposes of section 79(2)(a)—

    (a)  by transmitting it electronically, or

    (b)  by making it available on a web-site,

but only if it is transmitted or made available in accordance with subsection (3) or (5).

(3)  A document is transmitted electronically in accordance with this subsection if—

    (a)  the recipient has agreed that documents may be delivered to him by being transmitted to an electronic address and in an electronic form specified by him for that purpose; and

    (b)  the document is a document to which that agreement applies and is transmitted to that address in that form.

(4)  A document which is transmitted in accordance with subsection (3) by means of an electronic communications network shall, unless the contrary is proved, be treated as having been delivered at 9 a.m. on the working day immediately following the day on which it is transmitted.

(5)  A document is made available on a web-site in accordance with this subsection if—

    (a)  the recipient has agreed that documents may be delivered to him by being made available on a web-site;

    (b)  the document is a document to which that agreement applies and is made available on a web-site;

    (c)  the recipient is notified, in a manner agreed by him, of—

(i)   the presence of the document on the web-site;

(ii)  the address of the web-site; and

(iii) the place on the web-site where the document may be accessed.

(6) A document made available on a web-site in accordance with subsection (5) shall, unless the contrary is proved, be treated as having been delivered at 9a.m. on the working day immediately following the day on which the recipient is notified in accordance with subsection (5)(c).

(7) In this section—

"electronic address" includes any number or address used for the purposes of receiving electronic communications;

"electronic communication" means an electronic communication within the meaning of the Electronic Communications Act 2000 (c 7) the processing of which on receipt is intended to produce writing;

"electronic communications network" means an electronic communications network within the meaning of the Communications Act 2003 (c 21);

"electronically" means in the form of an electronic communication;

"working day" means a day which is not a Saturday or a Sunday, Christmas Day, Good Friday or a bank holiday in England and Wales under the Banking and Financial Dealings Act 1971 (c 80).

## 81 POWER TO MAKE FURTHER PROVISION ABOUT DOCUMENTS IN ELECTRONIC FORM

(1) Regulations may amend section 80 by modifying the circumstances in which, and the conditions subject to which, the delivery of a document for the purposes of section 79(2)(a) may be effected by—

(a) transmitting the document electronically; or

(b) making the document available on a web-site.

(2) Regulations may also amend section 80 by modifying the day on which and the time at which documents which are transmitted electronically or made available on a web-site in accordance with that section are to be treated as having been delivered.

(3) Regulations under this section may make such consequential amendments of this Part as the person making the regulations considers appropriate.

(4) The power to make such regulations shall be exercisable—

  (a) in relation to documents relating to complaints about hedges situated in England, by the Secretary of State; and

  (b) in relation to documents relating to complaints about hedges situated in Wales, by the National Assembly for Wales.

(5) In this section "electronically" has the meaning given in section 80.

## 82 INTERPRETATION

In this Part—

  "the appeal authority" has the meaning given by section 71(7);

  "complaint" shall be construed in accordance with section 65;

  "complainant" has the meaning given by section 65(5);

  "the compliance period" has the meaning given by section 69(6);

  "domestic property" has the meaning given by section 67;

  "high hedge" has the meaning given by section 66;

  "local authority", in relation to England, means—

      (a) a district council;

      (b) a county council for a county in which there are no districts;

      (c) a London borough council; or

      (d) the Common Council of the City of London;

      and, in relation to Wales, means a county council or a county borough council;

  "the neighbouring land" has the meaning given by section 65(5);

"occupier", in relation to any land, means a person entitled to possession of the land by virtue of an estate or interest in it;

"the operative date" shall be construed in accordance with sections 69(5) and 73(5) and (6);

"owner", in relation to any land, means a person (other than a mortgagee not in possession) who, whether in his own right or as trustee for any person—

(a)   is entitled to receive the rack rent of the land, or

(b)   where the land is not let at a rack rent, would be so entitled if it were so let;

"preventative action" has the meaning given by section 69(9);

"the relevant authority" has the meaning given by section 65(5);

"remedial notice" shall be construed in accordance with section 69(1);

"remedial action" has the meaning given by section 69(9).

## 83 POWER TO AMEND SECTIONS 65 AND 66

(1)   Regulations may do one or both of the following—

(a)   amend section 65 for the purpose of extending the scope of complaints relating to high hedges to which this Part applies; and

(b)   amend section 66 (definition of "high hedge").

(2)   The power to make such regulations shall be exercisable—

(a)   in relation to complaints about hedges situated in England, by the Secretary of State; and

(b)   in relation to complaints about hedges situated in Wales, by the National Assembly for Wales.

(3)   Regulations under this section may make such consequential amendments of this Part as the person making the regulations considers appropriate.

## 84 CROWN APPLICATION

(1)   This Part and any provision made under it bind the Crown.

(2) This section does not impose criminal liability on the Crown.

(3) Subsection (2) does not affect the criminal liability of persons in the service of the Crown.

# C10 Tribunal Procedure (Upper Tribunal) (Lands Chamber) Rules 2010, SI 2010/2600 (L15), Extracts

## PART 7
### APPLICATIONS UNDER SECTION 2 OF THE RIGHTS OF LIGHT ACT 1959

### 40 INTERPRETATION

In this Part "section 2" means section 2 of the Rights of Light Act 1959.

### 41 METHOD OF MAKING APPLICATION

(1) An application for a certificate of the Tribunal under section 2 is made by sending or delivering to the Tribunal an application which must be signed and dated and must state—

(a) the name and address of the applicant;

(b) the name and address of the applicant's representative (if any);

(c) whether the applicant is—

(i) the owner;

(ii) the tenant for a term of years certain and, if so, when the term will expire; or

(iii) the mortgagee in possession of the servient land;

(d) a description of the servient land;

(e) the name of the local authority that keeps the relevant register of local land charges;

(f) the names and addresses of all persons known by the applicant, after conducting all reasonable enquiries, to be occupying the dominant building or to have a proprietary interest in it; and

(g) if the application is for a temporary certificate, the grounds upon which it is claimed that the case is of exceptional urgency.

(2) The applicant must provide with an application under paragraph (1)—

(a) three copies of the application for the registration of a light obstruction notice under section 2 that the applicant proposes to make to the local authority in whose area the dominant building is situated and any attached plans; and

(b) the fee payable to the Tribunal.

## 42 NOTICES TO BE GIVEN

(1) Upon receipt of an application the Tribunal must send or deliver written directions to the applicant specifying—

(a) what notices are to be given to persons who appear to the Tribunal to be likely to be affected by the registration in the register of local land charges of a notice under section 2;

(b) the time by which such notices are to be given; and

(c) whether such notices should be given by advertisement or otherwise.

(2) The notices that the Tribunal directs shall be given under this rule must be given by the applicant who must—

(a) as soon as reasonably practicable notify the Tribunal in writing once this has been done; and

(b) set out full particulars of the steps taken.

## 43 ISSUE OF TEMPORARY CERTIFICATE

(1) If the Tribunal is satisfied that the case is one of exceptional urgency that requires the immediate registration of a temporary notice in the register of local land charges, the Tribunal shall issue a temporary certificate.

(2) A temporary certificate shall last no longer than 4 months.

## 44 ISSUE OF DEFINITIVE CERTIFICATE OF ADEQUATE NOTICE

The Tribunal shall issue a definitive certificate of adequate notice when it is satisfied that any notices which it has directed must be given under rule 42 (notices to be given) have been given.

# Index

*References are to page numbers.*